For Norman M. Fox

CONTENTS

BOOK ILLUSTRATED

TEXT, IMAGE, AND CULTURE
1770 – 1930

Edited by Catherine J. Golden

OAK KNOLL PRESS
NEW CASTLE, DELAWARE
2000

First Edition.
Published by **Oak Knoll Press**
310 Delaware Street, New Castle, Delaware, USA

ISBN: 1-58456-023-1

Title: Book Illustrated: Text, Image, and Culture
Editor: Catherine J. Golden
Typographer: Dianne Nelson, Shadow Canyon Graphics
Publishing Director: J. Lewis von Hoelle

Library of Congress Cataloging-in-Publication Data
Book illustrated: text, image, and culture 1770-1930 / edited by Catherine J. Golden.
　　p. cm.
　　Includes bibliographical references and index.
　　ISBN 1-58456-023-1
　　1. Illustration of books—History. 2. English literature—Illustrations. I. Golden, Catherine.
NC960.B67 2000
741.6'4'09—dc21
　　　　　　　　　　　　　　　　　　　　　　　　00-029844

Printed in the United States of America on 60# archival, acid-free paper meeting the requirements of the American Standard for Permanence of paper for Printed Library Materials

[ii]

LIST OF ILLUSTRATIONS

[ix]

Notes on Contributors

JONATHAN BATE is Leverhulme Research Professor of English Literature and King Alfred Professor of English Literature at the University of Liverpool. A fellow of the British Academy, he is both a Shakespeare scholar and a Romanticist. He is the author of *The Song of the Earth* (2000), *The Cure for Love* (1998), *The Genius of Shakespeare* (1997), *Shakespeare and Ovid* (1993), *Romantic Ecology: Wordsworth and the Environmental Tradition* (1991), *Shakespearean Constitutions: Politics, Theatre, Criticism, 1730-1830* (1989), and *Shakespeare and the English Romantic Imagination* (1986), as well as an edition of *Titus Andronicus* for the Arden Shakespeare (1995). He is writing the biography of John Clare.

RUTH COPANS is associate librarian, humanities and special collections, at Skidmore College and interim college librarian. She has co-curated two exhibitions at the Hyde Collection on "The Nuremberg Chronicle" and "Dream Blocks: American Women Illustrators of the Golden Age" and an exhibition on "The Artistry of Elfriede Abbe" at the Carl A. Kroch Library at Cornell University. She is also a rare-book binder; her bindings have been displayed in the Bibliotheque Historique de Paris and at Skidmore College. A member of the board of directors of SHARP, she has published in *Bulletin de Bibliophile* and *Visible Languages* and is a contributor to *Annual Bibliography of English Language and Literature*.

CATHERINE J. GOLDEN is associate professor of English at Skidmore College. She is co-editor of *The Mixed Legacy of Charlotte Perkins Gilman* (with Joanna S. Zangrando, 2000) and *Unpunished*, Charlotte Perkins Gilman's hitherto unpublished feminist detective novel (with Denise D. Knight, 1997), as well as editor of *The Captive Imagination: A Casebook on "The Yellow Wallpaper"* (1992). She is also the author of many essays and reviews on Victorian literature and book illustration published in *Victorian Poetry*, *Victorian Studies*, *Victorian Periodicals Review*, *Salmagundi*, *CEA Critic*, *Profession 95*, *Woman's Art Journal*, and books on the period. She is currently working on a book on women, reading, and illustrated fiction in nineteenth-century Britain and America.

SARAH WEBSTER GOODWIN is professor and chair of the English department of Skidmore College. She is the author of *Kitsch and Culture: The Dance of Death in Nineteenth-Century Literature and Graphic Arts* (1988) and co-editor of three collections: *Feminism, Utopia, and Narrative* (with Libby Jones, 1990); *The Scope of Words: In Honor of Albert Cook* (with Peter Baker and Gary Handwerk, 1990); and *Death and Representation* (with Elisabeth Bronfen, 1993). Goodwin has also published numerous scholarly articles on Romanticism and feminism in leading journals including *Tulsa Studies in Women's Literature*, *Salmagundi*, *L'Esprit Créateur*, and *Philological Quarterly*. This essay is part of a book in progress on Romanticism and the ballet.

JAMES A. W. HEFFERNAN is Frederick Sessions Beebe Professor in the Art of Writing at Dartmouth College. Recipient of fellowships from the Woodrow Wilson Foundation and the National Endowment for the Humanities and director of several NEH Summer Seminars, he is author of *Museum of Words: The Poetics of Ekphrasis from Homer to Ashbery* (1993), *Wordsworth's Theory of Poetry:*

The Transforming Imagination (1969), and *The Recreation of Landscape: A Study of Wordsworth, Coleridge, Constable, and Turner* (1985). He is also editor of *Space, Time, Image, Sign: Essays on Literature and the Visual Arts* (1987) and *Representing the French Revolution: Literature, Historiography and Art* (1992).

ELIZABETH K. HELSINGER is John Mathews Manly Distinguished Service Professor in the departments of English and art history at the University of Chicago. She is the author of *Rural Scenes and National Representation, Britain 1815–1850* (1997), *Ruskin and the Art of the Beholder* (1982), and co-author (with Robin Sheets and William Veeder) of the three-volume *The Woman Question. Society and Literature in Britain and America, 1837–1883* (1983; 1989). A co-editor of *Critical Inquiry* since 1985, she is currently working on a book on the Pre-Raphaelite arts of poetry and design in the 1860s.

ROBERT L. PATTEN, Lynette S. Autrey Professor in Humanities at Rice University, devoted thirty years to researching all aspects of Cruikshankiana in America and England, including the vast Cruikshank collections in the British Museum and at Princeton University. His two-volume biography entitled *George Cruikshank's Life, Times, and Art* (Rutgers University Press, 1992, 1996) was named by the *Guardian* (London) as the outstanding biography of the decade. Editor of *Studies in English Literature*, Patten also wrote *Charles Dickens and His Publishers* (1978) and has contributed essays to *The Oxford Reader's Companion to Dickens*, *The Cambridge Companion to Charles Dickens*, and the *New Dictionary of National Biography*.

DAVID H. PORTER, president of Skidmore College from 1987 to 1999 and former professor of classics and music at Carleton College (and president from 1986 to 1987), is currently teaching classics at

Williams College. His books include *Horace's Poetic Journey: A Reading of Odes 1-3* (1987); *"Only Connect." Three Studies in Greek Tragedy* (1987); and *The Not Quite Innocent Bystander. Writings of Edward Steurmann* (co-edited with Gunther Schuller and Clara Steurmann, 1989). He has in recent years published frequently on issues of higher education in the *New York Times*, the *Chronicle of Higher Education*, the *Boston Globe*, and *Higher Education and National Affairs*. His articles and reviews on the classics and on music have appeared in the *American Journal of Philology, Classical Philology, Harvard Studies in Classical Philology, Illinois Classical Studies, Music Review, Perspectives of Music*, and numerous other scholarly journals. A bibliophile and book collector, he has also published in *AB Bookman's Weekly* and *Biblio* and has lectured on the Hogarth Press as a Phi Beta Kappa Visiting Scholar in 1994-95.

PREFACE

This collection of essays is an outgrowth of the Hannah M. Adler Lecture series at Skidmore College. Upon Adler's death in 1990, Skidmore College received a bequest from her estate to initiate a yearly lecture, an occasion to discuss the importance of nineteenth-century literature and culture represented in the Hannah M. Adler Collection in the Lucy Scribner Library at Skidmore College. The genre of Victorian illustrated fiction primarily leaves its heritage in children's literature. However, the Adler Collection — which features the work of George Cruikshank among other seminal nineteenth-century illustrators and authors — recaptures the adult reading experience of the Victorian period by keeping alive a time when the pictures accompanying a serial novel often found more favor with the purchaser than the literary content to which they were wed. The series was inaugurated in 1991 with the generous support of the current owner of the Adler Collection, Norman M. Fox, a close friend of Hannah Adler, after whom the collection is named. The Adler Lecture series at Skidmore College has tapped into the rich visual literacy skills of the Victorian age and promoted the study of primary materials. Drawing from the excellent Adler Lectures delivered by leading scholars of nineteenth-century literature and culture over the past nine years, this volume gives particular emphasis to the book arts during the first wave of industrialization.

I am grateful to Norman M. Fox — a man with a vision, whose generosity gave life and spirit to what is now an established and important campus lecture series. From his admiration of old books and first-day covers, I have come to know Norman as one who shares a passion for rare books and truly appreciates the printed word. It is fitting that I dedicate this book to him.

There are other individuals I would like to thank for their invaluable help in bringing this project to fruition. The Office of the Dean of the Faculty of Skidmore College offered assistance in providing funds to support, in particular, the color illustrations for the volume. Robert L. Patten, a contributor to this volume, gave me unfailing encouragement in pursuing the idea of a collection based on the lecture series. I am particularly indebted to another contributor, Sarah Webster Goodwin, who offered me important advice on ways to shape the collection into a cohesive volume of essays. My husband, Michael Marx, too, served as a sounding board for the entire project. Ryan Kimmet, Skidmore Class of 1999, and Kristina R. Fennelly, Skidmore Class of 2002, provided excellent assistance in a range of production tasks. John von Hoelle, publishing director of Oak Knoll Press, offered helpful advice in all stages of this project. Anne Crookall Hockenos, editor, Office of College Relations, Skidmore College, offered invaluable assistance in the final stages of this project. I would like to recognize Dianne Nelson of Shadow Canyon Graphics for her care, craftsmanship, and vision in laying out this book. Finally, I would like to thank the contributors to this volume for their conscientiousness and promptness in responding to all of my requests and deadlines.

INTRODUCTION

Catherine J. Golden

Scholars of literature, focused as we often are on conventional literary periods and national cultures, can lose sight of the larger sweep, a profound coherence in the decades during which industrialization transformed Western culture (1770-1930). The reign of the image — in which we live — began with mechanical reproduction. We are familiar with the processes that brought this about. They include urbanization, industry, technological advances, expanded freedoms of the press, the emergence of the new class society, increased dissemination of money, and the rise of leisure. As printers reproduced better and cheaper images, the audience and market for them grew. This cultural change was a profound transformation, affecting, as we know, almost every aspect of social life.

Writing in 1936 about technical reproduction of art in "The Work of Art in the Age of Mechanical Reproduction," Walter Benjamin articulates a time when the fascination with the visual, the proliferation of images, and technical means of reproduction

[1]

(e.g., lithography, wood engraving, photography) attained previously unknown proportions in Western European culture. Works of art, Benjamin argues, increasingly designed for mass reproduction during the nineteenth century, became alienated from their roots in ritual, losing the "aura" that a unique art work possessed to serve a covert socio-political purpose.[1] The reproducibility of images emancipated art from ritual ("its original use value" [224]); likewise, the terms "authentic" and "autonomous" no longer applied to art, which became estranged from ritual. Benjamin regrets the loss of aura, a quality that, to him, only an original work of art possesses. And Benjamin's concerns still resonate in our mass media culture. In *The Rise and Fall of English* (1998), Robert Scholes recalls Walter Benjamin in his examination of the decline of the humanities: "In the age of mass media, literature has, as Walter Benjamin put it, lost its aura. We can either pretend, ostrichwise, that this has not happened, or decide what to do about it."[2] Benjamin cautions that the "uniqueness of a work of art is inseparable from its being embedded in the fabric of tradition" (223). Likewise, Scholes, recalling the wisdom of John Keats and Benjamin, argues that we must "change reading from a passive to an active process" (164); the human reader thus creates what Keats refers to as a "'tapestry'" (165), something new that is dependent upon a medley of previous texts and leads the reader back to what Benjamin refers to as "the fabric of tradition" — the life of the author and the literary sources that influenced his or her creation.

Many early-nineteenth-century mechanical reproductions, which I refer to as artifacts, arguably possess an aura, especially by comparison to digital reproductions conceived in the age of mass media today. Even Benjamin could not have foreseen the manifold turns mechanical and digital reproduction would take. Albeit designed for reproducibility, the artifact created during the first wave of industrialization returns us, then, to a time when the artist was, in some cases, intimately involved in the reproduction of art and, likewise, leads us back to the life of the creator and the original use value of the work. The illustrated books George Cruikshank, Dante Gabriel Rossetti, and Virginia and Leonard Woolf produced, for example, can be defined as authentic artifacts rather than mechanical reproductions. Examining artists who were actively involved in the process of reproduction brings us closer to the aura, in Benjamin's sense, of these early reproducible art forms, strengthening our understanding of our pictorial heritage.

Scholars of the book have expressed great concern over the preservation of primary materials. With the growth of new technology for creating reproductions, we must remember the importance of preserving the artifactual sources on which reproductions are based: "those artifacts provide the standard for judging the reproductions; they also contain, in their physicality, unreproducible evidence that readers (scholars, students, and the general public) need for analyzing and understanding, with as much historic context as possible, the writings that appeared and reappeared in them."[3] As this position statement from the Modern Language Association argues, we need access to printed artifacts of all kinds to study Western European and American culture during this important age of mechanical reproduction, ushering in modern culture. Accordingly, the authors of this collection have examined the book in its historical context with particular attention to illustrations, bindings, title pages, papers, and pictorial styles, considering as well related cultural arts, such as prints, paintings, and picture frames, which have bearing upon the book. These aspects of the book arts promote the study of primary materials, a vital window into past culture. The essays draw from materials in numerous archives including the Victoria and Albert Museum, the British Museum, the Delaware Art Museum, and many university libraries. Still, Benjamin cautions, "Even the most perfect repro-duction of a work of art is lacking one element: its presence in time and space, its unique existence at the place where it happens to be" (220). But in their examination of early mechanical repro-ductions, conceived prior to the age of mass media, the authors have returned us to the lives of illustrators and artists and the his-torical moments in which visual artifacts originated. They have explored the book in relation to political and social developments of a Western culture primed for the emergence of radio, television, video technology, and the Internet. These essays, thus, promote cultural studies and the continued use of primary materials as mediums of important cultural meanings, indispensable for research and teaching of the Romantic period through the Mod-ern Age in Britain and America.

Over sixty years have passed since Benjamin composed his seminal essay, "The Work of Art in the Age of Mechanical Repro-duction," which analyzes the impact of the cinema on traditional art. In our increasingly electronic age, sweeping technological changes have occurred in the arts, making not only cinema but radio, television, VCRs, CDs, and computers the norms of our world. But perhaps, as J. Hillis Miller argues in his exploratory book *Illustration* (1992), current interest in the interplay between word and image in film studies has changed the way we now view illus-trated books of the Romantic and Victorian ages; building upon Benjamin, Miller observes, "The new interest in the illustrations for nineteenth-century novels is a good example of Walter Ben-jamin's thesis in 'The Work of Art in the Age of Mechanical Reproduction,' that new technological means of reproduction have transformed the way we see artworks of the past," leading us to "a new recognition that nineteenth-century novels also combined two kinds of signs."[4] Digital availability and worldwide technolo-gies have rapidly broken down the boundaries of nationalism, as

Miller also notes, but this phenomenon was initiated during a precedent Western visual culture. Underlying this volume is the conviction that, if we examine aspects of the visual in English and American culture, we are led to a sense of powerful connections across genres and national boundaries.

Moreover, as Martin Meisel notes in his groundbreaking work *Realizations* (1983), the illustrated book, painting, and theatrical arts were mutually interdependent art forms. Meisel comments that "the play in the nineteenth century is the evident meeting place of story and picture."[5] In his study of British as well as French and German visual arts, Meisel also notes that "In the nineteenth century all three forms are narrative *and* pictorial; pictures are given to storytelling and novels unfold through and with pictures. Each form and each work becomes the site of a complex interplay of narrative and picture, rather than one member in a three-legged race to a synthesis" (3). In this rich interplay of the arts during the first wave of industrialization, visual forms multiplied and imitated each other. Theatrical tableaux vivants dramatically realized book illustrations. The press appropriated theatrical images, and the lithograph captured the fluid dancer. Book illustrations for children's and adult fiction influenced each other, and illustration emerged as a more legitimate art form. Children's literature, book design, and book production became art forms. A passion for the visual image pervaded western culture.

Our visual age of cinema and television has helped us begin to acknowledge the unprecedented fascination with these and other forms of the visual during the late-eighteenth through the early-twentieth century when, from a literary standpoint, it was important to read beyond the lines of the text. As Robert L. Patten urges us in this volume, if we "study graphic art once again with more intensity and less reliance on verbal preconceptions or on assumptions that only the verbal will 'explain' the visual, such readers will be in a better condition not only to understand our immense pictorial legacy but also to view critically the constructions of reality now so often provided by still, rapidly juxtaposed, or moving pictures" (110-11).

During the first wave of industrialization, literacy meant interpreting the details of an image as well as the words on a page. Testimonials abound in both fiction and literary history to the importance of studying our "pictorial legacy." The most memorable young heroines who transcend socially prescribed gender roles — Jane of Charlotte Brontë's *Jane Eyre* (1847), Maggie Tulliver of George Eliot's *Mill on the Floss* (1860), and Alice of Lewis Carroll's *Alice's Adventures in Wonderland* (1865) — as well as celebrated writers — including William Thackeray, Henry James, and George Du Maurier — attest to the importance of the image in picture-word collaborations. In the opening well-known scene of *Jane Eyre*, spirited ten-year old Jane sits "cross-legged like a Turk," reading her book in a window seat.[6] The raging November winds and rain draw her attention "[a]t intervals," but Jane is engrossed in Thomas Bewick's *A History of British Birds* (2 volumes, 1797 and 1804); she confesses, "the letterpress thereof I cared little for, generally speaking" (6). In the second chapter of *The Mill on the Floss*, we find Maggie Tulliver sitting on a stool by the fire, absorbed in the book on her lap. "There were few sounds that roused Maggie when she was dreaming over her book," Eliot assures us; however, it is the pictures she is "dreaming over."[7] To the shock of Mr. Tulliver's friend Mr. Riley, Maggie describes in detail the picture of a woman drowned as a witch from Daniel Defoe's *The Political History of the Devil* (1726). The unconventional Maggie admits to Mr. Riley that "'the reading in this book isn't pretty — but I like the pictures, and I make stories to the pictures out of my own head, you know'" (19). Sharing Maggie's preference for pictures, curious Alice sneers at her older sister's book without pictures and pronounces: "'and what is the use of a book . . . without pictures or conversations?'"[8] She promptly enters a dream world complete with copious — and significant — illustrations.

The predilections of these fictional characters also speak to the partiality of the writers of the age. *Alice's Adventures Under Ground* (1864), the first version of *Wonderland* that Carroll wrote and illustrated himself, reflects Carroll's privileging of pictures over words: he advises us to "look at the picture"[9] of the Gryphon to see this wondrous creature, not described at all. Carroll's own illustrations for *Alice* are interwoven with the text, demonstrating a close physical relation between word and image. Thackeray lauded Cruikshank (from whom he learned comic etching) for his contributions to *Oliver Twist* (1838), which he believed influenced the development of Charles Dickens's novel.[10] Even Henry James, a virulent critic of the late-nineteenth-century illustrated book, commented in *A Small Boy and Others* (1913) that George Cruikshank's pictures accompanying *Oliver Twist* made more of an impression on him than Dickens's text.[11] Writing in the 1890s, author-illustrator George Du Maurier reminds us that pictures accompanying adult serial fiction were examined "with passionate interest before reading the story, and after, and between."[12]

By the 1870s a web of economic and aesthetic factors led book illustration gradually to become excluded from adult fiction by the close of the century: changes in the nature of book illustration (images became more realistic, aesthetic, and easily absorbed), developments in the novel (a shift from Victorian realism to Modernism), the decline of serial fiction, rising labor costs, and influence and competition from other media (such as photojournalism and cinematography).[13] Nonetheless, "reading" illustrations as these real and fictional Victorians once did demonstrates that throughout most of the century the graphic image was an important means to convey the message of the artist, the author, and the author-illustrator. Moreover, if we conceive of illustration more inclusively, as this collection does, and see dance and theater as forms of visualization along with book illustrations, prints, and paintings, we witness an ongoing fascination with the visual and an emergence of interconnected visual art forms that explode exponentially during the electronic age.

To recall Patten's phrase, our "pictorial legacy" did not appeal simply to the uneducated or to children, although reading audiences welcomed illustrations in the growing market of mid-to-late nineteenth-century children's literature, which still carries on the tradition of the illustrated book. The wedding of literature and the visual and performing arts for an adult audience had diverse and ranging influences including the eighteenth-century (Hogarthian) tradition of graphic satire and caricature — a tradition which Cruikshank and Honoré Daumier, foremost among many others, continued in their caricatures — and the *ut pictura poesis* tradition, which became central to nineteenth-century culture. Even the intellectually sophisticated and economically advantaged reader studied "telling" details within graphic images, including clichéd gestures, theatrical allusions, popular figurines, classic portraits and paintings, and meaning-laden flowers as well as clever verbal captions (that the images often ridiculed or contradicted). As all the essays in this collection reveal, the image played a vital role in picture-word collaboration: images worked together with texts and, at times, at cross purposes with texts, creating complexities and tensions. Visual images and other forms of visualization, among other things, elaborated theme, symbolism, plot, and characterization; conveyed humor and satire; and pointed to gender confusions, political issues, and class values.

During the last three decades, the work of scholars such as Rudolf Arnheim, John Robert Harvey, Martin Meisel, W. J. T. Mitchell, J. Hillis Miller, and Wendy Steiner and the trend toward interdisciplinary studies have stimulated exploration of the relationship between the sister arts. Moreover, as Miller notes in *Illustration*, "A new branch of the interpretation of fiction has recently been opened up by the recovery, for example, of the graphic tradition to which Dickens's illustrators belonged and by the study of Dickens's novels as multi-media collaborative productions" (61).[14] This collection of eight new essays adds to this growing library of works devoted to "multi-media collaborative productions." The essays explore ideas ranging from feminism and political and social criticism to biographical investigation. They look before and beyond the nineteenth century in England and the United States, and they tap into the rich visual literacy skills of English and American readers during a span of 160 years when visualization reached previously unknown proportions. The essays are arranged chronologically to illustrate the ways visual culture evolved during the first wave of industrialization, prior to the electronic age.

In exploring developments in book illustration across the Romantic and Victorian periods and the complex interrelationship between the stage and the book arts, Jonathan Bate's essay, "Pictorial Shakespeare: Text, Stage, Illustration," makes a fitting opening to the collection. Looking back briefly to the early-eighteenth century, Bate returns us to the first illustrated edition of William Shakespeare by Nicholas Rowe (1709) to illustrate a central point: whereas a play is a dynamic performance art, an illustration of a play concentrates on but a moment in time. Bate then establishes: "It will be the argument of this essay that eighteenth- and nineteenth-century illustrations of Shakespeare, though they frequently drew from the stage tradition, took the plays into realms of experience far from the boards of the Globe. Illustration played a major role in the process whereby the Bard was novelized and historicized — a process that was itself crucial to his 'remaking' as universal genius, national and international Bard, rather than mere stage playwright" (34). His exploration features book illustration in works of Shakespeare including John Bell's 1773-74 edition (based on performance scripts, as opposed to Shakespearean texts), Alderman Boydell's 1790s edition, and Charles Knight's 1838-43 edition. Of particular interest is Bate's discussion of Boydell's Shakespeare gallery, established in the late-eighteenth century for a connoisseur market in an attempt to break from the "vulgarity" of the stage and to illustrate an "ideal" Shakespeare, according to principles of history painting. But he concludes: "A classical style is mingled with a sense of the long reach of native history in order to forge a sense of British cultural identity. Accretions of 'invented tradition' have been layered onto Shakespeare so thickly as almost to obscure the original" (43).

Bate's essay features the work of Charles Knight, a prolific and industrious Victorian publisher credited in helping to create a new class of reader by introducing cheap books and, thus, making knowledge more available to a mass market. Publisher to "The Society for the Diffusion of Useful Knowledge," Knight produced the *Penny Magazine* and numerous other popular works including illustrated histories of England, biographies of Shakespeare, and the *Pictorial Edition of the Works of Shakspere* (1838-43, later collected as the "National Edition" and the "Imperial Edition"). Focusing on the later "Imperial Edition" (1873, a more grandiose production aimed at the aspiring middle class), Bate notes how the illustrations in a popular edition geared for a mass market in some senses "novelized" and in other ways "historicized" Shakespeare paradoxically at a time when the theater was becoming more "pictorial" in its method of staging. From illustrations included in Knight's "Imperial Edition," Shakespeare emerges not as a mere playwright but an iconic genius part and parcel with Victorian imperial ambitions.

Bate's analysis raises salient questions that connect well to the issues Walter Benjamin raises in "The Work of Art in the Age of Mechanical Reproduction." The translation of Shakespeare from stage to illustration brings to light the difference Benjamin raises between the unmediated experience of a unique art — in this case performance art — versus the marketing of an authentic Shakespeare. The audience and dynamic art work supremely share the same time, space, and sound-world in the theater, but this aura cannot simply be encapsulated in a moment of time from a play depicted in a book illustration. Still, Bate's essay encourages us to question, to what extent can an edition of Shakespeare that attempts to offer an authentic rendition arguably draw some of the aura which the original stage production possesses as a unique work of art? Where lies the authentic Shakespeare in the complex relationship between stage and mass production of an original work of art? Bate's analysis fittingly raises the various negotiations and paradoxes between text, stage, and illustration across the Romantic and Victorian periods, ultimately demonstrating how illustrations often worked at cross purposes with the very books to which they were uneasily wedded.

Harkening to the discussion of stage and Romanticism raised in Bate's essay, Sarah Webster Goodwin in "Taglioni's Double Meanings: Illustration and the Romantic Ballerina" moves us to a different performance art: Romantic ballet. She principally explores illustrations of the celebrated Marie Taglioni, one of the founding dancers of Romantic ballet who graced the stages of London, Paris, and other European capitols. Noted for developing pointe technique and incorporating it into her performances, Marie Taglioni was the first dancer to demonstrate in a sustained way how a ballerina, on pointe, became ethereal. In the 1830s and 1840s, ballet became an important form of visual culture in London and Paris. Taglioni, in turn, became an international celebrity, and her image was widely publicized in the popular press.

[11]

Goodwin raises what happens when an illustrator attempts to reproduce the image of the dancer from the original stage production and thus, like Bate, recalls the ideas that Walter Benjamin raises in "The Work of Art in the Age of Mechanical Reproduction." Corresponding to Bate's discussion of the translation of a dynamic stage performance to a static illustration, Goodwin, in her exploration of Taglioni and other ballerinas depicted in *Julien's Album de L'Opéra* (1845?) and *The Exquisite* (1844), explores what happens to the authentic ballerina when her image is, as Taglioni's was, idealized, transformed, caricaturized, and marketed (through lithographs, sheet music, calling cards, paper dolls, and fans). The cult of the visual in French and British stage culture led to a rush of lithographs — mechanical reproductions — capturing the dancer in artificial landscapes. Images of the ballet made the dancer a commodity, focusing our gaze on the static or framed ballerina rather than her movement. Furthermore, the illustrations of the dancer reveal double cultural meanings that both destabilize and reinforce our conceptions about gender.

While the original art is the ballet performed in the theater, Goodwin argues that the volumes containing lithographs reproducing that original for a larger audience can also be considered "original" work, enriching our understanding of the Romantic ballerina. In this respect, Goodwin's stance is somewhat different from Bate's. She admits that the mechanical reproductions contained within these and other volumes, when removed from their bound volumes as collectors' items (as was often the case), may have little association with the authentic experience of art, as Benjamin contends. "But in tracing and interpreting some of the meanings of their original print contexts," Goodwin argues, "we open ourselves more fully to understanding some of the resonant contradictions they offer up to us" (63).

The contexts in which we find images of Taglioni become important sources to tap the complexities of cultural associations about her. Goodwin contrasts the features and illustrations of a bound edition of a twelve-month run of a weekly periodical, *The Exquisite*, directed at a male readership, to a handsome gift book of the same period, *Julien's Album de l'Opéra*, intended for a female audience and including sheet music. In doing so, she enhances our understanding of the book as an object of aesthetic pleasure (and practical use) as well as a representation of prevailing attitudes of gender. The preponderance of pink and gold and flowery decorations in *Julien's Album* reflects and contributes to our notions of feminine culture and "seems to define the female consumer's proper response to the ballet: commodify its beauty, contain its eroticism" (69). She concludes: "The ideal that is sold here in the form of the book is a fantasy of feminine power anchored in masculine desire. To be surrounded by garlands and floating tulle, to be the object of the adoring gaze, to exercise her power passively, demurely, chastely: these are the wishes that such a gift shapes and encourages" (71). Whereas soft-porn images targeted at a male audience eroticize the dancer, as Goodwin's analysis of *The Exquisite* suggests, the ballerina, through gift books like *Julien's Album*, came into the Victorian parlor and thus entered the world of respectable Victorian femininity.

While Bate's essay sweeps the Romantic and Victorian periods at the onset of industrialization, Robert L. Patten, like Goodwin, focuses his examination on a key person. Patten's biographical essay entitled "The Politics of Humor in George Cruikshank's Graphic Satire" centers on the inimitable George Cruikshank, a central figure in the book arts of the Victorian age. Patten uses the color plate entitled *Ah! Sure Such a Pair* (1820), depicting King George IV and Queen Caroline just before the queen was tried for adultery, as a point of departure to address the range of motivations

[13]

behind and influences upon Cruikshank's humor and graphic satire. Cruikshank's leading biographer takes us on a journey in search of George, prince of caricaturists, as his contemporaries called him, through the vantage point of this one compelling print and "its complex, contradictory, and perplexingly ambivalent iconography" (86).

Cruikshank's illustrations for a series of pamphlets produced by the radical publicist William Hone gave him an opportunity to engage in political warfare at home. Specifically, he attacked the political discontent of the rising middle class concerning the accession of George IV and the scandal surrounding his abortive attempt to divorce his wife Queen Caroline. The British Museum contains 565 satires dated 1820, and this 1820 design (issued in both colored and uncolored states) illuminates Cruikshank's career as well as political and social developments of the early-nineteenth century and the proliferation of political caricatures in a precedent visual culture. As Patten well reminds us in his two-volume *George Cruikshank's Life, Times, and Art* (1992 and 1996), Cruikshank was the leading political satirist of his day and the illustrator of Charles Dickens, then known as "the Cruikshank of writers." John Ruskin ranked him foremost among etchers, comparing the power of his art and his facility with etching to Rembrandt's. The Edwardians, however, considered Cruikshank second-rate, and his enormous output of single prints, caricatures, and book illustrations has never received proper curatorial attention. Cruikshank's contributions to Victorian fiction, recently reappraised, show illustration and text working together as one expressive art form. His style, modeled most notably by Hablot Knight Browne (Phiz), kept British book illustration distinct from Continental styles.

Akin to Goodwin's essay, Patten's opening discussion suggests how "original" might be applied within the context of print culture, a point that seemingly counters Benjamin's claim that "to ask for the 'authentic' print makes no sense" (224). At a time when Georgian graphic satire was being mass produced by dozens of etchers, designers, and publishers, George Cruikshank's graphic satires "developed brand-name identification, attracted copyists and plagiarists, and on occasions created a market demand for 'originals' printed from his etched plate that numbered upwards of 500 or more" (83), according to Patten. While reduced facsimiles lack the artist's touch, it is more likely the personal vision of the artist that marks an image with the artist's identity. Thus, finding the artist within the image is relatively easy in the case of Rowlandson or Gillray, but such is not the case, Patten argues, with George Cruikshank, who could satirize both sides of controversial political events and "issue devastating graphic satires for and against his best friend within the same week" (84).

At the outset of his examination of this seminal plate, Patten contemplates: "Where in this tangled story of royal infidelity and political expedience can Cruikshank's *own* opinions be located? What aspects of the imagery and fictions he deployed are *his*, not inherited from others or imposed by circumstances or his printseller patrons or reinforced by the sales of a particular strain of images?" (88) He ultimately locates this prolific caricaturist and illustrator whose popular imagery captured the essence of his time "as the artist who finds much to be said on both sides" (109). Cruikshank was only twenty-eight when he produced this plate; he was not yet married (though he did marry twice), and his parents, who quarreled, never separated. "Yet somehow," Patten ultimately concludes in his Coda, "drawing on the experiences and figurations of others and applying his own quirky line, keen eye, and assimilative sense of humor — hallmarks of a Cruikshank 'original' — the artist represented domestic discord as it might appear not just in high places, but everywhere" (112).

In reading the "layers of communication" (84) in Cruikshank's compelling print, Patten illuminates the origins of Cruikshank's caricature art, his treatment of gender, and his "subversive freedom of etching contradictions into the copperplate" (109), uncovering the complexity of an artist whose "politics can only be sought by looking for them not on one side, but on both, or many, sides" (109). But his claims are important not only to an understanding of the larger oeuvre of a leading Victorian book illustrator who was a household name by the mid-nineteenth century, but to this collection as a whole. Patten calls attention to central themes running across various essays — governing class values, gender conceptions and confusions, and theatrical allusions — ultimately to make an argument for the complexity of the role images play in modern culture: "our twentieth-century love-affair with print culture has effaced ways in which a precedent visual culture could conduct complex, persuasive arguments reaching deep into the collective psyche, using pictures only, or a combination of picture and text" (110).

To elevate the complexities of the book arts designed for a precedent visual culture, while continuing the focus on Cruikshank's art which Patten initiates, my essay entitled "Cruikshank's Illustrative Wrinkle in *Oliver Twist's* Misrepresentation of Class" explores the book illustrations for which Cruikshank is best known. A tension arises in the combination of picture and text that "wrinkles" Dickens's intentions in presenting governing class values. Analogous to Goodwin's and Patten's responses to Walter Benjamin's ideas, I argue that a nineteenth-century illustrated book designed during an age of mechanical reproduction can possess an aura, to recall Walter Benjamin's term, especially when compared to digital reproductions of the mass media age. Book illustrations were of consequence to Victorian reader-viewers. In inviting us to reexamine the contributions of its dual dueling creators, *Oliver*

Twist or *The Parish Boy's Progress* with George Cruikshank's "original" illustrations rekindles the creative collaboration between an artist and an author who quarreled over sovereignty and struggled to maintain their autonomy even while working within the realm of commercial publishing. As I advance: "The occasional opposition between text and illustration in *Oliver Twist* no doubt stems from the individualistic personalities of an author who wanted the upper hand with his illustrators and an artist who increasingly demanded autonomy as the illustrated novel progressed and became a commercial success" (141).

Oliver Twist first appeared serially in *Bentley's Miscellany*, a testimony to the fluid relationship between the periodical press and the book arts in the nineteenth century; serialization brought forth some of the best literature of the age.[15] I focus on the book version of *Oliver Twist*, which was printed in three volumes before it finished its serial run in *Bentley's Miscellany*. But the publication history preceding the issuing of the novel is of consequence: for two years, Cruikshank and Dickens battled to meet monthly deadlines (while both were working on other projects) and sparred over what images to include (e.g., the "Fireside" plate) or what scenes to depict (e.g., Cruikshank mightily ignored Dickens's guidance not to depict Sikes's demise). The essay records the tensions arising between the sister arts and ultimately demonstrates the ability of illustration to subvert its accompanying narrative and its political purpose.

Typical of Dickens's early works, *Oliver Twist* demonstrates Dickens's descriptive prose style that readily evokes visualization and so easily accommodates pictures as an integral part of the serial. *Twist* reveals Dickens's sympathetic treatment of thieves, prostitutes, and other outcasts; his commitment to improve the lives of unprotected, innocent children; his empathy for the afflicted; and his indignation against hypocrisy. But the work also reflects the self-contradictory yet mutually reinforcing attitudes of the middle class toward the lower class in its portrayal of lower-class life. Written early in Dickens's career, *Oliver Twist* dates to a time when the new class society was still evolving. As I argue, "Dickens inscribes documentable accuracy in the settings, behavior, and transactions among criminals, yet he retains an older attitude of contempt for the criminal element, particularly vicious Bill Sikes. In addition, at points Dickens distorts social reality not by estranging or vilifying, but by remaking the dominated class in the dominant class's own image" (119). Cruikshank's caricature illustrations of Sikes, for example, mirror Dickens's reactionary view of extreme villainy. Cruikshank also extends this view to his portrayals of Fagin and Nancy, whom Dickens misconstrues as more middle class. The ensuing opposition between text and image, appearing in certain plates depicting Fagin and Nancy, creates what I call an illustrative (and perhaps dialectical) "wrinkle." Such a tension amplifies Dickens's own authorial oscillation between two middle-class attitudes — one older, more reactionary view of contempt; one newly emerging, more philanthropically acceptable view preferable to the rising middle class, precariously applied to the preface and text of the novel.

The next two essays examine the illustrated book as an art object. In "Rossetti and the Art of the Book," Elizabeth Helsinger explores an aspect of this gifted Pre-Raphaelite poet-painter that looks beyond our knowledge of his sonnets "for a painting" and his monumental canvases of goddesses, dominated by the visage of Jane Morris, as Rossetti perceived her to be. She turns us, rather, to Rossetti's presentation of books, specifically his designs for bindings, frontispieces, title pages, end-papers, and other aspects of the visible form in which Victorians encountered contemporary poetry. Helsinger contends, "His published work is not adequately described as an art of words or of images or even of the two together: it is an art of the book" (147). Moreover, Rossetti defended his role as a creative artist even while he worked with commercial printers, binders, and publishers. He conceived the task of composing and printing a book as a process that involved the contributions of many hands — close friends in his artistic cir- cle, family members, printer, designer, and author. Rossetti attended to the particulars of the presentation of a book in its entirety — including the selection and arrangement of the con- tents, end-papers, binding, title pages, and illustrations. His artis- tic practice in the 1860s and his conception of "the book as a total work of art" (171) leads us to see fruitful connections between the aesthetic and the market that fuels our very appetites for art; like- wise, his artistic practice obscures the distinctions between "fine" art versus decorative, "commercial" art, produced for sale and domestic use, as well as the distinctions Benjamin draws between original art and mechanical reproduction.

Helsinger reexamines Rossetti's contributions to book design and picture framing in relation to changing Victorian attitudes towards artists and art objects, which Rossetti actively challenged and attempted to redefine. She argues that while Rossetti's few engravings for books have been appreciated as innovative and influential examples of design, they might also be explored as a reflection of his own interest in books and pictures as decorative craft objects in Victorian interiors, including his own home. His designs on bindings and picture frames — more often treated as specialized areas — are part of Rossetti's art, as Alastair Grieve's pioneering work has suggested. The decorative aspects of Rossetti's own work peaked during the decade when he was gathering and arranging furnishings for Tudor House. In the 1860s, Rossetti worked closely with publications for friends and family members — for example, he provided illustrations for sister Christina Ros- setti's *Goblin Market* (1862) — and this involvement culminated in the creation of *Poems* (1870), his first collection. Though *Poems* is not illustrated, "the line between poetic composition of a verbally satisfying work and the crafting of the book as a physical object is blurred in a fascinating way" (172). Helsinger argues that Rossetti's attention to every detail of the printing and publication of this work reveals his combined interests in domestic decoration, collecting, and book design, themes which resonate in the structuring trope of the major sonnet sequence of the collection, "The House of Life."

Much as Patten argues that Cruikshank's caricature art forces us to rethink our conceptions of the visual culture of the early-nineteenth century, Helsinger advances that Rossetti's art of the book in the 1860s — whether, to recall Benjamin, we conceive of it as an original artifact, as Rossetti would have, or a mechanical reproduction — "forces us to expand our ideas of what constitutes the work of art by embodying poems and pictures in material, historical forms that are the product of an extended social process. His books are collections in which he combines and oversees the work of poet, editor, designer, printer, and publisher" (185). Rossetti never underestimated the power and importance of the physical form of the book for the author or the buyer, and his book designs in the 1860s "attempt to embody in the bound and printed book something of the 'magical' effect" (169) his contemporaries heard when Rossetti read his poems aloud. Recalling the ideas of Benjamin, Helsinger aptly concludes: "Working already well within an age of mechanical reproduction, Rossetti finds a way to imbue his poetic objects with the kind of aura that neither craft nor commercial manufacture — and his books participate in aspects of both — is supposed to allow" (185).

James Heffernan continues Helsinger's aim to revise the ways we conceive of Victorian book illustration and augments the complexity of a field that has for too long been considered a "step-child" art. Aubrey Beardsley's riotously ornamented late-century illustrations might well, to recall Benjamin, be considered "original" artifacts. "Love, Death, and Grotesquerie: Beardsley's Illustrations of Wilde and Pope" offers a comparative reading of Oscar Wilde's *Salome* and Alexander Pope's *The Rape of the Lock,* texts that initially strike us as too dissimilar to compare. Both works, however, were illustrated in the 1890s by Aubrey Beardsley. "To view them side by side through Beardsley's eyes," Heffernan argues, "is to see not only what specific features they share but also how each of them represents the ambivalence of its heroine and the kinds of destruction generated by desire" (198).

As was the case with *Oliver Twist,* the play *Salome* — with nine drawings, including one sensational image by the precociously gifted twenty-one-year-old artist — first appeared in a periodical, *The Studio.* In April 1893, the London magazine formally introduced Beardsley as a new illustrator in its inaugural issue in an article written by Joseph Pennell. To recall Martin Meisel's distinctions between "illustration" and "realization," *Salome* radically revised the conception of a play as something to be "realized" on stage, as Bate treats the play in his essay: the publication of the script of *Salome* preceded the actual staging of the play by some three years. Heffernan notes that Beardsley in his drawing of "Salome with St. John's Head" thus depicted "a moment in the play that could never be visually 'realized' on stage because it is too grotesque to be seen; the stage directions call for total darkness" (196). Wilde then commissioned Beardsley to illustrate the first English edition of *Salome* — the focus of Heffernan's analysis; however, Wilde, in turn, complained that the illustrations hardly suited his work.

In illustrating Wilde and Pope with his startlingly original yet dangerously decadent illustrations, Beardsley thus took command of the pictures. Different from the Dickens and Cruikshank

[21]

collaboration of the 1830s that I explore in my essay, Beardsley did not work in close collaboration with the author but rather received the completed work and, thus, became its first interpreter or critic. Beardsley conveys this artistic independence in his illustrations for *Salome* and *The Rape of the Lock* in reading, as Heffernan contends, "not only the text but the life of its author: something unprecedented, so far as I know, in illustrated books before the nineties" (196). Beardsley's unmistakable style leaves an indelible mark on the texts of Wilde and Pope. While on the one hand Heffernan notes that Beardsley's style "seems not so much to serve the text as to appropriate it for its own idiosyncratic ends" (197), he advances that Beardsley's graphically self-indulgent illustrations for *Salome* offer a provocative gloss on Wilde's play, and his richly ornamented Art Nouveau illustrations for Pope's Augustan mock-epic, nonetheless, reach the core of Pope's poem.

Equally, as Heffernan points out, Beardsley, in his fascination with the grotesque and in his creation of text-affronting images, radically revised the conventions of book illustration in the late-nineteenth century by disrupting the rules of decorum. Beardsley's depiction of Salome kissing the severed head of John the Baptist illustrates this very point. The image of "Salome with St. John's Head" made visible the very last words that Wilde's necrophilic heroine utters in the play on a darkened set lit only by a shaft of moonlight. This image makes a striking contrast to William Holman Hunt's *Isabella and the Pot of Basil* (1867), which refrains from showing Lorenzo's severed head; however, a closer examination reveals that Wilde and Beardsley, in essence, expose the latent possibilities of grotesque eroticism evident in Hunt's work. In Beardsley's depictions of *The Rape of the Lock*, the act of cutting the lock becomes "an assault on the head — a form of decapitation" (211). The pair of scissors, an icon Beardsley foregrounds in the front cover design for the 1896 edition he illustrated, appears as an ominous assault weapon. Simply put, Beardsley's fin-de-siècle depictions of Wilde's play and Pope's poem convey that "we can never escape the grotesque" (233). Despite the dialogue engendered between Pope's and Wilde's texts and Beardsley's illustrations for each of them, Beardsley's work fittingly stands at a crossroads in the book arts in pushing the limits of collaboration between the sister arts at a time well into the age of mechanical reproduction. Heffernan's discussion encourages us to ponder whether Beardsley's late-century illustrations might be to blame, in part, for the eventual dropping away of illustration from adult literature, which occurs by century's end; illustration becomes more commonly associated with children's literature, as Ruth Copans's essay reveals.

Moving our discussion of illustration firmly into the twentieth century, Ruth Copans examines the potential for women to become visual artists in her essay entitled "Dream Blocks: American Women Illustrators of the Golden Age, 1890-1920." Whereas Golden's and Patten's essays concentrate on Cruikshank, and Heffernan's and Helsinger's also examine male artist-illustrators, Copans's essay speaks to a still neglected area in the history of the illustrated book and responds to issues of gender, raised by Goodwin. Copans laments that book illustrations for children's and women's texts designed by women artists including Jessie Willcox Smith have been relegated to calendars, not museums. Many collections offer but few fine representations of book illustration by women artists, yet the rise of women illustrators is central to book illustration in Victorian Britain and America. As Copans notes, "Clever at interpreting the commercial demands of the day and in responding to the pragmatic requirements of self-sufficiency, many of these women, despite their financial and artistic success, have again sunk into obscurity" (245). She argues in her essay that we need to reevaluate the illustrations produced by women artists during the golden age of illustration.

[23]

Copans initially explores how book illustration became one profession that formed a natural extension of a woman's domestic role. The proliferation of illustrated books and, in particular, magazines for women and children created a niche for women illustrators, who focused primarily on the themes of family and domestic life as well as romance and sentimental tales. Ironically, the changes in mechanical reproduction in the field of illustration that Benjamin laments actually fueled the market for illustrated books and magazines, creating a demand for women artists (who were welcomed also, in part, given the low status of illustration in the hierarchies of art). Numerous women artists came forward in the field of the book arts at the turn of the century, giving us access to visions of motherhood and childhood not previously represented. Although art education for women was not easily available in the nineteenth century, when Howard Pyle began to teach at Drexel Institute in 1894, women were among his students.

Copans discusses the most successful women illustrators who studied with Pyle: Jessie Willcox Smith, Elizabeth Shippen Green, and Charlotte Harding. She argues that other women illustrators, such as Alice Barber Stephens — considered a pioneer among American woman illustrators — and Violet Oakley, whose reputation rests on her murals, also played an important role in establishing illustration as a viable profession for women. Like Dante Gabriel Rossetti, many of these women recognized the importance of having an artistic circle: Oakley, Green, and Smith, for example, lived and worked together for fourteen years, and their work thrived in the supportive environment they created. Copans explores the lives of these women artists, the artistic friendships they formed, and the richness of their art, which, more than charming, cannot simply be dismissed as a "feminine" approach to illustration, as it was often admired in its day.

[24]

Primary materials are central to Copans's essay, which draws on archives from the Delaware Art Museum, the Pennsylvania Academy of Art, the Free Library of Philadelphia, and Drexel University. Although Copans agrees that — due to the neglect of the woman illustrator — we cannot readily find the voice of Stephens, Harding, Green, Oakley, and Smith, we can begin to find that voice by examining their lives, correspondence, and achievements in the book arts. Although these women artists also contributed illustrations to periodicals such as *Harper's* and *Scribner's*, Copans focuses her attention on their book illustrations for authors including Louisa May Alcott, Charles Kingsley, George MacDonald, Robert Louis Stevenson, and Kate Douglas Wiggin. Citing the cover Jessie Willcox Smith designed for Aileen C. Higgins's *Dream Blocks* (1908) as emblematic of both the persona of these women artists and the struggles they faced, she concludes: "Until the proliferation of magazines for women became an economic factor, women were blocked from achieving professional status in such fields as illustration. Finally, economic independence through dignified and profitable professional work was slow in coming to women and must, for a long time, to have seemed a dream, similar to the castle in the sky we see the day-dreaming child building with his blocks. The art produced by these women speaks eloquently of their talent, vision, hard work, and success, and they deserve to be remembered as more than a footnote in American illustration's golden age" (273). Her biographical essay emphasizes the talent of these American women illustrators, their vision, and their success.

The final essay by David Porter moves us from an examination of book illustrations by female and male artists back to the larger production of illustrated books, primarily from 1917 to 1927. In "'We All Sit on the Edge of Stools and Crack Jokes': Virginia Woolf and the Hogarth Press," Porter departs from previous accounts of the Hogarth Press in looking at Leonard and Virginia Woolf's own involvement in the production of books, especially those produced, often by hand, in the first few years. Porter first offers a brief history of how, in 1917, the Woolfs came to purchase a small hand printing press from a shop in Farringdon Road, then set it up in the dining room at their Richmond home, Hogarth House, after which the Press is named. At least one of the reasons for the purchase (its "original use value," to harken back to Benjamin) was the hope that the rote, even physical labor, involved in setting type, printing books, and assembling books would provide a beneficial change for Virginia Woolf from the intensity of writing, rewriting, and reading proof, activities which, at times, precipitated severe emotional swings. Between 1917 and 1927, the Press's first decade, the numbers document an ever-accelerating level of activity. Porter notes that "This 'Press of Her Own,' as we might call it, brought her [Virginia] a rare and valued degree of artistic freedom" (300).

Consonant with the aim of this collection to emphasize the significance of preserving primary records, Porter focuses his essay on the ways the Woolfs actively involved themselves in the art of book production at a time when this process was becoming mass produced and increasingly losing its connection to "art," as Benjamin conceived it. The Woolfs' stature as artists affects our sense of their books as artifacts and returns us to the problem of defining an original artifact: might their editorial comments as well as their bindings and dust jackets have an aura in Benjamin's sense?

Similar to Helsinger's exploration of Rossetti's involvement in the art of book production, Porter explores the labels and papers the Woolfs used, their use of woodcuts (e.g., Dora Carrington provided illustrations for *Two Stories*), and their involvement in the creation of entire texts, such as Hope Mirrlees's *Paris. A Poem.* Unlike Rossetti in this respect — the Woolfs, and particularly

Leonard, did not make full use of the help others offered them. Both were passionately involved: Leonard Woolf managed the Hogarth Press and was attentive to its minute operational details, while Virginia — recalling Rossetti's involvement in the creation of the book in its entirety — took part in virtually every aspect of book production from reading manuscripts, to typesetting and proofreading, to stitching the covers, and wrapping and mailing copies to purchasers. Porter points out that the books the Woolfs produced — in their inclusion of woodblock illustrations, line drawings, and photographic illustrations; but, more importantly, in the dust jackets they commissioned, and covers and labels they created for the smaller publications — fulfilled an intention Virginia expressed in a letter to Dora Carrington: "'we see that we must make a practice of always having pictures'" (282). Like Rossetti, the Woolfs recognized the importance of the physical form of the book, that the book's cover, in particular, would heighten its impact. Porter gives particular emphasis to book jackets, reproduced in color in this collection rather than black-and-white (as has been the custom). He examines, in addition, variations in cover designs of the earlier books as he offers insights into the ways the Woolfs put books together, noting, for example: Virginia Woolf's meticulous correction of misprints in Hope Mirrlees's *Paris: A Poem* in her characteristic purple ink; her binding of that same book in a distinct paper that Virginia also used for binding the notebook in which she wrote an early draft of the first portion of *Jacob's Room*; and the amusing, poignant, derisive, and penetrating comments that Virginia and Leonard Woolf made about the authors whose works they published.

Visualizations — conceived here as illustrations of plays, ballets, and novels as well as book bindings, dust jackets, book labels, and independent prints and frames — emerge as central to each essay in this collection examining text, image, and culture from

1770 to 1930. Reading the collection as a whole, the reader will traverse continents, artistic styles, literary periods, and genres and explore political satire, gender, social class, book illustration, painting, theater, and dance. The reader's journey will trace works by prominent male (e.g., Cruikshank) and still neglected female (e.g., Shippen Green) illustrators as well as noncanonical and enduring canonical works by, for example, Shakespeare, Dickens, and Woolf. Readers of this collection need to "read" the visual images accompanying each essay as avidly as their fictional Victorian sisters Jane Eyre and Maggie Tulliver. It is my hope that this collection will not only rekindle an examination of the pictorial legacy of the first wave of industrialization but spark further exploration of images and texts in late-eighteenth- through early-twentieth-century contexts. The essays collectively enable us to see how Western European and American culture was primed for radio, television, and the Internet but equally to appreciate and even lament the increasing alienation from the aura of original art, to recall Walter Benjamin, as new technologies of the visual have steadily evolved from the 1930s onward. Pointing to the evolving primacy of the visual in Western European and American culture from 1770 to 1930, these essays speak to the importance of keeping alive primary materials and recognizing the value of the artifact as a medium of important cultural meaning for scholarship and teaching.

Introduction

Notes

1. See Walter Benjamin, "The Work of Art in the Age of Mechanical Reproduction" in *Illuminations*, edited with an introduction by Hannah Arendt and translated by Harry Zohn (New York: Schocken Books, 1976), 217-51. Subsequent references to this work are cited parenthetically within the text. The scholars of this collection who refer to Benjamin's complex argument largely respond to his notions of aura and originality, not to his claim that a work of art reproduced for mechanical reproduction began to serve a covert socio-political purpose.
2. Robert Scholes, *The Rise and Fall of English: Reconstructing English as a Discipline* (New Haven and London: Yale University Press, 1998), 164. Subsequent references are cited parenthetically within the text.
3. Modern Language Association of America, "Statement on the Significance of Primary Records," *Profession 95* (1995): 28.
4. J. Hillis Miller, *Illustration* (Cambridge: Cambridge University Press, 1992), 61. Further references are cited parenthetically within the text.
5. Martin Meisel, *Realizations: Narrative, Pictorial, and Theatrical Arts in Nineteenth-Century England* (Princeton, N.J.: Princeton University Press, 1983), 3. Subsequent references to this work are cited parenthetically within the text.
6. Charlotte Brontë, *Jane Eyre*, edited by Richard J. Dunn (New York and London: W. W. Norton & Company, 1987), 5. Subsequent references to this work are cited parenthetically within the text.
7. George Eliot, *The Mill on the Floss*, edited with an introduction by Gordon S. Haight (Oxford: Oxford University Press, 1980), 16. Subsequent references to this work are cited parenthetically within the text.
8. Lewis Carroll, *The Annotated Alice*, with an introduction and notes by Martin Gardner (New York: New American Library, 1960), 25.
9. Lewis Carroll, *Alice's Adventures Under Ground*, with an introduction by Martin Gardner (New York: Dover Publications, 1965), 78.

10. See Robert L. Patten, *George Cruikshank's Life, Times, and Art*, Volume 2: 1835-1878 (New Brunswick, N.J.: Rutgers University Press, 1996), 56. Subsequent references to this work are cited parenthetically within the text.

11. See Henry James, *A Small Boy and Others* (New York: Charles Scribner's Sons, 1914), 119-20. James's privileging of Cruikshank's art over Dickens's is widely quoted; see, for example, J. Hillis Miller in *Illustration*, 70.

12. George Du Maurier, "The Illustrating of Books From the Serious Artist's Point of View," *Magazine of Art* (August-September 1890): 350.

13. For further discussion of the decline of illustrated fiction, see Jane R. Cohen, *Charles Dickens and His Original Illustrators* (Columbus, OH: Ohio State University Press, 1980), 230-32. Though her discussion is focused on Dickens's novels, it offers insight into the decline of Victorian illustrated fiction.

14. Dickens's illustrations have been explored more than those of other writers. See, for example, Jane R. Cohen, *Charles Dickens and His Original Illustrators*; Michael Steig, *Dickens and Phiz* (Bloomington, Ind.: Indiana University Press, 1978); Robert L. Patten, "Boz, Phiz, and Pickwick in the Pound," *Journal of English Literary History* 36 (September, 1969): 575-91; John Robert Harvey, *Victorian Novelists and Their Illustrators* (New Haven and London: Sidgwick & Jackson, 1970).

15. *Oliver Twist* appeared in *Bentley's Miscellany* from February 1837 to April 1839 (omitting June 1837, October 1837, and September 1838). *Master Humphrey's Clock* is a weekly periodical written wholly by Dickens to carry installments of his full-length novels *The Old Curiosity Shop* (1840-41) and *Barnaby Rudge* (1841). In 1859, *A Tale of Two Cities* appeared in Dickens's magazine *All the Year Round*. Other of Dickens's works, like *David Copperfield* (1850), *Bleak House* (1853), and *Our Mutual Friend* (1865), were published in monthly parts as was William Thackeray's *Vanity Fair* (1848).

Pictorial Shakespeare:
Text, Stage, Illustration

Jonathan Bate

The only illustration to the 1623 First Folio of Shakespeare is the famous frontispiece: Martin Droeshout's woodcut of the author, his forehead domed like the Globe, as if in allusion to the name of his theater and the universality of his genius. But once Shakespeare began to be edited and packaged for the burgeoning book market of the eighteenth century, the texts themselves began to be illustrated.

A paradigm was established by the dramatist Nicholas Rowe, in his six-volume edition of Shakespeare's plays, published in 1709. Here, each individual work was "Adorn'd with cuts" in the form of copperplate frontispieces that visualized a key scene. These illustrations were predominantly shaped by painterly traditions — baroque classicism in particular — but a handful of them incorporated details garnered from celebrated stage productions. Most notably, the *Hamlet* frontispiece (fig. 1), which illustrates the closet scene, places a knocked-over chair prominently in the foreground, whilst the figure of Hamlet has one garter loose and a

Figure 1.
Frontispiece to *Hamlet* from Nicholas Rowe's 1709 edition,
copperplate engraving, courtesy of British Library.

[32]

stocking half-down. Thomas Betterton, the most renowned Shakespearean actor of the Restoration, used to appear as Hamlet in accordance with Ophelia's description, "his stockings fouled, / Ungartered, and down-gyvèd to his ankle,"[1] and as a dramatic sign of his discomposure upon the ghost's reappearance in Gertrude's chamber, he always knocked over a chair, a piece of stage business so admired that several generations of subsequent stage Hamlets were expected to replicate it.

When translated from stage to page, the image of the over-turned chair changes in meaning. On stage, the key thing is the act of knocking it over — the effect is dynamic, symbolic of the sudden charge introduced by the ghostly apparition and the flurry of emotional intensity which results. In the illustration, what counts is not the action but the shape of the composition. The empty chair lies across the bottom of the picture, forming the base line of a triangle which points upward, via the symmetrically placed figures of Hamlet and the ghost, to a portrait of Old Hamlet which forms the apex of the image, above the central figure of Gertrude. The chair she sits in is like a throne, while her late husband, in both the portrait on the wall and in the hand of his ghostly form, bears a sceptre. Once the viewer pauses to take in these connections, then Betterton's overturned bedroom chair begins to look like an empty throne, out of which the rightful king has been unceremoniously turfed. The question at the center of the image thus becomes "how much responsibility for Old Hamlet's death is borne by Gertrude?"

An illustration of a dramatic text is a peculiar thing. It makes meaning by freezing a single moment, whereas the unstoppable motion of time, the piling of action upon action upon reaction, is the very essence of drama. Statuesque though the pace of Betterton's performance would have been if judged by modern standards, in his theater there would have been no time to pause upon the symbolic meaning of the fallen chair — the eye would soon have been drawn to the body of Polonius falling from behind the arras. By arresting the moment, the act of illustration absorbs the play through the eye of the beholder into the dimension of imaginative interiority. *Hamlet* is a play, not a novel; but an illustration of a moment in *Hamlet* is formally no different from an illustration of a moment in a novel. It will be the argument of this essay that eighteenth- and nineteenth-century illustrations of Shakespeare, though they frequently drew from the stage tradition, took the plays into realms of experience far from the boards of the Globe. Illustration played a major role in the process whereby the Bard was novelized and historicized — a process that was itself crucial to his "remaking" as universal genius, national and international Bard, rather than mere stage playwright.[2]

By the middle of the eighteenth century, Shakespeare was being given what may be described as a "French" treatment. The 1740 edition of Lewis Theobald's text included frontispieces to all the plays by Hubert Gravelot, a pupil of François Boucher. Gravelot brought to English literary book illustration the rococo style characteristic of editions of Racine and Molière. Four years later, Thomas Hanmer's handsome Oxford edition appeared in a larger format (quarto as opposed to Theobald's duodecimo) and with higher-quality engraved frontispieces, some by Gravelot and others by Francis Hayman, an artist who played a key role in the visualization of Shakespeare both inside and outside the theater — on the one hand, he was a scene-painter at Drury Lane, while on the other, he undertook four large historical paintings of scenes from the plays for display in the Prince of Wales's pavilion in the Vauxhall pleasure gardens.[3] Hanmer's preface was explicit about the importance of quality illustration of the national Bard: "Since therefore other nations have taken care to dignify the works of their most celebrated Poets with the fairest impressions beautiful with the ornaments of Sculpture, well may our Shakespeare be thought to deserve no less consideration."[4] Having been edited and annotated like a classical author, Shakespeare now had to be illustrated like one. Only then could "our" British Shakespeare be made to rival the French classics, those epitomes of high art and hence of national cultural sophistication. Frenchified illustration of the English Bard helped answer the strictures of Voltaire and others, who at this time were mocking Shakespeare's plays for their lack of classical decorum.

An expensive edition such as Hanmer's was meant for a gentleman's library. It was a book to be read at leisure, and to be displayed and admired. Its illustrations were painterly, while its text and annotation were literary. It had little to offer the theatergoer. There was, however, an alternative tradition of eighteenth-century Shakespeare volumes: low cost, designed for sale in the theater or by pedlars, poorly produced and small format, aimed at the "popular" as opposed to the "gentle" end of the market. The texts printed in these volumes often took the form of the plays as they were performed in the contemporary theater, rather than as they were written by Shakespeare.

In the 1770s, then, we find two very different kinds of edition. The gentlemanly and scholarly tradition is epitomized by a set published in 1778, *The Plays of William Shakespeare. In Ten Volumes. With the Corrections and Illustrations of Various Commentators; to which are added Notes by Samuel Johnson and George Steevens. The Second Edition, Revised and Augmented.* "Illustrations" here means textual and glossarial notes. The sparse visual accompaniments to the edition are confined to the ample preliminary matter in the first volume: a reproduction of the Droeshout frontispiece to the First Folio, a cut based on a drawing of the Globe theater (taken from "the long Antwerp View of London in the Pepysian Library"), and a fold-out facsimile of the signatures

[35]

appended to Shakespeare's will. The clear aim of the whole project, from both its textual principles to its supporting scholarly apparatus, is the historical reconstruction of Shakespearean originals.[5]

Contrast this with an eight-volume production of 1773-74, *Bell's Edition of Shakespeares Plays, As they are now performed at the Theatres Royal in London; Regulated from the Prompt Books of each House By Permission; with Notes Critical and Illustrative; by the Authors of the Dramatic Censor*. Whereas editors such as Edward Capell and George Steevens had set about restoring Shakespeare's original text of, say, *King Lear* and *Romeo and Juliet*, by means of a scrupulous comparison of Folio and Quarto variants, Francis Gentleman, who was mainly responsible for the introductions and notes in Bell's edition, pronounced with confidence that he was presenting the public with, in the case of *King Lear*, a "judicious blending" (as performed at Drury Lane) of the Shakespearean original and Nahum Tate's rewrite with a happy ending. And with regard to *Romeo and Juliet*, Gentleman writes, "There have been many alterations of this play, but we make no scruple to pronounce Mr *Garrick's*, which we here present the public, to be the best."[6] The printed text reproduces Garrick's many alterations to the play, including his major revision of the ending, whereby Juliet awakes just *before* Romeo's death, allowing for a brief and passionate reunion before the final severance of death. A footnote commends the innovation:

> The waking of *Juliet* before *Romeo's* death is exceedingly judicious; it gives an opportunity of working the pathos to its tenderest pitch, and shows a very fine picture, if the performers strike out just and graceful attitudes. What Mr GARRICK has wrote of this scene, does him and the stage great credit, as it affords a fine and extensive scope for capital powers.[7]

[36]

It is notable here how the stage is compared to a "picture" and acting to the striking of graceful "attitudes" analogous to those adopted in portraiture. The picture-frame stage of the proscenium arch and the attitudinizing style of acting were in their way as substantial "revisions" of the original Shakespearean stage — with its bare thrust platform and fluid pace of acting — as were the textual alterations that characterized the eighteenth-century theatrical tradition.

Given the greater resemblance suggested here between the impression created by a painting and the style of the eighteenth-century — as opposed to the Shakespearean — theater, there is a certain rightness about the inclusion in Bell's edition of an engraved frontispiece for each play, evocative of a moment in the performed text. That for *King Lear*, captioned "Thou art the thing itself / —— Off, off, you lendings," shows Lear, the disguised Kent and Poor Tom outside the hovel in the storm (fig. 2). In the original Shakespearean text there are four characters on stage at this moment: it is the Fool who first goes into the hovel and is scared out again by the presence of Tom. Lear says to Tom, "here's three on's are sophisticated! Thou art the thing itself; unaccommodated man is no more but such a poor, bare, forked animal as thou art. Off, off, you lendings! Come unbutton here."[8] But Nahum Tate had cut the Fool from the play altogether, deeming his presence indecorous to tragedy (he was not restored to the stage until William Charles Macready's production of 1838), so the text in Bell's edition has "here's two of us are sophisticated,"[9] and the illustration accordingly leaves out the Fool.

Here, then, we have an illustration which is closer to "stage Shakespeare" than "text Shakespeare." But it still offers a very different experience from that of the stage. The theatrical impression at this moment would have been dominated by the *sound* of the storm — the thunder-sheet in the wings — whereas the illustration

Figure 2.
Frontispiece to *King Lear*, painted by E. Edwards,
engraved by J. Hall, from John Bell's 1774
"theatrical" edition, copperplate engraving.

offers an *image* of the storm in the form of the zigzag of lightning. The technology of copperplate engraving is eminently suited to the visual effect: cloud is represented by a honeycomb of black and white, which is split apart by the thick white line of the lightning. In the theater, on the other hand, it is only in the age of electricity that lightning can be mimicked: in both Shakespeare's theater and Garrick's, it was the sound-effect that was all important. That would have been true at the level of verbal mimesis as well as stage-effect: Lear's "Rumble thy bellyful!" (3.2.13) is written to be spoken like a deep thunder from within.

The point alerts us to something peculiar about live performance: it offers a place where artwork and audience share not only a spatial and temporal experience, but a sound-world.[10] Books and paintings are alike in that they have no sound-worlds. Plays, operas, and ballets are special because they appeal to the ear as well as the eye. They approximate to the Wagernian *Gesamtkunstwerke*. Their sensual totality, combined with their temporal immediacy, gives them what Walter Benjamin termed an "aura."[11] They are *experienced*, participated in, rather than reflected upon. They live on the edge of risk — a "retake," a painting-over, or a revised edition are not options in the event of error. And for all these reasons, they are unreproducible. Anyone who has been in a theater audience and then later seen a video recording of the production will know that the event and the reproduction are very different experiences.

Bell's edition made unusual efforts to give the reader something of the experience of the theater. In 1775-76, that is to say in the two-year period following the completion of the text,[12] Bell issued a series of thirty-six Dramatic Character plates, one for each play. Where the original frontispieces illustrated moments of interaction in a scenic background, these offered full-length portraits of contemporary actors and actresses against a blank background.

[39]

They were available for individual purchasers either to keep as a discrete collection — rather in the manner of cigarette cards of baseball players in a later time — or to bind into their edition, at relevant moments in each play. Each image was captioned so as to associate it with a particular moment, as had been the case with the "scene" plates, but the style of the images belongs more to the studio than the stage.

Consider "Mr Shuter in the Character of Falstaff" (fig. 3).[13] Though meant for *Henry IV Part Two*, act five scene eight (the rejection scene), and subtitled with the line "My King, my Jove, I

Figure 3
"Mr. Shuter in the Character of Falstaff," by J. Parkinson, from John Bell's *Dramatic Character Plates*, copperplate engraving, 1776.

speak to thee my Heart," this could really be Falstaff at any moment in either part of the play. The image is of interest to theatrical historians for what it shows us about the look of an eighteenth-century actor, about stage gesture and costume, but its principal effect is to make Falstaff into a self-contained character, to take him out of his plays and transform him into an iconic figure. It is an approach commensurate with Maurice Morgann's near-contemporaneous *Essay on the Dramatic Character of Sir John Falstaff*, which attempts to vindicate the fat knight from the charge of cowardice by considering his whole life-story, every bit as much as if he were a person in real life or at the very least a character in a novel. A generation later, Charles Lamb's friend Jem White would be penning a set of imaginary *Letters from Sir John Falstaff*. And a couple of generations after that, Mary Cowden Clarke, the wife of Keats's schoolmaster, would novelize the major plays still more comprehensively in a book called *The Girlhood of Shakespeare's Heroines*.

A parallel development to that which gave imaginary past histories to individual Shakespearean characters — the process I have called "novelization" — was that which reimagined the plays in terms of the traditions of "history painting." For Shakespeare to be elevated to the status of a "classic," he had to be not only edited but also painted as the classics were. Painters such as Nicolas Poussin remained immensely admired throughout the eighteenth century for their large canvases portraying scenes from classical history and myth. Biblical material continued to be given similar treatment. Modern history became a favored subject, too, as in Benjamin West's celebrated *Death of General Wolfe*. It was therefore only a matter of time before vernacular literary texts were given the same treatment.[14] William Hogarth's famous painting of David Garrick as Richard III in his tent on the night before the battle of Bosworth Field, now in the Walker Art Gallery, Liverpool, made certain references to Garrick's stage

Richard, but it was really a studio portrait garnished with the appurtenances of historical painting. It paved the way for John Boydell's extraordinary project to create a Shakespearean school of English history painting.

Alderman Boydell, entrepreneur and printseller, opened his Shakespeare Gallery in Pall Mall in May 1789. He had commissioned the leading artists of the day to produce paintings on Shakespearean subjects, which would be exhibited in the gallery, then sold in engraved form. The enterprise collapsed within a decade, largely because the international print market dried up as a result of the European wars following the French Revolution, but two remarkable illustrated book projects emerged from it: *A Collection of Prints, from Pictures Painted for the Purpose of Illustrating the Dramatic Works of Shakspeare, by the Artists of Great-Britain*, in two atlas folio volumes, containing a hundred prints from the large paintings in the gallery (published in 1805, but with the year 1803 on the title page), and an edition of the *Dramatic Works* of Shakespeare with the Steevens text — specially printed with magnificent leaded type and extra-wide margins — adorned by copperplate engravings from the one hundred smaller paintings in the gallery (published serially in eighteen parts between 1791 and 1802, and as a nine-volume collected folio in 1802).[15]

The distance of this project from the contemporary theater is apparent from a canvas such as James Barry's rendition of the moment in the final scene of Lear, where the king enters with Cordelia dead in his arms (fig. 4). In the version of the play which held the stage at this time, Cordelia did not die: she was paired off with Edgar, and Lear was happily restored to his throne. Nor is Barry's image really an illustration of the Shakespearean text: the composition of the figures owes more to the *Pietà* tradition in religious art than to any Shakespearean stage-direction, while the setting, with its Stonehenge or Avebury-like structure

[42]

Figure 4.
"*King Lear*. Act V. Scene III. A Camp Near Dover,"
painted by James Barry, engraved by F. Legat,
from Alderman Boydell's *Collection of Prints*,
stipple engraving, 1805.

in the background, is much more pointedly evocative of primitive, quasi-Druidic British history than the Shakespearean text ever is. A classical style is mingled with a sense of the long reach of native history in order to forge a sense of British cultural identity. Accretions of "invented tradition" have been layered onto Shakespeare so thickly as almost to obscure the original.

There was, however, a two-way movement between painting and the theater. In the first half of the nineteenth century, many of the principles of "history painting" were applied to theatrical costume and scenic design. As Martin Meisel has demonstrated, in

[43]

both the theater and painting, the Victorian age was dominated by forms of pictorial realism in which historical subjects were invested with moral, sentimental, and nationalistic purposes aimed at the present; the freighting of both fictive and historical representations with the thick texture of the "real" was a means of making the past answer to contemporary concerns.[16] The Shakespearean stage was central to this process. One key figure was Charles Kean, who interpolated magnificent historical tableaux into his productions. The proscenium-arch stage was like a picture frame, the elaborate scenery like the background in a historical painting. The costumes in a Kean production were neither "Elizabethan" nor "modern-dress": they were of the age in which the play was set. The assumption was that Shakespeare was a historical realist — like, say, Sir Walter Scott, whose invention of the historical novel owed so much to his reading of Shakespeare. The historical-realist approach was bound up with Victorian Britain's sense of its own historical identity. This was the period when the city fathers of Liverpool, one of the ports upon which the British empire was built, erected a great civic hall in the high Roman style, named it St. George's after the nation's patron saint, and adorned it with the initials S.P.Q.L. — Senatus Populusque Liverpudliensis. The clear implication was that the British Empire was a second Roman Empire. And for Britain to be a second Rome, Britain's poet had to be mediator of the national sense of destiny. He was made to take on the epic grandeur of Virgil. Hence the epic production style of Charles Kean.[17] This theatrical style had its bookish counterpart in the work of the author and publisher Charles Knight.

Between 1838 and 1843 Knight published his *Pictorial Edition of the Works of Shakspere* in fifty-six parts, to be gathered into eight volumes — two of Histories, two of Comedies, two of Tragedies and Poems, one of "Doubtful" works (which the recent German critics A. W. Schlegel and Ludwig Tieck had been busy attributing to Shakespeare), and the other a biography of the playwright. This edition included introductory notices, notes, glossary, music to the songs and hundreds of wood engravings. Both textually and visually, Knight sought to "illustrate" as much as he could of Shakespeare's "historical" meaning. He uses the word "illustration" in both the sense of explaining historical details and allusions, and that of providing visual images. Thus the mention of "Brownists" in act three scene two of *Twelfth Night* is glossed by way of reference to Neal's *History of the Puritans*, while the line in the following scene, "Big enough for the bed of Ware in England" (3.3.39), receives the note "We have given a representation of this famous bed, which is more interesting than any description" — a half-page engraving of the enormous four-poster heads the "Illustrations of Act III" of *Twelfth Night*.[18] The representation is certainly more evocative than the sort of dry verbal note that is characteristic of modern editions: "Famous Elizabethan bedstead, nearly eleven feet square, now in the Victorian and Albert Museum, London."[19]

Knight's treatment of costume and locality are more problematic. He concluded his introduction to *Troilus and Cressida* with a tail-piece illustrating "Phrygian Tunic, Bi-pennes, Bow, Quiver, Helmets, &c." Shakespeare himself would not have had the vaguest notion of the nature of Phrygian battle gear; the Greek and Trojan warriors on his stage would have looked classical in only the most general sense. But Knight took the opportunity to bring modern archaeological research into play. Ideologically, the combination of modern British scholarship — one suspects that it was partly for patriotic reasons that Knight expressed considerable scepticism over the German contribution, particularly in the area of authorship attribution — with the enshrinement of the National Poet himself served to make the case for Britain as a great cultural power akin to classical Greece and Rome.

[45]

More practically, Knight was seeking to assist historically minded men of the theater such as Charles Kean by giving them tips on "accurate" staging. He suggested, for instance, that in *Troilus and Cressida* the Trojans should wear greaves and the Greeks sandals. And, indeed, his "illustrations," both verbal and visual, were used by producers in preparing set-designs and deciding on costumes.[20] There are, however, notes on costumes for most of the plays, including such infrequently staged ones as the *Henry VI* trilogy. An illustration such as "Costume of the Commonality of the Period" (fig. 5), the tailpiece to the introduction to *Part II*, would therefore have been designed less for the stage producer than for readers, with the intention of allowing them to imagine the play as historically "authentic," in the manner of a Scott novel.

The processes of what I have termed novelization and historicization are also apparent from the many topographic illustrations in the *Pictorial Shakspere*. The Shakespearean theater, with its bare boards and its reliance on word-pictures to conjure up locations, was even further from "realistic" stage-settings than it was from "authentic" costumes. But the technical capabilities of artificial lighting, dioramas, flats, screens, and backdrops in the Victorian playhouse created a theater of highly specific scene location. The Rialto and the Roman Capitol were lovingly recreated for numerous productions of *The Merchant of Venice* and *Julius Caesar*. Analogously, Knight's edition included engravings, many based on drawings by G. H. Harvey, of scores of places mentioned in the plays.

So it is that the introduction to *Othello* explains the "Period of the Action and Locality" as follows:

> The republic of Venice became the virtual sovereigns of Cyprus, in 1471 . . . [the island] was retained by the Venetians till 1570, when it was invaded by a powerful Turkish

Figure 5.
"Costume of the Commonality of the Period,"
tailpiece to introductory note to *Henry VI Part II*,
from Charles Knight's *Pictorial Edition of the Works of Shakspere*,
woodcut, 1838-43.

force . . . Leikosia, the inland capital of the island, was taken by storm; and Famagusta, the principal sea-port, capitulated after a long and gallant defence. It is evident, therefore, that we must refer the action of Othello to a period before the subjugation of Cyprus by the Turks. The locality of the scenes after the first Act must be placed at Famagusta, which was strongly fortified, — a fact which Shakspere must have known, when in the second Scene of the third Act he says, —

[47]

"I will be walking on the *works.*"

The interesting series of sketches, of which we have been fortunate in obtaining copies from the portfolio of Mr Arundale, exhibits to us the principal remains of the old fort and town of Famagusta, in which the towers and colonnades of the Venetians are mingled with the minarets of the Turks, and where the open space in which stands the half ruin of a fine old Christian church is now called "the Place of the Mosque."[21]

When the reader reaches Act Two of the text, he or she finds it duly headed by a cut of the citadel at Famagusta. Act Three is topped by "Venetian Remains at Famagusta," four by the afore-mentioned "Piazza of the Mosque," and the final act by a "General View of Famagusta" (fig. 6), which gives a good sense of the "works," the sea-bordering fortifications, but includes the distraction of a rather un-Venetian sailing boat in the foreground. This kind of illustration may be of historical interest, but it creates the false impression that Shakespeare was in the business of "realistic" staging in the manner of the nineteenth-century theater.

For the remaining thirty years of his life, when not busy with his work as publisher of the *London Gazette* or with the publication of such mass-market productions as his *The Land We Live In: A Pictorial and Literary Sketch-Book of the British Empire* (1847) and *Popular History of England* (1862), Charles Knight devoted his publishing career to the constant updating and repackaging of his pictorialized Shakespeare. A second edition (1842-44) was started before the first was even finished; it extended to twelve volumes and was known as the "Library Edition," later rechristened the "National Edition" (eight volumes, 1850-52). The seven-volume "Standard Edition" of 1847 abridged the biography and left out the "doubtfully" attributed (or "apocryphal") plays, but increased the

Figure 6.
"General View of Famagusta," headpiece to Act V of *Othello*,
from Charles Knight's *Pictorial Edition of the Works of Shakspere*,
woodcut, 1838-43.

number of woodcuts. In the same period (1847-48) Knight produced a massive "Cabinet Edition" in sixteen volumes. Then in the
1850s there were various versions of the "Stratford Edition" (begun
in monthly parts in 1853, completed as a ten-volume set in 1857).

The original *Pictorial Shakspere* had been practical rather than
handsome. At the end of his life, Knight capped his career with a
more grandiose production, which had a suitably elevated title:
the "Imperial Edition" (1873). Whereas the previous editions had
been published by Knight himself, this was given maximum
impact in the marketplace by way of the distributional capacities
of the major house of Virtue & Co of Fleet Street. This handsome

two-volume folio set was aimed at the well-to-do aspirant middle classes. This was the edition for the self-respecting, decent home — a showpiece item to keep with the family Bible. Partly under the inspiration of such earlier collections as *Shakespeare Portfolio: A Series of ninety-six Graphic Illustrations of the Plays of Shakespeare, after Designs by the Most Eminent British Artists* (1829) and Charles Heath's set of steel engravings, *The Shakespeare Gallery, containing the Principal Female Characters in the Plays of the Great Poet* (1836), Knight brought together a wide range of post-Boydell Shakespearean paintings as a visual feast to accompany his text, while reprinting a somewhat stripped-down version of his explanatory material. The volumes were thus a showpiece for modern British art as well as the national poet.

Knight included engravings of many paintings that had been published in earlier collections, such as the highly sentimental "Olivia" of C. R. Leslie from the "female characters" of the 1836 *Shakespeare Gallery*, but he also commissioned new engravings from paintings not hitherto reproduced for mass circulation. The technological evolution from copperplate engraving into steel plates facilitated the mass production of comparatively inexpensive copies (steel being much more durable than copper), ensuring that the *Imperial Shakspere* was within reach throughout the nation, and for that matter the empire, in contrast to Boydell's *Collection of Prints* which had been aimed at the connoisseur market.

The frontispiece to the "Imperial Edition" takes the form of an engraving of the "Chandos" portrait of Shakespeare. With his beard and his earring, he cuts a figure much more responsive to the Romantic notion of genius than did the wooden-looking fellow in the Droeshout engraving. There is a further gesture to the Romantic apotheosis of the Bard in the title-page vignette in volume one: the birthplace house in Stratford-upon-Avon is shown together with an imaginary representation of the procession for

Figure 7.
"The Globe Theatre, Bankside — 1593,"
title-page vignette from Vol. 2 of
Charles Knight's *Works of Shakspere: Imperial Edition*,
steel engraving, 1873.

Garrick's Shakespeare Jubilee of 1769, an event traditionally seen as the launchpad for Bardolatry. The volume two title-page vignette offers an equally romanticized image: it purports to show "The Globe Theatre, Bankside — 1593" (fig. 7). The year was presumably chosen in order to be symbolic of the beginnings of Shakespeare's fame (a similar choice was made in the film *Shakespeare in Love*), though it was in fact a year when the theaters were mostly closed because of plague and the acting companies were in a state of considerable flux (it was the following year, 1594, that the Lord Chamberlain's Men were formed, with Shakespeare as in-house writer). Shakespeare probably spent most of 1593 away from the London theater world, perhaps in the household of the earl of Southampton, to whom he was dedicating his narrative poems around this time. As for the Globe, it was not built until 1599. In 1593, the nucleus of actors who were to become the Chamberlain's Men, and who would eventually build the Globe on Bankside, were working well to the north of the river in Shoreditch. But the purpose of Knight's illustration here is to conjure up an idealized image of the Shakespearean theater as part of merrie England: the names Globe Theatre and Bankside, together with the year 1593, have a talismanic quality. The idealization of the image extends to the figures peopling it, some of whom are on horseback, some on foot. This mixture symbolizes the social inclusiveness of the Shakespearean theater, the idea that it appealed to all ranks and thus unified the nation. The subtext of the image is that Shakespeare can — through such works as this edition — again be the means of unifying a nation and indeed an empire.

The imperial ambition of the project is also apparent from the prominence and elaboration of the illustrations to the plays set in classical Rome. The illustrations to both *Julius Caesar* and *Antony and Cleopatra* are extravagant in their emphasis upon Roman architecture and imperial power. They offer a Victorian, not an Elizabethan, image of the ancient world. So too, in less historical vein, with *A Midsummer Night's Dream* and *The Tempest*: here we have a Victorian, not an Elizabethan image of the "faery" world. *The Tempest* is accompanied by an engraving of Robert Huskisson's painting envisioning Ariel's song "Come unto these yellow sands" (fig. 8). Originally painted in 1847, but not exhibited, this is Huskisson's earliest extant work. He was a contemporary of Richard Dadd, who shared an interest in the fairy genre — and whose Shakespearean illustrations in this genre are better known today. Huskisson's pretty visualization, all swirls and gossamer, is

Figure 8.
"Come unto these yellow sands," painted by R. Hukisson,
engraved by T. A. Prior, from Charles Knight's *Imperial Edition*,
steel engraving, 1873.

many miles from the Elizabethan stage, but of a piece with the
Victorian theater's sentimentalizing approach to Shakespeare's
magical plays, which treated them as opportunities for flights of
unworldly fancy, regressions to childhood. Not until the postwar
theater of Peter Brook and others were these plays restored to
intellectual toughness.

Where the Roman plays were re-envisioned with the masculine moral uplift of imperial historical writing and the magical
plays rendered softly fanciful, Victorianly feminine and dream-
like, the tragedies tended to be "novelized." An especially notable
example is the frontispiece to *Othello*, by Charles West Cope. He
was a painter well-known not only for his dramatic subjects but

[53]

also for his genre scenes, typically of almsgiving and acts of charity. The *Times* of 30 April 1859 lauded him as the chief painter of modern domestic life. *Othello* is undoubtedly the most domestic of Shakespeare's tragedies, but it is also a work of great political and civic scope. In Cope's hands, however, it becomes merely domestic: the scene chosen for illustration is "Othello Relating his Adventures" (fig. 9), painted as an interior of family life, with the civic context of Renaissance Venice removed to the background. This is a picture of not a mercenary general but a man seeking the hand of a well-to-do woman, knowing that her father is the key player in the transaction. In accordance with the norm of the age, Othello himself is represented as a noble figure of mildly Oriental demeanor, not a threatening out-and-out Blackamoor. But the most striking thing about the illustration is that what it is visualizing is not actually a scene in the play. Othello does not relate his adventures on stage. That has happened before the action begins. He *recollects* that relation in act one scene three, as part of his "trial" in a very public setting before an audience of the duke and senators. Cope is illustrating not the play as staged, but the world of the play's action as it might be imagined by a public for whom the novel has become the most influential mode of artistic representation of reality.

The tradition of "pictorial Shakespeare" confronts us with a number of paradoxes. Boydell's attempt to yoke Shakespeare to an emergent school of English "history painting" was intended to lift the plays above the tawdriness and ephemerality of the stage, yet its main effect was to contribute to a more historical and pictorial approach to staging in the nineteenth century. The emergence of the historical novel furthered this development: the Waverley novels of Sir Walter Scott, illustrations to those novels, stage dramatizations of them, illustrations of Shakespearean texts, Shakespearean paintings in the exhibition room, and picture-frame productions of Shakespeare on the proscenium-arched Victorian

Figure 9.
"Othello Relating His Adventures,"
painted by C. W. Cope, engraved by T. Vernon,
from Charles Knight's *Imperial Edition*, steel engraving, 1873.

stage all tended to share one and the same histrionic style — a style that was from a Shakespearean point of view pseudo-historical insofar as it sought the kind of "accuracy" with regard to which Shakespeare himself, self-conscious anachronist, was gloriously irreverent. Text, stage, and illustration were also closely related in their emphasis on "moments": as Matthew Arnold judged literary works by the "touchstones" of key speeches of poetic intensity, so Charles Kean directed his stage productions toward formalized tableaux which would suspend the action and provoke applause from the auditorium, while a whole array of painters and book

Figure 10.
"Malvolio," painted by Daniel Maclise, engraved by R. Staines,
from *Charles Knight's Imperial Edition*, steel engraving, 1873.

illustrators set about freezing and immortalizing moments in the
plays — though, as we have seen, these were often, as with "Othello relating his Adventures" and "Come unto these yellow sands,"
moments at more than one remove from the actual visual experience of the Shakespearean drama. This latter tendency had the
effect of collapsing the distinction between the modes of imagining appropriate to drama and to novel.

From the point of view of our own versions of historicism —
our respect, say, for the bareness of the Elizabethan stage — pictorial Shakespeare might be thought to have done damage to its great
original. But a century from now, our own approaches will seem
equally limited and bound to their own time. Pictorial Shakespeare is a very different beast from our Shakespeare, but the very
extent of the difference points to the extraordinary power of the

plays to continue adapting to fresh environmental circumstances. This is the key to their cultural survival. They undergo a constant process of reinvention and diversification. If we now value Shakespeare especially because of the self-consciousness of his mobility and sense of *play* — the idea that we are all role-players, that our identities are constantly shifting, that even our sexuality is something that, Viola/Cesario-like, we can put on and take off like a costume — then it is instructive to recall in contrast that he spoke equally powerfully to the nineteenth century because of his stability and sense of *reality*. Pictorial Shakespeare reminds us how richly the language of the plays can conjure up a world textured with both everyday and exotic *things*. In the hands of a truly accomplished painter such as Daniel Maclise, a scene such as Malvolio's cross-gartered posturing before the Lady Olivia (fig. 10) can impress and amuse as much when frozen in the elaborate setting of a painted garden with cool paving, clipped hedge, and peacock as it does in motion on the bare boards of the Shakespearean or the modern playhouse.

Notes

1. *Hamlet*, 2.1.80-1. All Shakespearean quotations are followed by line reference to *The Norton Shakespeare, based on the Oxford Text*, gen. ed. Stephen Greenblatt (New York and London: W. W. Norton, 1997).
2. On this process more generally in the eighteenth and nineteenth centuries, see chapters 6-9 of my *The Genius of Shakespeare* (London: Picador, 1997 and New York: Oxford University Press, 1998).
3. There is an important discussion of these in T. S. R. Boase, "Illustrations of Shakespeare's Plays in the Seventeenth and Eighteenth Centuries," *Journal of the Warburg and Courtauld Institutes* 10 (1947): 83-108.

[57]

4. Quoted, W. Moelwyn Merchant, *Shakespeare and the Artist* (London, New York and Toronto: Oxford University Press, 1959), 56. This highly informative book remains the best survey of the subject, but we badly need a more up-to-date study.

5. Though this policy does not extend to the retention of "old spelling." The desire for authenticity revealed by the inclusion of such illustrative material as the facsimile of the will calls into question the argument of Margreta de Grazia, in her *Shakespeare Verbatim: The Reproduction of Authenticity and the 1790 Apparatus* (Oxford and New York: Clarendon Press, 1991), that the historicizing "authentication" of Shakespeare was the unique innovation of Edmond Malone's 1790 edition.

6. *Bell's Edition of Shakespeares Plays* (London: John Bell and York: C. Etherington, 1774), 2: 3, 85.

7. Bell's edition, 2: 148.

8. Conflated text in Norton edition, 3.4.97-101.

9. Bell's edition, 2: 44.

10. For an attempt to reconstruct the "soundscapes" of Shakespeare's England, see Bruce Smith's innovative work of "acoustemological" criticism, *The Acoustic World of Early Modern England: Attending to the O-Factor* (Chicago and London: University of Chicago Press, 1999).

11. Walter Benjamin, "The Work of Art in the Age of Mechanical Reproduction," in *Illuminations,* edited with an introduction by Hannah Arendt and translated by Harry Zohn (New York: Schocken Books, 1976), 217-51.

12. As was often the case with eighteenth- and nineteenth-century editions of Shakespeare at the popular end of the market, the plays were issued individually (title pages dated some 1773 and some 1774), but could then be bound up into a collected edition (for which through pagination was introduced and special title pages printed for each volume).

13. Bell's *Dramatic Character Plates* have been usefully reprinted in facsimile (London: Cornmarket Press, 1969). Shuter was a well-known

comedian and an appropriately Falstaffian figure: in 1772 Mrs. Griffith's play *A Wife in the Right* flopped on its first production at Covent Garden largely because Shuter, by his own admission, had been drunk for three days and nights prior to the opening.

14. On this, see Ronald Paulson's excellent *Book and Painting: Shakespeare, Milton and the Bible: Literary Texts and the Emergence of English Painting* (Knoxville: University of Tennessee Press, 1982).

15. The best accounts of the Boydell project are Winifred H. Friedman, *Boydell's Shakespeare Gallery* (New York and London: Garland, 1976) and *The Boydell Shakespeare Gallery*, ed. Walter Pape and Frederick Burwick (Bottrop: Pomp, 1996). *The Boydell Shakespeare Prints* have been published in facsimile (New York: Arno Press, 1979), introduction by A. E. Santaniello.

16. See Martin Meisel, *Realizations: Narrative, Pictorial, and Theatrical Arts in Nineteenth-Century England* (Princeton: Princeton University Press, 1983).

17. A concise introduction to the theater of Charles Kean is provided by Russell Jackson in "Actor-Managers and the Spectacular," chap. 6 of *Shakespeare: An Illustrated Stage History*, ed. Jonathan Bate and Russell Jackson (Oxford and New York: Oxford University Press, 1996). See also Meisel, 42-45.

18. *The Pictorial Edition of the Works of Shakspere*, ed. Charles Knight (London: Charles Knight, n.d. [1838-43]), *Comedies: Vol.II*, 171.

19. Norton edition, 1798.

20. See, for example, the account in Merchant, 119-26, of the use of Knight editions of *Lear* as promptbooks for productions at Sadler's Wells in 1855 and the Surrey Theater in 1873.

21. *The Pictorial Edition of the Works of Shakspere*, ed. Charles Knight (London: Charles Knight, n.d. [1838-43]), *Tragedies: Vol.I*, 257.

Taglioni's Double Meanings: Illustration and the Romantic Ballerina

Sarah Webster Goodwin

I n "The Work of Art in the Age of Mechanical Reproduction," Walter Benjamin argues,

> Even the most perfect reproduction of a work of art is lacking in one element: its presence in time and space, its unique existence at the place where it happens to be. This unique existence of the work of art determined the history to which it was subject throughout the time of its existence. This includes the changes which it may have suffered in physical condition over the years as well as the various changes in its ownership.[1]

The work of art, for Benjamin, cannot be reproduced, because its very essence inheres in its uniqueness. For all its prophetic power, Benjamin's essay — as the editor's introduction to this volume points out — does not anticipate that the terms "reproduction" and "work of art" would eventually take on a second meaning. A

[61]

reproduction itself can now also be considered an "original" work that, digitally or otherwise reproduced, sheds what he calls its "presence in time and space, its unique existence at the place where it happens to be" (220). Thus a nineteenth-century book containing lithographed illustrations, when reproduced by a press such as Dover in an inexpensive paperback format, loses the traces of its "presence in time and space": its binding and endpapers, the impress of hands that have held it, the weight of its original paper. We may borrow an insight here from reader-response criticism and suggest that the early owners and readers of a book in a sense have helped to create it. When we read and observe a book with a history, we can read traces of that history in its material form. In fact, we cannot help but read those traces: a book's form unavoidably mediates our understanding of it, bearing meanings that may be as weighty as those conveyed solely by the text and illustrations, those parts of the book that most lend themselves to reproduction.

Two illustrated British volumes from the mid-1840s richly exemplify the point. *Julien's Album de l'Opéra* (1845) and *The Exquisite* (1842) both contain images representing the celebrated Marie Taglioni, one of the founding dancers of Romantic ballet on the stages of Paris, London, and other European capitols. In both cases, the images show her, ostensibly, as she appeared on stage, posed as in the midst of a dance. The "original," then, in Benjamin's terms, was a performance in a theater; these two volumes attempt to reproduce that original for a much larger audience. The volumes themselves, however, are in turn significant artifacts, contributing richly to the cultural meanings of Marie Taglioni, ballerina. When images of the ballerina are lifted from such volumes and reproduced, we lose the "original" artifact, its presence and its history.[2] The lithographs, as mechanical reproductions, may appear to have little in common with the work of art whose authenticity Benjamin goes so far as to associate with quasi-religious experience.

But in tracing and interpreting some of the meanings of their original print contexts, we open ourselves more fully to understanding some of the resonant contradictions they offer up to us.

These two volumes show us Marie Taglioni as glamorous commodity, in one case ethereally elegant, in the other associated with a kind of eroticized London demi-monde. Together they reveal the interconnected economy of theater, book arts, the popular press, and lithography at mid-century; the ways the lines of gender clearly operated in the world of ballet images as disseminated in books and periodicals; and, implicitly, the ways the ballerina in her performance and her life helped to destabilize her contemporaries' assumptions about gender even as she also reinforced them. Although Marie Taglioni was not the first star of the ballet, she was the first whose fame spread through the new and extensive networks of the reproduced image. The iconography of her images reveals, I argue, a double cultural meaning: she continues the traditional role of ballerina as seductress, but also generates a new one, the ballerina as powerful high priestess of a new art form.

MARIE TAGLIONI AND ROMANTIC BALLET

The distinguishing feature of Romantic ballet is that it defies gravity. Marie Taglioni, in developing pointe technique and incorporating it thematically into her ballet narratives, inaugurated a new art form. Before her, a number of dancers — men and women — had gone up on pointe as part of a dance; she was the first to show in a sustained way that the dancer on pointe seems ethereal, other-worldly, because she conveys the illusion of weightlessness as she moves on her toes. After she made her debut in Paris in 1827, images of her began to proliferate in the popular press. In 1832, she caused a sensation with a new ballet, *La Sylphide*, choreographed for her by her father, and the ballerina as international superstar emerged as a new phenomenon. Many other dancers followed, no more than a dozen of them attaining similar status. By mid-century, their admirers could find hundreds of lithographs depicting the stars of the Romantic ballet.

Ballet thus swept in during the 1830s and 1840s as one of the most important forms of visual culture in London, Paris, and other European cities. More, the rush of images depicting dancers that appeared in just about every conceivable context participated in what Charles Baudelaire called a "cult of the image," an obsession with the visual.[3] Audiences flocked to the ballet to watch dancers perform in narratives that themselves enacted visual themes: the sylph, in Marie Taglioni's first major ballet, appears explicitly as the object of the gaze, her beloved doing little more on stage than partnering her lifts, observing her longingly, and wishing he could see her when he cannot. The audience, of course, shares his obsession with the sight of his sylph. They know her from the countless images they have seen: in newspapers, lithographs, and sheet music, on calling cards, paper dolls, and fans. Marie Taglioni enacts in her performances and illustrates in her reproduced images the interconnected components comprising the cult of the visual at mid-century.

That cult, as exemplified in ballet, centered on the ballerina, the woman who was there to be seen. Again and again, in the reproduced images, we notice how the dancer poses for our benefit. We have only to compare any of these illustrations with a painting of dancers by Edgar Degas to remember how strikingly the images differ. Degas's dancers seem to turn inward toward themselves as they put on their shoes, stretch, or rest. The popular images, in contrast, show us ballerinas whose body parts seem mass-produced: long necks, rounded but graceful arms, indistinguishable legs and waists, all turned in formulaic ways toward the viewer. This is "to-be-looked-at-ness," as Laura Mulvey has called it, in one of its most pervasive early forms, a precursor of the cinematic image she identifies with the quality that female characters have in cinema as they present themselves to the male characters, the "man as bearer of the look."[4]

Indeed, just as Benjamin draws a direct line from lithography to film, we might see a similar lineage from Romantic ballet to popular cinema. Benjamin may have been the first to argue that the film audience necessarily identifies not with the actors but with the camera (228); ballet too has come to seem almost designed for the camera. What Mulvey proposed, with such far-reaching influence, is that the camera is masculine, its gaze directed towards the actress in a gendered relationship.[5] Romantic ballet, with its emphasis on the ballerina as the object of visual desire, may in this respect be the most influential theatrical precursor of popular cinema.

It is easy to forget, as we study the lithographs and illustrations, the key element that they omit: the dancer's movements. Images of the ballerinas are often collected and referred to as though they showed us the dancers themselves. Instead, it is those images that defined and circumscribed the dancers, assigning them meanings they could not control even as they elided the most important sources of the dancers' power. Creating the ballerina as an icon of stillness, posed for the observer, endlessly available to the gaze, the images effectively counteract the force of the dance. It was her movement that gave her power — of a multifaceted kind. Dancing, the ballerina assumed a freedom of movement that was forbidden to most of the women in her audience. She transformed movements that could be construed as eroticized, hence taboo, into a form of artistic expression. But a tension remained, surrounding the ballet with an aura of forbidden pleasures. There is no question that part of the marketing of Romantic ballet, especially in Victorian England, involved discreetly managing this aspect of its public image.

[65]

Perhaps no clearer evidence exists of this tension between erotic entertainment and high art than the kinds of testimony offered by poet and critic Théophile Gautier, whose reviews articulated the enthusiasm and discerning appreciation felt by much of the ballet audience. He wrote repeatedly about Marie Taglioni, lavishing praise on her performances and revealing his complex ideas about the forces informing ballet as art. In one review, for example, he writes excitedly about her return to Paris in 1844 after a four-year absence:

> Happy woman! She still has the same slender and elegant figure, and the same sweet, intelligent and modest expression. Not a feather has dropped from her wings, not a hair has lost its sheen beneath her coronet of flowers! At the rise of the curtain she was greeted with thunderous applause. What lightness, what rhythm of movement, what nobility of gesture, what poetry of attitude, and above all, what sweet melancholy, what chaste abandon! Nothing could be more delicate or coquettish than her poses in the *pas de trois* . . .[6]

Chaste and modest, but also coquettish, Gautier's Taglioni is a true poet, bringing together in a dynamic tension two opposed ideas of femininity and seduction. (And seduce she did: taking her bows, she was "greeted with a hurricane of bouquets and a floral cloudburst. For one moment we feared for her life, so heavy, intense and prolonged was the bombardment," Gautier writes. He regrets that she is to give only six further performances: "all too few, considering that a million Parisians and three hundred thousand tourists want to see her again" [133].) It is part of Marie Taglioni's extraordinary power that she can be both chaste and coquettish, at once proper and subtly, though unmistakably, eroticized.

That doubled nature appears, too, in her personal life, in which she both married into nobility (a marquis) and, subsequently, conducted her affairs much as she chose, bearing two children long after separating from her husband. Taglioni continued a long-standing tradition in which dancers conducted their private lives with much greater freedom than middle-class women; indeed, in that tradition dancers belonged to the social category of expensive courtesan, and both principals and members of the *corps de ballet* routinely supplemented their income by forming liaisons. But Taglioni did not simply subscribe to these traditional freedoms. She took advantage of her unprecedented popularity to travel widely and perform throughout Europe and in Russia, commanding dramatic fees and building ever greater audiences.[7] Furthermore, Taglioni redefined ballet as a serious and decidedly respectable art form: even the future Queen Victoria was such an ardent fan as a young girl that she painted a series of watercolors representing her.[8] Taglioni made available to the principal ballerinas, at least, a new category with considerably more power and mobility than that of the courtesan, one that transcended limits traditionally imposed on female performers.

The reproduced images of Marie Taglioni and other ballerinas after her augmented that power by increasing their popularity. However, they also challenged or circumscribed it. Without the popular press, the lithographs, and the many other disseminated images, the dancers' relationship with their audience would have been quite different. By metonymy, the dancers were commodities, like their images, subject to powerful marketplace forces. They were also subjects controlling some aspects of their own commodification. More, they were artists, poets of movement, whose performances drew comparisons to Johann Wolfgang von Goethe and Lord Byron; Gautier wrote that Taglioni was "as great a genius, using the word to mean a faculty carried to its furthermost limits,

[67]

as Lord Byron. Her *ronds de jambe* . . . are, by themselves, the equal of a long poem" (2). From the poet Gautier, this is the highest possible praise. He encouraged audiences to see her this way, of course, but he was also reflecting the public's wild enthusiasm. Marie Taglioni was one of a group of women who occupied an unstable position in mid-nineteenth-century culture. Her dances could not be reproduced mechanically by the means then available, but the contexts in which we find some of her images reveal some of the contrasting cultural ideas about her.

JULIEN'S ALBUM AND THE EXQUISITE

It is hard to imagine two more radically different contexts for the ballerina's image than the two volumes I will compare here: *Julien's Album de l'Opéra* and *The Exquisite*. The latter is a twelve-month run (1844) of a near-weekly periodical, published in London, that survived just three years; it is directed at a male readership and combines racy stories and jokes with nonfiction articles.[9] In contrast, *Julien's Album de l'Opéra* is a handsome gift book that combines lithographs of ballerinas with decorative pages and a substantial collection of music from ballets, adapted for piano.[10] These two volumes both contain images of Marie Taglioni and other ballerinas. But they differ completely in material form, in content, in intended audience, and in significance. The differences align themselves along the line of gender, and they evidence very different kinds of response to the provocation that Marie Taglioni can be seen to represent to middle-class culture.

Most striking, and most important for this essay, are the differences in form. *Julien's Album* is oversized (12 in. x 18 in.), slim, bound in ivory silk with a gold stamped title, the hefty pages edged with gilt. The title page is printed in gold ink with an elaborate floral design; it is followed by a two-page gold and rose-colored "Plan of HER MAJESTY'S THEATRE," a bird's-eye view indicating stage, seats, and boxes complete with curtains. After two blank pages, there follow five detailed, full-page, colored lithographs representing four different ballets. All are well-known lithographs by J. Brandard, beautifully printed here in clear lines with subtle coloring. In each case, the ballerina does not appear alone; all dance pas de deux, with one exception. Marie Taglioni appears as one of four dancers in a celebrated image: the "Grand Pas de Quatre" staged specifically to bring her together with three other stars, Lucile Grahn, Carlotta Grisi, and Fanny Cerrito (fig. 11). The *pas de quatre* is the third of the five lithographs. A dedication page follows the lithograph: in the copy I saw, it had been inscribed to "Edith Sheppard on her birthday," in a space designed for such an inscription. After the inscription page there is a table of contents listing eleven pieces of ballet music, followed by the music itself.

This handsome volume is clearly a gift intended as an object of aesthetic pleasure as well as some practical use. Its recipient can play the music, and thereby participate metonymically in the world of the ballet whose glamour lends itself to the gift book. Even without the inscription, we would guess that the recipient was female: the flowery decorative motifs and the preponderance of pink and gold convey clearly the feminine culture this object both reflects and contributes to. It seems to define the female consumer's proper response to the ballet: commodify its beauty, contain its eroticism, participate in its refined aesthetic pleasures.

The book does nod faintly to the ballet's implicit eroticism. Its first two lithographs represent the "'Mazurka d'extase' danced by Monsr. Perrot & Mad*lle* Lucile Grahn, at her Majesty's Theatre." In the second of the two, entitled "L'Extase," the ballerina falls backwards into her partner's arms, apparently fainting in ecstasy. But her partner is far from taking advantage of her, and the image remains completely discreet.

Figure 11.
"Grand Pas de Quatre," *Julien's Album de l'Opéra,*
lithograph, 1845?
courtesy of Harvard Theatre Collection.

In contrast, the "Grand Pas de Quatre" shows a stylized, abstract pose, each of the four ballerinas in turn displaying a graceful arc of the arm and turn of the head. Marie Taglioni reigns over them, her arms raised in a slightly angled fifth position, her eyes turned demurely downward. Though there are faint differences in their features, the ballerinas are almost indistinguishable: dressed alike, coiffed alike, all wear decorative flowers that correspond to the flowers scattered at their feet and to the garland draped curiously over a branch in the background. A gentle pink color shades the ballerinas' skin, the flowers, and the costumes, echoing the rose tints in the earlier picture of the theater. The landscape behind them is shaded with a soft green, and a small white tempietta appears tucked into a hillside. Despite the flowers and trees, the effect is of a completely artificial — indeed, clichéd—pastoral stage setting. Here, nature is tamed; it does not threaten to break out of its controls. The most exquisite detail in the image appears in the dancers' hands, all eight of which are posed gracefully in the air.

The ballerinas are icons here of a chaste and civilized femininity. Everything about the book that encloses the image reinforces the sense of containment and grace. Marie Taglioni, as the senior member of the foursome, appears in a superior position, conveying her own kind of majesty. But this is no haughty queen. Instead, she symbolizes perfectly the proper woman as the object of the gaze. The ideal that is sold here in the form of the book is a fantasy of feminine power anchored in masculine desire. To be surrounded by garlands and floating tulle, to be the object of the adoring gaze, to exercise her power passively, demurely, chastely: these are the wishes that such a gift shapes and encourages.

The Exquisite could hardly present a more complete contrast to *Julien's Album*. The London weekly, apparently launched in 1842 for a three-year run, is printed on lightweight, inexpensive paper.

Its purchase price appears on the title page: a mere fourpence. The title page also tells us a bit more about this journal: "A collection of Tales, histories, and Essays, Funny, fanciful, and facetious, interspersed with anecdotes, original and select. Amorous adventures, piquant jests, and spicey [sic] sayings, illustrated with numerous engravings, published weekly."

Despite the editor's claims, there were few illustrations; these were printed separately and enclosed for readers to afix on their own. They were limited to two kinds. A weekly illustration by Honoré Daumier accompanied the serialized translation of *Robert Macaire*, usually representing various male characters in conversation taken from the story. In addition, from No. 3 on, an almost-weekly picture of a ballerina was meant to be affixed to the title page; in the copy I studied, all but one of the images had indeed been glued on. The images are crudely engraved copies of well-known lithographs and portraits (figs. 12, 13). There is no pretense of artistry. Nor do the ballerinas serve as illustrations to any enclosed articles. They are simply there to decorate the cover.

It is only when we study the contents of *The Exquisite* more closely that we understand just what those cover illustrations signified. A few titles give some sense of the journal's range: "The Victim of Love," "Nights at Lunet," "Stars of the Saloons," "Manners and Customs of the Courtesans of Ancient Greece," "Where Shall I go to Night," "On Prostitution in Paris" (this last a translation of Du Chatelet's famous study). The final stanza of "Nights at Lunet" conveys the nature of the material. The speaker records a poem he wrote, ostensibly on his wedding night:

> Then by the taper's flickering ray
> I well can note her eyes, that say
> Flow on thou stream of love, till day.

Figure 12.
"Taglioni, in the Ballet l'Ombre," *The Exquisite*, no. 24,
lithograph, 1844, courtesy of Harvard Theatre Collection.

[73]

Figure 13.
"Duverney [sic], in 'The Krakoviack,'" *The Exquisite*, no. 17,
lithograph, 1844, courtesy of Harvard Theatre Collection.

Ten times ere dawning of the morn
Was virgin fancy ript and torn.
She scattered her pearls, and I scattered mine,
Enough to have moulded [sic] heroes nine,
Pushing, wriggling, squirting, ducking
Oh the joys, the charms of —
At the conclusion of this rhapsody, I was so excited
that I rolled on the bed, and determined in my own
mind, to act as I have described. (No. 11, 124)

A modern reader feels a bit caught unaware here: the journal lacks the pornographic images that might cue us to expect such "literature." There are more surprises throughout the pages of *The Exquisite*: short biographies of notable prostitutes, including addresses; discourses on venereal disease; frankly raunchy jokes; and countless tales of seduction. In short, it is a Victorian precursor of *Playboy*, minus the photographs.

In this context, there can be little doubt what the ballerinas' images signify. Out of thirty-six issues bound in one volume, twenty-five included portraits of women. Three are actresses. Marie Taglioni appears in ten images; the others vary, though Pauline Duvernay and Fanny Elssler appear four times and three times, respectively. All but four of the dancers' plates show them alone, in costume, posed more privately for the viewer, in contrast to the pairs and the *pas de quatre* in *Julien's Album*. The images do not appear the least bit pornographic, though clearly their role in the journal is to signify the female object of desire around which the articles circle so relentlessly. In the copy I saw, a reader — there is no way to know when — pencilled in two nipples on one ballerina, thereby simply rendering explicit what seems everywhere assumed.

One brief article in The *Exquisite* connects a ballerina more explicitly, though still discreetly, to the journal's erotic material. A brief biography of the dancer Pauline Duvernay recounts that her mother made an agreement to accept money from an old gentleman in exchange for her young daughter's favors. At the time, the dancer was in love with the Marquis of Lavelette, the story reports, and he had sent the gentleman as a go-between. Duvernay refused the money, but unwittingly drank a potion that made her unconscious, and Lavelette had his will. Afterwards, the old gentleman ran off with the money, "leaving the lost girl's parent without a single sou of reward for the sale of her daughter's chastity" (No. 35, 395). Later, we are told, Duvernay became the mistress of a wealthy Englishman, Lyne Stephens,

> who has settled upon her a handsome annuity. She is now in Paris, and, unknown to Stephens, constantly sees Lavalette, with whom all her former intimacy is renewed. Again does he press that fair creature in his arms; again does her voluptuous bosom heave against his heaving breast; again are her lips glued to his in all the tender dalliance of love's delights . . . . (No. 35, 395)

I quote this at some length because it follows the general pattern established by the ballerina's images in this journal: at first apparently discreet, if gossipy, this story's real raison d'être lies in the fantasy of sexual ownership, a fantasy that erupts in the prose at the end. (It bears some, but not much, resemblance to Duvernay's life as recounted by Parmenia Migel.)[11] The Exquisite informs us of the various transactions — Lavelette pays 1,600 louis for the privilege he winds up simply appropriating, and Duvernay receives a "handsome annuity" from her Englishman. Effectively, this anecdote places the ballerina seemingly almost within reach of the reader: no longer an ethereal, evanescent being, she is a very real woman. We are not surprised that one image of her is the most coquettish of all the prints included in *The Exquisite*: her hand behind her back, she seems to beckon the viewer (fig. 13).

One final aspect of the prints in *The Exquisite* bears mentioning: the title page's frame (figs. 12, 13). From the very first issue, the frame shows two dancing girls at the top, and two men at the bottom, one raising a toast and the other lifting a lorgnette to his eye. Both look upward toward the dancing girls and toward the space occupied by the ballerinas when the prints are afixed. They bear a distinct resemblance to a famous print by Robert Cruikshank, "The Green Room" (fig. 14), which shows gentlemen inspecting, chatting with, and attempting to seduce a room full of dancers. Cruikshank's print, it must be noted, dates from 1824, three years before Taglioni made her Paris debut; but two distorted copies of it, both with Taglioni's image inserted, did appear in 1831 (fig. 15).[12] The dancers depicted on *The Exquisite*'s frame, despite a certain resemblance to Cruikshank's figures, are not ballerinas. The contrast between their poses and the ballerinas' images in *The Exquisite* shows just how much a shift in the angle of the legs can signify for a woman, and suggests that even for this audience there is a nuanced shift toward greater authority in the ballerinas' cultural significance. The man with the lorgnette — it is impossible to resist suggesting the Freudian meaning of that extra eye — will see more of the dancing girls than he will of Marie Taglioni. As if the lorgnette were not enough to reinforce the motif of the gaze, the journal's motto is *"Veluti in Speculum,"* or "As if into a mirror": lorgnette or mirror, the journal turns its eye possessively toward the women in London's streets, theaters, and bedrooms.

What is particularly interesting about Marie Taglioni is that she appears to have opened up other possibilities, at least for principal dancers. *Julien's Album de l'Opéra* illustrates the shift. Through lithographs and other forms of reproduced images, ballerinas were able to

Figure 14.
Robert Cruikshank, "The Opera Green Room, or Noble Amateurs
Viewing Foreign Curiosities," engraved by Robert Cruikshank, 1824,
courtesy of Harvard Theatre Collection.

Figure 15.
"Premières Danseuses and Their Admirers: The Green Room
of the Opera House (King's Theatre) 1822," 1831,
courtesy of Harvard Theatre Collection.

enter the virtual parlor of the gift book, the world of proper Victorian femininity. Because of the bargaining power she accrued through her popularity, Taglioni became a kind of mediating figure, moving between roles enacting a passive, chaste femininity and a life in which she was neither passive nor chaste. And because of her vision, her disciplined regime, her talent, and her ability to effect the changes she saw as possible, she also mediated between concepts of high art and the demands of a large and greedy public.

Earlier in this essay, I asserted that the distinguishing feature of Romantic ballet was that it defied gravity. That is a simple statement about the nature of pointe technique; it also summarizes the great romantic themes articulated by the ballerina. To defy gravity was to defy the body, and everything associated with it (weight, but also time, death, sexuality). The Romantic ballerinas, led by Marie Taglioni, performed that defiance as a powerful fantasy; countless contemporary reports attest to their effectiveness.[13] To possess them, whether in the form of a gift book or of a soft-porn journal, must have seemed in some sense to appropriate some of that heady power. The very dichotomy of the two volumes we have considered — one very "feminine," the other equally associated with "masculine" culture — also informs the balletic narratives, which, in their focus on the ballerina, enforce gender distinctions much more emphatically than did the decorous eighteenth-century ballets that preceded them. It is almost as though the battlefield for what came to be called the "New Woman" was the ballerina's own body: dancing, living, and mechanically reproduced. We can see her as trapped within the paradigm of the obsessive and possessive masculine gaze; we can also see her as making that gaze her high theme, her instrument and her challenge, which she met with an unprecedented freedom and autonomy of movement, as well as discipline and artistry.

Notes

Work on this essay was generously supported by Skidmore College. I would also like to thank Susannah Harris, who introduced me so unforgettably to Romantic ballet, and the staff of the Harvard Theatre Collection, especially Heather Ahlstrom and Annette Fern, for their generous assistance.

1. Walter Benjamin, *Illuminations*, edited with an introduction by Hannah Arendt and translated by Harry Zohn (New York: Schocken Books, 1969), 220. Further references are to this text.
2. In fact, lithographs of ballerinas became such collectors' items in the early decades of this century that many appear to have been removed from bound volumes, leaving little trace of the context in which they originally appeared. Many of those images appeared later in reproduced form, either as illustrations to ballet histories or, in at least two cases, in dedicated collections.
3. In Baudelaire, *Mon coeur mis a nu*, quoted in Beatrice Farwell, ed., *The Cult of Images: Baudelaire and the 19th-Century Media Explosion*, exhibition catalogue (Santa Barbara, CA: University of California at Santa Barbara Art Museum, April 6-May 8, 1977), 7. As Farwell points out, lithography, which emerged as the primary medium for mass-producing images during the nineteenth century, was the key element in the explosion of images that took place from about 1820 to 1860. These were the very decades that saw the emergence and decline of Romantic ballet in France and England.
4. Laura Mulvey, "Visual Pleasure and Narrative Cinema," 1975, rpt. in *Visual and Other Pleasures* (Bloomington: Indiana University Press, 1989), 14-26: see p. 19.
5. Benjamin, not surprisingly, does not address gender explicitly, but he does so implicitly. He identifies the camera with "testing," arguing, "The camera director in the studio occupies a place identical with that of the examiner during aptitude tests" (246n). It is hard to imagine a presence more implicitly masculine than the "committee of experts" he associates with that examiner.

6. Théophile Gautier, *Gautier on Dance*, edited and translated by Ivor Guest (London: Cecil Court, 1986), 132. Further references are to this edition.

7. Binney's excellent brief biographical essay mentions specific sums: for example, a benefit performance (to raise money for the ballerina) at the Paris Opera in 1837 raised the "enormous sum" of 36,970 francs; Taglioni was thirty-three, and though she retired from the Paris Opera with that performance, she performed in many other lucrative ballets before her final retirement ten years later. Edwin Binney, *Longing for the Ideal: Images of Marie Taglioni in the Romantic Ballet, A Centenary Exhibition* (Cambridge, MA: Harvard College Library, Harvard Theatre Collection, 1984), 23 ff.

8. "The little princess was passionately attracted to the ballet, and Marie Taglioni became her idol. She had a Taglioni doll, named her fastest horse after the dancer, and noted in her diary, 'I dressed myself up as La Naiade, as Taglioni was dressed, with corals in my hair'" (Binney, 18).

9. *The Exquisite*, Vol. I: 1-36 (London: H. Smith, 1844). Further references are to this edition.

10. *Julien's Album de l'Opéra.* (London: Hanhart Lith. Printers, n.d.; 1845?). This gift-book format seems to have been somewhat unusual in England, though not unique; several similar "albums" were published in Paris at the height of the Romantic ballet, sometimes appearing first as a series of lithographs with accompanying text, then ultimately bound as a souvenir volume. The traditional mid-Victorian gift-book series (such as *The Keepsake* and *Forget-Me-Not*), interestingly, do not include pictures of ballerinas. Further references are to this edition.

11. Parmenia Migel, *The Ballerinas: From the Court of Louis XIV to Pavlova* (New York: Da Capo Press, 1972), 225-29.

12. Binney, 18.

13. See especially Ivor Guest, *The Romantic Ballet in England* (Middletown, CT: Wesleyan University Press, 1972).

THE POLITICS OF HUMOR IN
GEORGE CRUIKSHANK'S
GRAPHIC SATIRE

Robert L. Patten

While Georgian graphic satire was churned out in hundreds of multiples by dozens of different designers, etchers, and publishers, prints often had the cachet of being by identifiable artists. James Gillray was probably the most successful in establishing an "aura" for his vision, though Thomas Rowlandson ran him a close second, and after 1810 George Cruikshank's graphic satires developed brand-name identification, attracted copyists and plagiarists, and on occasions created a market demand for "originals" printed from his etched plate that numbered upwards of 500 or more. The originality of a graphic satire inhered more in the characteristic visual language (line, gesture, topics, and imagery) of particular artists than in the uniqueness of the print; but reduced facsimiles produced by journeymen etchers, or copies hastily manufactured by rival dealers, do generally lack the verve, the touch, the brio, of the artist's own execution. Nonetheless, when one examines the etchings of a Gillray or a Rowlandson it is the personal vision of the artist that, more than the "touch," stamps an image with its artist's identity. Even copies of a Rowlandson or Gillray will be recognizably of a Rowlandson or a Gillray, because they deployed such identifiable and distinct modes of expression.

Thus it would seem as if finding the artist within the image would be a relatively easy task, and that inferring an artist's views on passing events from his political satires could be accomplished with a fair degree of certainty. That turns out not to be the case with George Cruikshank, whose multiple satires on various sides of controversial political events confound efforts to identify a single and consistent political or ideological commitment within his etchings and wood engravings, his dealers, and his associations.[1] The layers of communication that accrete to visual figures and situations being adapted from other verbal, pictorial, architectural, and sculptural sources on an almost daily basis during heated crises and scandals produce apparently edged and focused critiques that, upon close inspection, bespeak multiple contradictory affiliations and implications energetically discoursing within a single frame.

It is puzzling to late-twentieth-century commentators, especially those trained in history or theory, to find omnidirectional politics throughout an artist's work. In George Cruikshank's case, the fact that he could issue devastating graphic satires for and against his best friend within the same week seems explicable only in terms of insincerity, disloyalty, or lack of principle.[2] Cruikshank doesn't help to identify his center of political consciousness: late in life he reflected that his grandfather had been a Whig and his father a Tory, that he had been radical as a youth, and was by 1867 a Conservative, so in short he was "a Tory-Whig-Liberal [suppressing the subversive side of radicalism]-Conservative."[3] Moreover, during his long life he adhered rather stubbornly to certain convictions, including an Enlightenment belief that a person's life was directed by willpower. Consequently he found himself in his later years skeptical of policies that were justified by conceptions of social construction — for instance, that human beings are evil or dissolute because their conditions of existence are imperfect. "Nonsense," the octogenarian Cruikshank would thunder. To go right, one only needs to engage one's willpower — abstain from alcohol, save money, develop a craft, hold a job, work hard, and behave. After studying Cruikshank's oeuvre for a quarter century, I concluded that the artist holds a medley of opinions more Whig than Tory, more lower-middle class than upper class, more liberal than radical, and definitely cautious, even suspicious, about extreme claims for progress (cf. 1.151-52).

So to read the politics of a graphic satirist into his life, or vice versa, is not always an easy or valid task. Of George Cruikshank's great contemporaries, Gillray's life and art are probably better understood in terms of sectarian politics than Rowlandson's; and while our knowledge of Isaac Cruikshank's output may be less complete and systematic than in the other cases, from what we know it seems probable that partisan political convictions were not a central motivation for many of Isaac's graphics. Politics and humor are not easy bedfellows. The wholesale appropriation of visual and verbal imagery that characterizes the marketplace for exfoliating products in Georgian print shops often confounds attempts to isolate a particular target of attack. When satirists had to make a fresh image once a week or more and to keep the market for these evanescent products stimulated, they grafted images from other artists' work, from pamphlets and popular theater and classics and any other oblique source currently in circulation, and reformulated the formula. In so doing, the disparate origins and implications of the appropriated materials complicate simple, stable, politically univocal readings of the resulting images. Popular imagery remains popular in part because it speaks to many different audiences.

[85]

An image exemplifying the ramified and contradictory voices of an apparently simple and characteristically Cruikshankian satiric print is one of the many produced by graphic satirists during the frenzied months between the accession of George IV in January 1820 and the death of his estranged consort, Caroline of Brunswick, on 7 August 1821. The feud between the mismatched royals extended to their political supporters and outward into the public, and the two sides had their cases sharpened by the partisan rhetoric and graphics of superb publicists. The episode has been much studied as a moment in history when revolutionary fervor and discontent dissipated through the spectacularization of a long-running marital spat, so instead of dealing with the historic origins and political consequences of these events, which had constitutional implications, I will focus on a representation of the king and queen ostensibly etched by Cruikshank for the queen's side and examine its complex, contradictory, and perplexingly ambivalent iconography.[4]

Ah! Sure Such a Pair was issued in colored and uncolored states on 23 June 1820 (Plate 1 fig. 16).[5] Caroline, who had been exiled to Europe for years, had, according to inquiries the Prince of Wales instituted on several occasions, misbehaved herself badly, elevating her major-domo to a factitious barony and, according to many, the favors of her bed, and shocking the public by her antics and décolletage. She, on the other hand, was seen by her admirers as affectionate, impulsive, spoilt, a rattle and a railleur, a "kindly, generous, tactless woman" who, during her long persecution, "showed that the leonine nature of a Brunswicker was a real hereditary attribute and not merely a courtier's myth."[6] Throughout her married life, she was subjected to surveillance by the prince's minions, who infiltrated her retinue and sent to the estranged husband scandalous — and apparently unfounded — tattle about Caroline's supposed affairs and illegitimate children.

But it had never been possible to prosecute the princess because her husband was such a notorious profligate himself that the countercharges would have been ruinous.

When George III died on 29 January 1820, his eldest son determined that his hated, adulterous wife would never be crowned queen. He insisted on an Order in Council preventing her name from being inserted into the Church of England liturgy. To assert her rights, Caroline returned to England, where radical politicians, city merchants, Londoners, and the common people remade her, for a few months during the summer of 1820, in the image of a lily-white heroine cruelly abused by an immoral husband. The king directed his ministers to introduce into the House of Lords a bill depriving Caroline of her rights and granting a divorce; the resulting "trial" of the queen paralyzed the government and captivated the public through the autumn of 1820. Nothing else was thought of until, after the third reading on 10 November, the bill received a bare majority of nine; at that point Lord Liverpool withdrew the action and the public rejoiced in the "vindication" of their heroine. The following year, on 19 July 1821, Caroline tried to force her way into the Westminster Abbey during the coronation ceremony; refused entrance, she returned to Brandenburgh House in humiliation. The public had veered round to the new king and now found Caroline meretricious, foolish, and bawdy. She was excoriated for having accepted earlier that spring a Parliamentary grant of £50,000 per year and giving up many of her other claims. Some who knew her did not hesitate to pronounce her as mad as her relatives — insanity ran in the Hanoverian line, and she was the child of George III's favorite sister. (The queenite version held that she had the same tenacity as her famous warrior father, the duke of Brunswick.) A few months later Caroline was dead, probably of intestinal cancer but in the popular mind killed by shame and conjugal cruelty.

[87]

During the most intense phase of this affair, newspapers, broadsides, pamphlets, and prints (plain or colored) proliferated at a staggering rate — the British Museum houses 565 political satires dated 1820. George Cruikshank, Britain's leading graphic caricaturist, and his brother Robert churned out dozens of broadsheet etchings and hundreds of designs for wood engravings illustrating inexpensive pamphlets about the affair. In effect, they lived off the royal marital scandal for nearly a year. Most of George Cruikshank's prints took the queen's side, portraying the king as a rake, a debauched villain, a paunchy and infantilized victim of his mistress's ambitions, and so forth.[7] But some plates attacked the queen, her lover Bergami, her lawyer Lord Brougham, and her supporters — radical MPs, independent city merchants, and the lower classes.[8] Whichever side they took, Cruikshank's lampoons worked powerfully to articulate public opinion, to engage, shape, and incite it. Of some of these images, over 100,000 were sold within a few weeks. Thus on this point at least, it ought to be possible to ascertain which side a particular image supported and then to determine whether Cruikshank's political satire abetted the king or the queen.

But we face at the outset of our quest to define Cruikshank's politics a host of unanswerable questions. Where in this tangled story of royal infidelity and political expedience can Cruikshank's *own* opinions be located? What aspects of the imagery and fictions he deployed are *his*, not inherited from others or imposed by circumstances or his print-seller patrons or reinforced by the sales of a particular strain of images? When he borrows from others, does the source control the implication of the image, or can Cruikshank delimit the resonances of his materials to the single note he wants to sound?

In this strikingly simplified print, the king and queen are portrayed as green bags; the king wears his crown, but the queen

Figure 17.
R. Cooper after William Derby,
*Caroline, the Injured Queen of
England*, engraving, 1820,
courtesy of British Museum.

wears the "Regent's cap" with which she had often been identified (fig. 17).[9] Its ostrich plumes may indicate to some that she is still princess of Wales, the feathers being a characteristic part of that insignia and often depicted as tattered peacock feathers when the Prince of Wales was lampooned. She seems to be demurely taunting the king, while he appears simultaneously furious and terrified.

We might start by interrogating the origins of these simplified forms — the almost pure shapes through which the iconography and bodies are rendered. The political caricatures of many of Cruikshank's predecessors, and especially of the greatest of these artists, James Gillray, often depended on complex emblematic allegories. Gillray's 11 Jan. 1798 print, *The Apotheosis of Hoche*, converts the panoply of symbols associated with the divine right of the *ancien régime* into symbols of a secular, rational, citizen state: the triune deity, for instance, becomes a rational, mathematical, equilateral triangle.[10] General Lazare Hoche was an ardent Republican, an inveterate enemy of Britain, and victor over the Vendée revolt and at Quiberon; he died mysteriously at the age of thirty-one. Gillray depicts him playing a guillotine instead of a

[89]

lyre, about to be transported heavenwards not by flights of angels but by a noose.

Diana Donald has recently concluded that during the 1780s the elaborate allegorical and emblematic graphics transmitted from Renaissance emblem books migrated downward into prints for semiliterate customers, while the upper classes patronized images increasingly dependent for satiric thrust on deviations from Old Masters and other works known only to the cognoscenti.[11] While there may be some truth to this bifurcation of imagery in the late-eighteenth century, the relationship between icono-graphic style and audience class does not operate in any very sys-tematic way in British caricatures. Caricaturists are likely to meld iconography from disparate sources, "high" art and "low," to make inventive use of popular images and children's games, to draw on the patent and non-patent theaters and on any source, domestic or foreign, that provides a striking pictorialization of an event or issue. And the audiences for these prints were very broad in num-bers and classes, ranging from dukes to dustmen. In the case of the Hoche print and Gillray's other work of the time for the *Anti-Jacobin*, his patrons and advisers were aristocrats and members of the prime minister's inner circle. So evidently parodies of the emblematic tradition still in 1798 spoke to the governing classes as well as the middle classes.

The nonemblematic imagery of Cruikshank's green bags prob-ably owes much to the importation of Russian prints into Britain in 1812. These were designed simply; characteristically they used large figures and bright colors. Cruikshank adapted many of them for his anti-Napoleon plates of the next few years. In one, he depicts the Allied hero, a Russian Cossack, snuffing out a tiny flat candle in the shape of Napoleon (fig. 18).[12] Above the candle is a picture resembling a print by another graphic satirist, William Elmes, who makes Napoleon a farthing rush light instead of a flat

Figure 18.
George Cruikshank, *Snuffing Out Boney*, colored etching, 1814.

candle.[13] Both Cruikshank and Elmes had adapted the virile Cossack from Russian originals.

Admittedly, Cruikshank might have learned this lesson about simplification from Gillray, who by 1812 was a victim of mental illness and could no longer etch anything. In addition to the complex allegorical prints such as the one about Hoche, Gillray did sometimes design wonderfully simple squibs: the 1791 picture of the intertwined feet of the duke of York and his new wife imaged the gossip about the duchess's tiny feet and implied, without graphic vulgarity, their conjugal delights.[14] And whether Gillray taught him the lesson, or his father Isaac Cruikshank, or his print dealer, Cruikshank knew well that a simple image took less time to etch and color, and if cleverly imagined, could strike the public fancy just as remuneratively as any imitation of a high-art engraving. So the bold, simplified forms of this print may indicate the class of audience Cruikshank targeted, his indebtedness to Russian prints or to his fellow artists Gillray (a negative and positive example) and Elmes, or his publisher's request that he make an image easily and quickly produced for rapid turnover in the agitated market for propaganda about the royals.

Caricature bodies often represent recognizable persons; indeed a whole branch of caricature specialized in distorting the features of well-known figures. But these bodies also often represent personality and moral character. Cruikshank's image of the king and queen as green bags renders only their heads anatomically. The rest of their bodies are stuffed into, or converted into, green bags. This caricature print, like most, was issued in hand-colored state for two shillings six pence and in uncolored state for a shilling: only the colored state would in this case make clear what those bags were. Green bags were simply the Georgian equivalent of briefcases, containers into which documents were put. Two years before this print, in 1818 the prince regent had been anticipating his reign and thinking of marrying again. To secure the throne, he needed to produce an heir, since his only child Charlotte and her first-born son had died in childbirth. So the regent dispatched three officials to Milan, "and from thence to all other places at your discretion for the purpose of making enquiries into the conduct of Her Royal Highness the Princess of Wales."[15] Over the next two years the Milan Commission spied on the princess, suborning her servants (especially those she dismissed) and sending home "evidence" of her infidelity with her majordomo Bartolomeo Bergami (or Pergami). On 7 April 1820, the day the queen arrived in London, the king sent two green bags full of the Milan Commission's "evidence," one to the House of Lords and the other to the House of Commons. The bags were placed upon the table as evidence. The one sent to the Commons was not opened, pending negotiations with the queen's representatives. But that sent to the Lords was investigated by a secret committee, which reported a month later that the green bag contained sufficient grounds to proceed with a trial for adultery.

Cruikshank delights in the double-edged pun: he has the bags "ordered to lie" — rest upon the table and prevaricate — , but he changes the verb to "lay," which both partially cancels the accusation of falsehood while calling attention to it and also implies the sexual improprieties that are alleged to be at the base of these proceedings. Are lying and laying, then, etymologically distinct though often confused, both different and the same?

The queen's counsel, Henry Brougham, quipped on 7 June, "If the King had a Green Bag the Queen might have one too," a warning that he was prepared, if necessary, to bring out the king's illegal marriage to a Catholic widow, Mrs. Fitzherbert.[16] To the public, a "green bag" had been for some years a symbol of tainted evidence; in popular figuration the green bag stands "for a conspiracy by means of perjurers, sometimes of assassins."[17] Green bags were alluded to in virtually every print supportive of the queen during the remainder of the "trial." In the margin Cruikshank gives credit for inventing the image to Brougham — his name, characteristically, simplified in spelling to that of a household utensil used to sweep out dirt. He also dedicates the print to *"Old Bags,"* that is, Lord Chancellor John Scott Eldon (created the first earl of Eldon in 1821), who had been one of Caroline's admirers until the prince was named regent in 1811. Then Eldon switched sides, hoping for preferment; as lord chancellor he presided over the "trial."

So the bodies of the monarch and his consort have been reduced to bags. To be sure, signs of their nobility remain: both are belted with the highest honor the crown can bestow, the Order of the Garter, the king's literally a belt to cinch his girth, the queen's the totemic blue velvet ribbon of the order inscribed with its all-too-appropriate motto, *honi soit qui mal y pense* (that is, "may he be shamed who thinks ill of it"). Because the limbs of both persons have been contained or squashed or cut off in the bags, these garters cannot go around the calf as they should; instead they girdle the overflowing waists, figures for their sexual, financial, alimentary, and administrative excesses. One other word shows: "Droit," that is, "right" — as in the right of a monarch to order or the right of his spouse to be prayed for and crowned. "Right," too, connotes correct, proper, righteous, senses that would justify the power which is another aspect of "droit" and which have not been applicable to either bag's behavior.

These baggy shapes inscribe the body of the king struggling to get out of his bag and pummel his antagonist and the body of the queen withdrawing, both coy and provocative. That we sense the shape of bodies beneath the cloth is due to Cruikshank's superb draughtsmanship. But that skill in drawing is deployed for other effects as well. The king had been the greatest sportsman of his time, a champion whip, fencer, and hunter; he patronized the ring and the racecourse. But over time, gourmandizing swelled his body to grotesque proportions. Cruikshank drew him as the *Prince of Whales* in 1812.[18] The prince's thick natural hair was eventually replaced by what William Makepeace Thackeray remembered years later as "one of Truefitt's best nutty brown wigs reeking with oil," while his face was framed by mutton-chop sideburns and his body encased in tight-fitting, elaborately embroidered uniforms.[19] An 1816 Cruikshank print, *Gent, No Gent, and Regent*, illustrates the declension of body and character from "Gent," when the prince was a handsome young colonel of the 10th Light Dragoons, to "No Gent" reveling in a tavern with Mrs. Fitzherbert and two radical members of Parliament, Charles James Fox and Richard Brinsley Sheridan, and finally to "Regent," enthroned in Oriental splendor at Brighton.[20]

As soon as the regent became king, he attempted to suppress unfavorable pictures of himself by buying off caricaturists and publishers. He paid £100 to George Cruikshank "not to caricature His Majesty in any immoral situation."[21] Cruikshank signed the receipt so stipulating only four days before he published his green-bag print. And the artist went on caricaturing his majesty, using the king's ungainly bulk as a sign of his licentiousness, gross appetites, and enormous expenditure. Following another of Gillray's brilliant images, a portrait of the prince in 1792 as *A Voluptuary under the Horrors of Digestion*, Cruikshank designed in August 1820, two months after the green bags, a wood engraving depicting the king as tipsy, stupefied, lolling in a chair with the Order of the Garter dangling from his left calf.[22] This image comes at the start of a little inexpensive pamphlet, *The Queen's Matrimonial Ladder*, co-invented, written, and produced by the radical publisher William Hone. This was both an illustrated verse-satire and a cardboard toy ladder that, with different images

[95]

and words, both trace the rise and fall of the prince's courtship and marriage. It is a brilliant adaptation of nursery rhymes and play-things, one of many nineteenth-century instances of childhood materials being put to adult uses.[23] Forced by Parliament to marry (despite his secret, unlawful marriage to Mrs. Fitzherbert) in order to settle his debts, the prince's "qualification" to propose to his cousin Caroline was, in the words of the verse, that he was "In love, and in drink, and o'ertoppled by debt; / With women, with wine, and with duns on the fret." Thus the very bulk that lies concealed within the green bag in Cruikshank's caricature expresses the unmanning of a former sportsman and soldier, the gross physical contours of a debauched voluptuary. And yet, true to the letter of his word, Cruikshank has not depicted the king in any immoral situation.

So far the caricature seems to side with the queen, using her counsel's threat for its principal trope and alluding to the king's obesity and misbehavior. Indeed, the king's sins are so gross that his bag is far larger than the queen's. But the queen is also baggy. Already overweight when George first met her, Caroline had grown more corpulent and outré in dress, until her décolleté-dropped to alarming depths. Allegedly she appeared at one European ball costumed as Venus, naked from the waist up. Writing about Cruikshank's career many years later, Thackeray, who had learned comic etching from Cruikshank, declared that the artist "most certainly believed, along with the great body of the people whom he represents, that the Princess was the most spotless, pure-mannered darling of a Princess that ever married a heartless debauchee of a Prince Royal."[24] But Thackeray had forgotten much, including Cruikshank's earlier prints attacking Caroline for her flagrant sexuality. Caroline had worn a Turkish peasant's cos-tume to a ball she gave in 1814 for Murat, prince of Naples. More-over, at least according to the Milan Commission spies, she had taken Napoleon's former courier, Bergami, as her lover. Not too subtly, in an 1817 print of Caroline's *Royal Condescension*, showing her introducing Bergami to Prince Metternich, Cruikshank hints at the phallic attractions all men allegedly had for Caroline.[25] Allegations that Caroline bedded her chamberlain and behaved indecently with him in public continued to circulate in private letters home from Europe, in the government packets containing the testimony of paid spies, and in the prints and pamphlets produced for home consumption. In a broadsheet caricature issued just a week prior to his more even-handed green-bag print,[26] Cruikshank shows Caroline in four compromising situations: in the first, accompanied by Bergami in a Naples opera box, she is wearing a Turkish turban and décolleté dress; they were hissed out of the theater by patrons outraged at her effrontery. A second incident alludes to Caroline's ennobling her chamberlain; a third represents their unchaste conduct; and the last attacks her for consorting with Napoleonic hangers-on such as Murat and Pauline Borghese. In all cases Caroline's outlandish and revealing dress is emphasized. It contains her body barely more than the green bag does.

On the other hand, as is so characteristic of the layered imagery of caricature, "much may be said on both sides," as Robert Cruikshank once observed in a print.[27] Turkish or Oriental dress was ridiculous, un-English, licentious. The princess from Brunswick was definitely not English, not hypocritical, not repressed; her costume connotes display, immodesty, sexual energy, and the overflowing breasts that were also possessed by the succession of maternal women who nursed the prince's body and ego. But the non-Western, non-Christian, Turkish or Oriental style also connoted strangeness, a kind of cultural sophistication, romance; it suggested the power of something other, power often troped through the nineteenth century as the fantasy of British men's control over their women.[28] This power was notably wielded by a great patron of Orientalia, the prince regent, in his

[97]

Figure 19.
George Cruikshank, *The Court at Brighton à la Chinese!!*, colored etching, 1816.

Orientalized Brighton pavilion. An 1816 Cruikshank caricature of *The Court at Brighton à la Chinese!!* alludes to the regent's "oriental" tastes, to the dragons, pagodas, and bells being added to the pavilion at Brighton as well as to his increasing girth and resemblance to the Chinese emperor (fig. 19).[29] The imagery also picks up tropes from Lord Stanley's recent speech in the House of Lords opposing an income tax to finance the regent's extravagance: Stanley deplored any revenue that would support "the pomp of a Persian satrap, seated in the splendour of oriental state, [rather] than the sober dignity of a British prince, seated in the bosom of his subjects."[30] If these baggy bodies are signs of dissipation and impotence, they are also signs of a gross appetitive luxury unknown to sober domestic Britons nurtured at a more mannerly bosom.

Moreover, even though the bulky shapes may connote appetitive vitality, they are so alike as to be androgynous, asexual. If it were not for their hair — but they are wigs in both cases — ; if it were not then for the crown and the hat — but hers is very mannish and sports the Prince of Wales's feathers; if it were not then for the belts — but they are almost alike; if then it were not for Caroline's ruff, we would hardly know which was the man-bag and which the woman-bag. The king was drawn to maternal mistresses, older, bosomy women, who were often depicted as leading him around like a baby on a leash. In their hands he was thought to revert to infantile orality. The queen was imaged not only as seeking phallic power for self-gratification but also as wielding it herself by wearing trousers and by conducting her own campaign to be crowned alongside her spouse. Sir Walter Scott wrote to his son that if Caroline "had as many followers of high as of low degree (in proportion), and funds to equip them, I should not be surprised to see her fat bottom in a pair of buckskins, and at the head of an army."[31] Cruikshank's blurring of genders in these baggy bodies thus speaks to the reality of their perceived behavior.[32]

That blurring of gender distinctions also speaks, though perhaps less overtly, to a division between the king's two bodies known to iconographic portraiture for centuries. Since it was disloyal, even treasonous, to criticize the divine right ("droit") of kings, a political and pictorial fiction was generated in which the king's royal body does no wrong while the king's physical body is misled by evil councilors or, in this case, motherly mistresses who infantalize him. Such a strategy was invoked during the reign of George III.[33] And as he grew older and more eccentric, farmer George, the kindly old man living frugally at Kew, began to be depicted as a lovable old body, a portly human being whose figure is nearly assimilated into that of John Bull. One of the most famous transformations of oppressive royalty into benignant royalty was Gillray's sympathetic portrait of George III as the king of Brobdingnag, examining a Lilliputian Gulliver/Napoleon and pronouncing him "one of the most pernicious, little — odious — reptiles that nature ever suffer'd to crawl upon the surface of the Earth."[34] Against such portrayals of the royal family, what are we to make of Cruikshank's bodily deformations? Do they speak to his contempt for the person, for the character, for the morals, for the advisors, or for the office? Does he advocate diet to condition the person, reform to amend the character, abstinence to correct the morals, a change of government to admonish the advisors, or regicide? And whose body rules — the king's or the queen's?

Indeed, does Cruikshank depict two bodies here or a doubled view of one? There were two green bags, but each contained the same Milan Commission evidence. There were two houses of Parliament, two tables to lay the bags on, and two parties to the dispute. But only Parliament acting as one body could sever the one body made by marriage back into two gendered bodies.

Cruikshank's plate has another kind of two-in-oneness. It depends not only on graphic images but also on words. The title is

[100]

part of the total communication. That title is a phrase, "Ah! sure such a pair was never seen so justly form'd to meet by nature." This phrase comes from a song in a play, *The Duenna* (1775), by Richard Brinsley Sheridan, the playwright and member of Parliament who was one of the regent's boon companions when he was courting Mrs. Fitzherbert. The play is set in Spain, where a Portuguese Jew, Isaac Mendoza, who is notable for his ugliness and who finds ugly women consoling, meets the equally ugly duenna Margaret pretending to be her young mistress Louisa and angling to marry the Jew for his money. Isaac's friend Carlos can think of nothing complimentary to say about the allegedly enamored couple, so he sings:

Ah! sure such a pair was never seen,
So justly form'd to meet by nature.
 The youth excelling so in mien,
 The maid in ev'ry grace of feature.
  O how happy are such lovers
  When kindred beauties each discovers.
   For surely she
   Was made for thee,
And thou to bless this lovely creature.[35]

Cruikshank had used the tag line for the title of an 1818 social satire.[36] In that plate, a remarkably ugly pair meet in profile, the dandified man's misshapen features and upswept hair dovetailing into the woman's face and décolleté dress. They are clearly yin and yang, two parts of a composite whole. And they correspond to Isaac and Margaret in Sheridan's play. However, the same tag line had been picked up by the popular press and adapted to Princess Caroline's liaison with the whiskered Bergami on the banks of Lake Como:

Never sure on earth was seen a
Pair, so formed the eye to charm,
Whiskerandos, Tilburina,
Queen and Lacquey, arm in arm.[37]

Bergami was a handsome, virile man, much admired by the females in his retinue, and Caroline was, off and on, a favorite of the men. So in this instance the lovers are, if of different ranks ("Queen and Lacquey"), still attractive and not mismatched.

What then are we to make of Cruikshank's applying the line to the king and his consort? What meanings might be found in the chain of substitutions, from Isaac Mendoza to ugly dandy to Bergami to Whiskerandos to equally bewhiskered king; from elderly duenna masquerading as young heiress to ugly female to princess to Tilburina to queen? If Brougham, punningly present as the originator of the print's trope, is identified as the queen's spokesperson, can we suppose that for some portion of Cruikshank's audience Sheridan, implicitly present as the author of the print's title, becomes spokesperson for the king's side? And is Eldon, formerly one of the queen's courtiers, then the king's, and now presiding over their divorce, a spokesperson for "both" sides? Might we — or Cruikshank and his fellow artists, or his purchasers and viewers — read the object of the queen's coy look as both the king (who spent their wedding night passed out on the floor of the bedchamber but who nevertheless fathered a daughter born nine months later) and Bergami (who may or may not have slept with Caroline, but certainly never fathered a child by her)? In this squib tag line and image together set up unstable relationships: multiple persons are conflated in each member of the "pair," and the binaries of beauty and ugliness, youth and age, Portuguese Jew and Spanish duenna, major domo and king, princess and queen, are present in the same image. Here is another instance of the duplicity of pairing and singleness, one-in-twoness, and an excellent example of the way in which a physical shape, alone or allied with a text, may simultaneously present more than one figure.

Let us back off these dizzying binaries for a moment and look more closely at Caroline, whose beauty or blowsiness depends on the observer. When Sir Thomas Lawrence painted her portrait in 1816, after her separation but before her European exile, she was in her forties, corpulent but not gross (fig. 20). If his depiction seems to flatter her, that may be because he, like other courtiers, fell in love with her and was, allegedly, one of her paramours. By the time of her "trial" in 1820, the fifty-two-year-old Caroline was bloated and raddled, probably suffering from the first stages of intestinal cancer. She was, however, still phenomenally energetic. To some she seemed deranged. Lady Brownlow was "shocked and disgusted with her appearance. She had exchanged her long fair hair for a black wig with a mass of long curls hanging on each side of her face, her eyebrows were painted black, her cheeks were plastered with rouge, and the expression of her countenance was most disagreeably bold and stern."[38] Others saw her differently, though her principal publicists, Brougham and William Cobbett, of course overdid their flattering rhetoric in order to paint a picture of a "spotless, pure-mannered darling." Has Cruikshank contributed to this public relations effort by lightening the paint on the eyebrows, thinning the cheeks, and dressing the hair more becomingly, because he too believes in her purity?

He may have liposucked the jowls a bit, but both faces are notably puffy around the jaws, and their "justly form'd" shapes resemble a pair of unripe (green) or overripe (aged) pears. There is clever visual comedy in the way Cruikshank has taken the jowly faces and replicated them on an enlarged scale for the bodies. But there is a further meaning to these shapes. High and low artists, oil painters and caricaturists alike, subscribed to general principles of

Figure 20.
Sir Thomas Lawrence,
Caroline Amelia Elizabeth of Brunswick,
oil painting, 1804,
courtesy of National Portrait Library.

representation that equated physical types with temperaments. The most elaborately worked out of these equations concerned the head and the ways in which it revealed character. In a famous etching of 1798, *Doublûres of Characters*, James Gillray illustrated how little alterations of contour could convert a realistic portrait of a living public figure into the essential character he resembles — the "arch fiend," in the case of the radical M.P. Charles James Fox, or "Judas selling his Master," Gillray's charge against the perennially bankrupt Sheridan.[39] There is no ambiguity about Gillray's politics here; he was in the government's pay and hit the opposition hard. But he cited an unimpeachable authority for his doubles of character, his two-in-oneness. "'If you would know Mens Hearts, look in their faces' — *Lavater*." Johann Caspar Lavater, a Swiss, had in four volumes worked out the implications of each facial feature: his *Essays on Physiognomy* established a vocabulary of physiological psychology for three generations of European artists and writers.[40] Of the pear-shaped head, Lavater writes:

> Large bulky persons, with small eyes, round full hanging cheeks, puffed lips, and a chin resembling a purse or bag; who are continually occupied with their own corpulence, who on every occasion consult their own ease without regard to others, are, in reality, frivolous, insipid, power-less, vain, inconstant, imprudent, conceited voluptuous characters, difficult to guide, which desire much and enjoy little — and whoever enjoys little, gives little.[41]

This diagnosis is not wide of the mark for either the king or the queen, at least insofar as they have been represented by their detractors. By graphically portraying the Lavaterian somatotype, Cruikshank implies through shape his characters' personalities.

[105]

And once again, by making each of them pear-shaped, he implies that this pair is the same, two as one.

Such conflation erases Gillray's partisan bias. Insofar as Cruikshank's bags represent character, they bespeak a plague on both houses. By contrast, when the great French publicist Charles Philipon carried on his war against Louis-Philippe by drawing the devolution of a portrait bust of the "citizen king" into a pear, the attack was confined to the king. *"Poire"* in French slang means dimwit, fool; soon radicals and youngsters were chalking up "the Pear" on walls everywhere. Philipon's drawing and variants of it by Honoré Daumier and others, including one of the pear-headed king as a bare-chested fat Oriental statuette, were considered so injurious that Philipon and Daumier were prosecuted and jailed. Cruikshank got away with a charge Philipon could not make with impunity a decade later because in 1820 the British government was paralyzed by rival factions and because its efforts to prosecute libelous caricatures, to jail their publishers, and to buy up harmful plates had all failed to shut down the market. The July Monarchy inherited the state machinery of the Bourbons and the Bonapartes. In the early 1830s it could suppress, if not extinguish, opposition criticism ruthlessly.

Cruikshank continued to attack both king and queen, though his plates appealed to a London public generally queenite in sympathy. When after his coronation George IV enjoyed a few months of popularity, Cruikshank lampooned Caroline. And throughout the whirligig of transient opinion, Cruikshank worked for the premier, and conservative, dealer, George Humphrey, known for his support of the king. Humphrey inherited his aunt's shop just a few steps from St. James's Palace, and with the shop came the inventory of coppers and prints etched by Gillray, who lived upstairs as an artistic pensioner of Hannah Humphrey until his death, and the patronage of many within the governing class.

Publishers' biases and the customer base responding to those biases have much to do with which side a political cartoonist takes. What, then, can we conclude about Cruikshank's, or Humphrey's, or their customers' politics when Cruikshank etches two plates for George Humphrey within five weeks, one queenite and one kingite? The first, *Royal Rush Light*, published 3 March 1821, uses that imagery Cruikshank had applied to the Cossack extinguishing the flat candle Napoleon.[42] Here the king and his ministers cannot blow out the little farthing rush light of the queen, who prevails. The picture would seem to side with the queen. Ambiguity arises, however, when this picture is juxtaposed to its predecessor and model, *Snuffing Out Boney*. The king here is in the position of the Cossack, Britain's ally against Bonaparte in the earlier picture, and the queen here replaces Napoleon, the far-thing rush light or flat candle. So is the king/Cossack good, though unable to extinguish the queen/Napoleon who is bad? A month later, on 7 April 1821, Humphrey published *The Royal Extinguisher, or the King of Brobdingnag and Gulliver*.[43] Here Cruik-shank, using his brother Robert's idea, combines the imagery of *Snuffing Out Boney* with Gillray's plate of George III pronouncing judgment on a Lilliputian Gulliver/Napoleon. And here, past iconography seems to reinforce present usage: the king, like his father and the Cossack, prevails over Britain's enemies foreign (Bonaparte) and domestic (Caroline).

The politics of a caricaturist are thus not easy to discern; they are inflected by many forces, and the resultant images often recon-cile in lines and shapes and colors warring convictions and parties and ideas. The nineteenth century reintroduced the criterion of "sincerity" as a measure of an author's or artist's work, but it is a concept inappropriate to apply to Georgian-era satirists. Thus, if we cannot identify very specific and particular political programs to which George Cruikshank gave unswerving support, we must not convict him of insincerity or expediency or weakness of intellect but instead look elsewhere for what he, as the inheritor of the great tradition of Georgian satire, valued in his vocation.

Cruikshank can be identified first of all by his art. His primary aim throughout his lifetime was to produce good quality pictures that would catch the public's eye and sell. In the case of the green bags, Cruikshank did three or four other full-sized satiric etchings in the same month, June 1820, and was preparing thirteen designs for wood-engravings illustrating a pamphlet entitled *The Green Bag*, published early in July.[44] So he had to be economical in detail. He drew a plate that was easy to etch and print and color, easy to read, easy to market, and easy to assimilate into public consciousness — into the whole range of figuration, from Old Master images to Gillray's caricatures to children's games and toys and verses — that had been employed to represent the king and queen and would be used in the future about them and the "trial." Cruikshank was an artist, and his triumph in the first instance was to meld within a graphic vocabulary a miscellany of feelings, opinions, words, appearances, characters, and actions, and to make the result instantly recognizable to his public.

Second, Cruikshank can be identified by the economy of that meld. The essence of art, and especially of humorous art, is economy, as Freud explains in his treatise on jokes and their relation to the unconscious. The subject of much of Jack Benny's humor was his stinginess; but his miserliness was also the genius of his craft. No one ever wrested more purchase from a penny or more laughter from a pause. Analogously, Cruikshank's humor springs from his economy, from the simplicity and condensation of his shapes and puns. He focuses multiple meanings onto a single element, a bag, or a word. The trouble with explaining this print, or any joke, is that the joke gets buried under the wordiness of the explanation. No matter how many subsidiary and contributing bits the

[108]

joke may contain, its central point must register immediately. And Cruikshank's does.

Third, Cruikshank can be identified by his absence. That is, he was a popular artist working for his publishers and his public, and in some sense speaking for them in all their variety. Thackeray indicates as much when he speaks of "the great body of the people whom [Cruikshank] represents." I am convinced, after looking at thousands of political prints for a half century, that art is more likely to be popular if it mixes up lots of programs and ideas than if it enunciates one unambiguous doctrine in every line and shape (supposing such a thing could ever be done). The latter becomes propaganda and usually stales. But the former lasts because different ages see different aspects of its meaning. Pierre Macherey, in *Theory of Literary Production*, argues that "no ideology is sufficiently consistent to survive the test of figuration."[45] I subscribe to the converse, that no significant figuration can consistently express a simple ideology. Popular imagery is too incorporative and widely appealing to have an edged, bounded message. Caricature prints tapped a larger market when, over and under the pictorial surface, counterthemes and undercurrents were allowed to play that enrich, deepen, complicate, contradict, and universalize the design. Insofar, therefore, as Cruikshank can be "found" in this or any other major picture, he can be found as the artist who finds much to be said on both sides, and who prefers, even in drawing for a particular patron, the subversive freedom of etching contradictions into the copperplate. So Cruikshank's politics can only be sought by looking for them not on one side, but on both, or many, sides.

To dilate on this last point: many contemporary critics would deny that aesthetics is an appropriate aspect of criticism and judgment, though the pendulum may be swinging back toward a postmodern version of "connoisseurship." Aesthetic concerns, these detractors maintain, are elitist and conceal, through the appeal to standards and taste, the domination of the powerful few over the powerless many. Besides, for bureaucrats passing out money, "taste" and aesthetic standards are unquantifiable. They can't be entered into a utilitarian calculus of public or charitable "good." Other contemporary theorists and commentators, looking at ideologies and politics through neo-Marxist lenses, may ignore the physical object and all that pertains to it — the contractual and economic and productive/reproductive technologies that make making an image possible and profitable. There are lots of discussions of commodity exchange and capitalist fetishism that never consider an object in all its materiality or think about that particular object and the ways in which it engages with other objects. To maintain that if we cannot locate an artist's partisan politics we have not read the art responsibly neglects the object itself — which has its own agenda, power, formal relations, ideological incorporations, rhetorical effects, and purposes within the economy of material signs and commercial products.

Moreover, as I hope the foregoing discussion has implied, our twentieth-century love-affair with print culture has effaced ways in which a precedent visual culture could conduct complex, persuasive arguments reaching deep into the collective psyche, using pictures only, or a combination of picture and text. Often, even in sophisticated theorizing about pictures, we assume that the visual image is a representation of a prior reality or verbalization: pictures are good if they "really look like" the primary subject on which their secondary representation is based.[46] If the argument of this paper convinces readers to study graphic art once again with more intensity and less reliance on verbal preconceptions or on assumptions that only the verbal will "explain" the visual, such readers will be in a better condition not only to understand our immense pictorial legacy but also to view critically the constructions of reality now so often provided

[110]

by still, rapidly juxtaposed, or moving pictures. The nineteenth-century dialogue between picture and text testifies first to what John O. Jordan and Carol Christ have established, that "nineteenth-century aesthetic theory frequently makes the eye the pre-eminent organ of truth."[47] Beyond that, the visual-verbal interchanges articulate in two languages, and in the translations between them, the ways different mediums present human life and ideas. Some things can be presented better, or only, in nonverbal mediums. If we lose our ability to read images, we lose historical comprehension and limit our understanding of alternative representational systems, ontologies, epistemologies, and forms of expression and authority. Pictures don't necessarily bespeak politics in the same ways or to the same degrees that texts do; pictures may, however, express in their own terms the politics of their visual and intellectual inheritance, patronage, construction, production, and consumption.

CODA

But there is even more to Cruikshank's feuding royals than has been hitherto elucidated. While writing this paper I happened to hear Jimi Hendrix's song, "The Wind Cries Mary." When Hendrix sings "Somewhere a Queen is weeping; / Somewhere a King has no wife," I thought again of *Ah! Sure Such a Pair.* The picture of an alarmed, baffled, and furious king who has no wife in fact and wants to put her away, and a queen smiling in public but weeping in private, might be not just a specific configuration of royals in 1820 Britain but an archetypal situation. Although Cruikshank's etching depicts royalty, as the figures merge with other characters within the program of the plate and within our reading of their expressions and situation, the deeper representation seems to be of a situation common to human life and stories. Cruikshank etches into this portrayal of domestic strife the outlines of a situation we all may know first- or second-hand. He was only twenty-eight when he issued this plate, and he was unmarried. His parents had fought and made up, but they had never separated. So Cruikshank had not experienced the agonies of marital discord or the fleshly encumbrances of age or the baggage of misbehavior that I suspect many of us carry with us and sometimes fling against our partners. Yet somehow, drawing on the experiences and figurations of others and applying his own quirky line, keen eye, and assimilative sense of humor — hallmarks of a Cruikshank "original" — the artist represented domestic discord as it might appear not just in high places, but everywhere. "Somewhere a Queen is weeping; / Somewhere a King has no wife."

I cannot end on such a portentously elegiac note. Looking at the picture again reminds me how very funny we may appear in our furious impotence or smug feigned indifference. Cruikshank's resolution of the pity and terror of royal and domestic discord passed through an Aristotelian catharsis. The sorrow and pain and anger that an audience identifying with a king or queen may feel is released and assuaged by laughter. If humor contains aggression, it also offers reconciliation. And in such successive emotions provoked by brilliant images George Cruikshank's art both addresses politics and disperses the factional by making fun.

Notes

1. When the first of my two volumes about Cruikshank, *George Cruikshank's Life, Times, and Art* (New Brunswick: Rutgers University Press; Cambridge: Lutterworth Press, 1992, 1996) was published, Celina Fox, the curator of paintings, prints, and drawings at the Museum of London, chided me in her *Times Literary Supplement* review for my "timid judgment" about what I called Cruikshank's "moderate radicalism" (1.234): she declared that I lacked "historical

grip" and that I should have been more specific and searching in my analyses of Cruikshank's politics. References to this biography will appear hereafter parenthetically in the text by volume and page number.

2. In the following discussion, I incorporate material from *George Cruikshank's Life, Times, and Art*, esp. 1: 170-72. I hope that the more elaborated discussion of a single image and the broader argument about the ambiguity of graphic satire's politics revised in the light of more recent publications, will justify occasional repetitions.

3. George Cruikshank, *The British Bee Hive* (London: W. Tweedie, 1867), n.p.

4. A classic, prize-winning treatment of these events is Thomas Laqueur, "The Queen Caroline Affair: Politics as Art in the Reign of George IV," *Journal of Modern History* 54 (Sept. 1982): 417-66. For the caricaturists' responses, see M. Dorothy George, "Introduction" to vol. 10, *Catalogue of Political and Personal Satires* (London: British Museum, 1952), esp. xx-xxviii. Entries in this catalogue are hereafter identified by a number preceded by "BMC." A recent reconsideration of Cruikshank and William Hone's pamphlet collaborations about this and other political issues of the period 1817-24 is Marcus Wood, *Radical Satire and Print Culture 1790-1822* (Oxford: Clarendon Press, 1994). E. A. Smith usefully collects and prints many of the documents relating to the "trial" in *A Queen on Trial: The Affair of Queen Caroline* (Stroud, Gloucestershire and Dover NH: Alan Sutton Publishing, 1993).

5. BMC 13735, published by George Humphrey.

6. Sir Edward Parry, *Queen Caroline* (London: Ernest Benn, 1930), 31.

7. For an authoritative analysis of radical political strategies, consult J. Ann Hone, *For the Cause of Truth: Radicalism in London, 1796-1821* (Oxford: Clarendon Press, 1982): "It could be argued, in view both of the assumptions underlying this analysis and of the radicals' aspirations for a better world, that their ideological solidarity was not to their advantage. In the terms of most twentieth-century ideologies, these men did not get to the heart of the matter" (321-22).

Libertarian, individualistic, committed to a belief in "truth" and "improvement," most radicals thought that changes in politics, not more fundamental changes in the economic structures of society, were all that were needed to bring about utopia.

8. BMC 13895 (October 1820), BMC 13902 (28 October 1820), and BMC 13975 (11 November 1820), all by George Cruikshank, initiate the organized propaganda against the queen, according to Dorothy George (10.xxv).

9. See Sir Thomas Lawrence's portrait of her (National Portrait Gallery), reproduced as frontispiece to Joanna Richardson, *The Disastrous Marriage* (London: Jonathan Cape, 1960).

10. BMC 9516. The best survey of Gillray's work is Draper Hill, *Mr. Gillray The Caricaturist* (London: Phaidon Press, 1965).

11. Diana Donald, *The Age of Caricature: Satirical Prints in the Age of George III* (New Haven: Yale University Press, 1996), 44-74.

12. BMC 12254, 1 May 1814.

13. BMC 12097, 10 November 1813.

14. *Fashionable Contrasts*, BMC 8058, 24 January 1792.

15. Sir John Leach, vice-chancellor, to William Cooke K. C., Lieutenant-Colonel Browne, and John Allan Powell, 8 August 1818, quoted in Richardson, 112-13.

16. Not recorded in *Parliamentary Debates* according to Dorothy George but in the *Examiner*, p. 379; see discussion of BMC 13735.

17. George, 10.xxiii.

18. BMC 11877, 1 May 1812.

19. William Makepeace Thackeray, *The Four Georges* (London: Smith, Elder, 1876), 94.

20. BMC 12791, 5 July 1816.

21. Royal Archives 51382 (a)/21.

22. Gillray, BMC 8112; Cruikshank, BMC 13791.

23. Marcus Wood's analysis of the Hone-Cruikshank pamphlet collaboration details ways popular images were invoked in these publications.

24. William Makepeace Thackeray, "Essay on the Genius of George Cruikshank," *Westminster Review* 34 (June 1840): 1-60, 11.

25. BMC 12890, 15 September 1817.

26. BMC 13731, 15 June 1820, a print sold by George Humphrey, who was royalist in sympathy.

27. BMC 14194, June-July 1821.

28. Edward Said, *Orientalism* (New York: Pantheon Books, 1978), argues that in the nineteenth century everything in the Orient "was, if not patently inferior to, then in need of corrective study by the West. The Orient was viewed as if framed by the classroom, the criminal court, the prison, the illustrated manual" (41). And yet persistently through graphic satire and in fiction of the nineteenth century — George Meredith's *The Egoist* is a representative instance — fantasies of a kind of male "Oriental" despotism circulate; these are, in the instances I have encountered at least, usually reframed in the end to privilege British cultural values as superior.

29. BMC 12749, March 1816; the imagery also draws on caricatures done at the time of Lord Macartney's 1792-94 mission to the Emperor Chien Lung, as in Gillray's *The Reception of the Diplomatique and his Suite*, BMC 8121?, 14 September 1792.

30. Speech delivered on 12 March, recorded in *Parliamentary Debates*, 33.201; quoted in commentary on BMC 12749.

31. Sir Walter Scott to Paymaster Thomas Scott, *Letters, 1819-1821* (London: Constable, 1934).

32. Early in the divorce campaign, Robert Cruikshank had designed and etched a brilliant print commenting on the ambiguity of who wears the crown, Brunswick's daughter or George's son: in *Reflection. To Be, or Not to Be??* (BMC 13661, 11 February 1820), the king (as a dithering Hamlet trying on his crown just a few days after his father's death) looks into a pierglass, which startles him by reflecting his wife, crowned, massive, and contemptuous.

33. Vincent Carretta, *George III and the Satirists from Hogarth to Byron* (Athens and London: University of Georgia Press, 1990).

34. BMC 10019, 26 June 1803.

35. Richard Brinsley Sheridan, *The Duenna*, in *Dramatic Works*, ed. Cecil Price, 2 vols. (Oxford: Clarendon Press, 1973), 1: 254 (II.ii). This particular song was set to music by Michael Arne, originally for Allan Ramsay's "The Highland Laddie": Roger Fiske, "A Score for *The Duenna*," *Music and Letters* 42 (1961): 132-41. *The Duenna*, which premiered at Covent Garden Theatre on 21 November 1775,

was one of the most popular operas ever produced in Britain; it was performed regularly in London and the provinces until the 1840s (see Roger Fiske, *English Theatre Music in the Eighteenth Century* [London: Oxford University Press, 1973], 414).

36. BMC 13131, 10 March 1818.
37. Anonymous, *The New Pilgrim's Progress; or, a Journey to Jerusalem*, 5th edn. (London: Wright, 1820), quoted in Richardson, 102.
38. Emma Sophia, Countess Brownlow, *The Eve of Victorianism* (London: John Murray, 1940), quoted in Richardson, 149.
39. BMC 9261, 1 November 1798. George Cruikshank etched a reduced facsimile of this plate for William Hone's never-published "History of Parody" (BMC 9261 B).
40. For Lavater's European influence on literature, see Graeme Tytler, *Physiognomy in the European Novel: Faces and Fortunes* (Princeton: Princeton University Press, 1982); for his effect on art and theater, consult Judith Wechsler, *A Human Comedy: Physiognomy and Caricature in Nineteenth-Century Paris* (Chicago: University of Chicago Press, 1982).
41. Johann Caspar Lavater, *Essays on Physiognomy*, trans. Henry Hunter, 4 vols. (London: G.G.J. and J. Robinson, 1789): 4: 380.
42. BMC 14130.
43. BMC 14145.
44. BMC 13771.
45. Pierre Macherey, *A Theory of Literary Production*, trans. Geoffrey Wall (London: Routledge and Kegan Paul, 1978), 195.
46. One place to start wrestling with issues of "representation" is Murray Krieger, *Ekphrasis: The Illusion of the Natural Sign* (Baltimore: Johns Hopkins University Press, 1992).
47. Carol T. Christ and John O. Jordan, eds., *Victorian Literature and the Victorian Visual Imagination* (Berkeley, Los Angeles, and London: University of California Press, 1995), xix-xx.

Cruikshank's Illustrative Wrinkle in *Oliver Twist's* Misrepresentation of Class

Catherine J. Golden

The multiplot novels of Charles Dickens unfolded through and with illustrations integral to plot, characterization, and setting. A vital part of the reading experience even of sophisticated Victorians, illustrations of serial novels were studied, as author-illustrator George Du Maurier has put it, "with passionate interest before reading the story, and after, and between."[1] Modern editions of Dickens, however, have erased — or at best eroded — the complexity of the Victorian illustrated book by eliminating most or all of the original illustrations.[2] *Oliver Twist* (1838) without the twenty-four plates George Cruikshank designed for the novel[3] is a book different from the one Dickens intended and the Victorian readers experienced. An avid reader of Dickens, Henry James, as a child, was transfixed by Cruikshank's illustrations for *Oliver Twist* that imprint the personal vision of the artist on the novel. He concedes that the novel "perhaps even seemed to me more Cruikshank's than Dickens's."[4] The experience of James, among others, leads J. Hillis Miller to conclude that book illustrations be regarded an integral part of the texts they illustrate since "For many readers Fagin, Sikes, Nancy, Oliver, Mr. Brownlow, and Rose Maylie live even more in Cruikshank's etchings than in Dickens's words."[5]

Responding to Walter Benjamin's "The Work of Art in the Age of Mechanical Reproduction," this analysis takes as its starting point that a nineteenth-century illustrated book designed during an age of mechanical reproduction can possess the aura of an "original" work, in Walter Benjamin's sense, especially in comparison to digital reproductions conceived in the mass-media age.[6] Only with its "original" illustrations can *Oliver Twist* be considered an authentic Victorian artifact, recording the intimate involvement of and struggles between its illustrator and author in the presentation of social class.[7] In inviting us to reexamine the collaboration of its creators, which forms a vital part of what Benjamin refers to as a work's "unique existence at the place where it happens to be" (220), the "original" illustrated *Oliver Twist* brings us closer to the distinct visions of a recently reclaimed middle-aged artist who was a household name by the mid-nineteenth century and a rising young author whose reputation still endures.

Oliver Twist reveals the struggles between an artist and an author who quarreled over sovereignty and equally exposes the Victorian society it openly criticizes in text and illustrations, for which Cruikshank is best known. While others have noted what Cruikshank's leading biographer, Robert L. Patten, refers to as the "'apples of discord'"[8] between author and artist in the creation of *Oliver Twist*, one contentious "apple" has been hitherto unharvested: Cruikshank's and Dickens's differing perceptions of social class, resulting in conflicting visual and verbal presentations of lower-class characters within *Twist* itself. Such a tension in the presentation of the lower class preserves the conflict between two strong-willed individuals who struggled to maintain their autonomy as creative artists even while working within the realm of commercial publishing.

[118]

I

Written when the new class society was still evolving and middle-class ideals were gaining ascendance, *Oliver Twist* or *The Parish Boy's Progress* demonstrates the self-contradictory attitudes of the middle class in its portrayal of lower-class life. Dickens inscribes documentable accuracy in the settings, behavior, and transactions among criminals, yet he retains an older attitude of contempt for the criminal element, particularly vicious Bill Sikes. In addition, at points Dickens distorts social reality not by estranging or vilifying, but by remaking the dominated class in the dominant class's own image. Dickens's characterization of his parish foundling and some members of Fagin's world offers an emerging, more philanthropically acceptable, middle-class attitude toward the lower class. The text shares a fantasy of upward mobility with other contemporary fiction, such as William Thackeray's *Vanity Fair* (1848) and Charlotte Brontë's *Jane Eyre* (1847), with a slight "twist." Oliver is actually returning to his rightful class affiliation. Occurring long before his education with Brownlow or the Maylies, Oliver's received standard English has been judged inconsistent with Dickens's satirization of the system that brought him up "by hand"[9] and with Dickens's general adherence to the theory that misery and poverty cause vices,[10] as his characterization of Oliver's paired "idle apprentice," charity-boy Noah Claypole, confirms.

Cruikshank's illustrations for the novel call attention to the opposition of middle-class attitudes toward the lower class that Dickens inscribes within the text of the novel. Illustrations were of consequence to an audience who appreciated Cruikshank's caricature art and commonly "read" the plates to derive nonvisual significance from them. Cruikshank's art promotes Dickens's reactionary attitude toward the extreme villainy of Monks and Sikes, in particular. Sikes the "robber," "housebreaker," and "murderer," as Dickens alternately refers to him in the text, appears repeatedly committing violent acts — gripping Oliver with brute strength in "Oliver Claimed by His Affectionate Friends," animalistically growling at Oliver in "The Burglary," and endeavoring to kill his loyal dog Bull's-eye in "Sikes Attempting to Destroy His Dog" (an act of consequence to a Victorian society that vehemently opposed animal cruelty). However, Cruikshank displays this same reactionary attitude toward the sympathetic criminal characters, particularly Nancy and Fagin, whom Dickens mistakenly construes to be more middle class, like himself.[11] This opposition between Dickens's text and Cruikshank's illustrations, though occurring only occasionally, magnifies Dickens's own authorial oscillation between these two opposite yet mutually reinforcing middle-class attitudes. Thus, it is my contention that the resulting tension in verbal and visual depictions of social class recorded within the illustrated pages of *Oliver Twist* leads us back to the lives and conflicting views of its dual creators.

Cruikshank and Dickens present similar ideologies in the opening workhouse section. They jointly satirize the misappropriation of charity funds for the "rising parochial generation" (4) to serve a moral. Transposing the Romantic conception of the child onto the novel, Dickens identifies Oliver as a victim of social injustice. Although Dickens personally showed uncertainty in his regard for charity in relieving the condition of the poor,[12] in *Oliver Twist* he excelled in exposing the parish system's dietary allotment of "one porringer, and no more" (9).[13] To his class-conscious readership, Dickens presented Oliver's now famous request for more gruel for the children of the poor through a middle-class child temporarily rotated downward in class affiliation. Adhering to the traditional clear-cut class distinctions based on birth, the text retains ambiguity regarding Oliver's true class origins; of his mother, "'where she came from, or where she was going to, nobody knows'" (2), and of Oliver, "Wrapped in the blanket which had hitherto formed his only covering, he might have been a child of a nobleman or a beggar" (3). But the request is uttered by a middle-class child who has gone undercover to serve a moral purpose; as Mark Spilka notes: "Dickens seduced his original class-conscious readers into putting their own children, if not themselves, in Oliver's place — as well they might in an age when social slippage was so common that societies were often formed against it."[14]

Dickens softens the request through its middle-class accent.[15] Although not in virtue or speech, Oliver descends into the lower class as Dickens himself did as a child in an age when social slippage was feared enough that Evangelical societies sprang up to prevent it. The outrageous request for more gruel is firmly couched in politeness; Oliver utters: "'Please, sir, I want some more'" (10). "Oliver Asking for More" (fig. 21) crystallizes the text's attack on the abuse of the newly amended Poor Laws of 1834, exacerbated by the government's decentralization and laissez-faire principles. The rounded belly of the master, whom Dickens describes as a "fat, healthy man" (10), calls attention to Oliver's emaciation. The dramatic backdrop of hollow-eyed, sunken-cheeked, thin-ankled parish workhouse children strengthens Dickens's commitment to dietary and sanitary reform; Cruikshank shows the boys with shaved heads, a preventative measure against ringworm, common among workhouse children. Cruikshank also validates Oliver's middle-class origins by dramatically flooding him in light, accentuating his inner goodness, which survives because he is seemingly protected in a special state of grace.

For Victorian readers who readily associated external beauty with inner goodness, the improved appearance of Oliver in the third plate, "Oliver Plucks Up a Spirit," makes him an even more sympathetic character. Cruikshank declares this was his intention: "'I earnestly begged of him [Dickens] to let me make Oliver a nice

Figure 21.
George Cruikshank, "Oliver Asking for More," from Charles Dickens,
"Oliver Twist," in *Bentley's Miscellany*, etching, February 1837,
courtesy of Hannah M. Adler Collection, Skidmore College.

pretty little boy, and if we so represented him, the public — and particularly the ladies — would be sure to take a greater interest in him and the work would then be a certain success.'"[16] While the truth of this claim is debatable,[17] Cruikshank calls our attention to Oliver's improved appearance, which is unmistakable. Oliver looks wan and timid in "Oliver Asking for More" and even more pained and haggard in "Oliver Escapes Being Bound Apprentice to the Sweep." But the pathetic Oliver, who is reduced to beggary in these first two plates, emerges anew in "Oliver Plucks Up a Spirit" as he rises to defend his dead mother's honor. Oliver's light wavy locks and slightly fuller and evenly formed features transform him into — what Mario Praz has gone so far as to claim — "'the fair, long, sad face of a neo-classic angel.'"[18] His angelic features were of consequence to Victorian viewers. In creating an appealing child protagonist of unsuspected gentle birth, Dickens and Cruikshank seduce their progressive middle-class readers to fall prey to their own sentimentality: to turn against or at least question their own preconceptions about the poor — that a benevolent gift must "pauperize" and that the "theory of self-dependence" (as John Stuart Mill was to call it) obliterated the need for any action.[19]

The workhouse section becomes almost incidental to the novel's design as the reader follows "The Parish Boy's Progress" into urban London. Dickens mediates the criminal element through the eyes of an innocent middle-class child — a textual lens which distorts some of the characters he encounters. In his preface to the third edition of 1841, Dickens discloses both his intention "to draw a knot of such associates in crime as really do exist" (xxvi) alongside what is frequently pounced upon as an acquiescence to his middle-class audience: "I saw no reason, when I wrote this book, why the very dregs of life, so long as their speech did not offend the ear, should not serve the purpose of a moral" (xxv). In one familiarly long Dickensian sentence, he presents the two middle-class attitudes toward the lower class, which he oscillates between. The "very dregs of life" — who are not worth caring about — will reassuringly be contained and condemned; however, when they "serve the purpose of a moral," their speech will "not offend the ear" of the middle-class audience. In his 1867 preface, Dickens places this critical phrase "so long as their speech did not offend the ear" in parentheses, but its presence, nonetheless, remains undiminished in the text. Despite Dickens's avowal, "I will not, for these readers, abate one hole in the Dodger's coat, or one scrap of curl-paper in the girl's dishevelled hair" (xxvii), Dickens mistakenly construes the language and behavior of Dodger, Nancy, and Fagin to be more middle class.

At the end of the workhouse section, Oliver tells the more unfortunate little Dick, "'I am going to seek my fortune'" (44). The path to fortune begins with a reconstitution of family, first in the criminal element with Fagin and Nancy, and finally in a higher social milieu with Brownlow and the Maylies. The misrepresentation of class intersects with the most reassuring of moral themes for his intended audience: the Victorian home, the center of Victorian middle-class life. As Dickens moves close to the heart of his middle-class readers, an opposition emerges between his verbal misrepresentation and Cruikshank's reactionary visual presentation of lower-class characters, which draws distinctions between the reconstituted families along class lines.

Through Dickens's pen, characters within Fagin's den desire middle-class values — a sense of community and emotional warmth — as conveyed by their treatment of Oliver. The "perverted" family over which the maternal Fagin presides imagines the fundamental desire of the poor to be for middle-class forms of domestic insularity and well-being. Artful brings the "'jolly green'" (56) Oliver to a den of fellowship and gaiety, which dissolves as

Fagin gives way to greed, conspires with Oliver's evil stepbrother, and ultimately brings about Sikes's murder of Nancy. The text adopts an attitude of contempt for Fagin, who swings to disfavor and finally to condemnation. Although Fagin's evilness is immediately revealed through the description of his "villainous-looking and repulsive face" (50), Dickens initially undercuts this impression by referring to Fagin as "the merry old gentleman" (53) and describing his maternal manner. Fagin provides Oliver with sizzling sausages and drink, shelter where "he sunk into a deep sleep" (53), and the first real enjoyment Oliver has ever known: "Oliver laughed till the tears ran down his face" (57). Playing the part of a gentleman whose pocket is picked, a role which Brownlow actually plays, Fagin stands as an ironic complement to Mr. Brownlow, Oliver's adopted father who offers him a home at story's end.

Of Oliver's first reconstituted family of Jacob's Island, Nancy, in Dickens's text, emerges as a saintly "double" of Rose, Oliver's real aunt and sister by preference: "'Not aunt,' cried Oliver . . . 'I'll never call her aunt — sister, my own dear sister, that something taught my heart to love so dearly from the first!'" (337). Something also taught Oliver's heart to care for Nancy "from the first": "Oliver thought them [Nancy and Bet] very nice girls indeed" (57). Like Oliver, Nancy enjoys a special state of linguistic grace, particularly in her interview with Rose, which Cruikshank elected not to illustrate.[20] Though Nancy delivers Oliver to Fagin, she achieves this by pretending to be his sister and ultimately helps to return him to his rightful station by divulging information about his parentage. Dickens soothes his middle-class readers by creating a romantic image of a saintly prostitute whose occupation he suggests, but never names in the text. Risking her life to save her "'Nolly, dear'" (79) while remaining devoted to Sikes, Nancy, through Dickens's pen, achieves an introspective, individualized personality structure that is private, moral, conscientious, and reassuring to his middle-class readership. Her demise becomes an evangelical message for readers in an age undergoing a resurgence of religious feeling. Holding Rose Maylie's own white handkerchief "as high toward Heaven as her feeble strength would allow" (303), Nancy exits the novel as Rose's "double," bonded to her through their loyalty to and love for a middle-class child.

Although Dickens mistakenly construes Nancy to be more middle class, her death triggers textual contempt for the "vilest evil" from which Dickens drew this "lesson of the purest good" (xxv). The murder of Nancy scatters the merry gang of thieves and reassuringly contains deviant behavior. Nancy's eyes work for the side of law, order, and social good and lead Sikes to turn against his body to become his own executioner.[21] Moreover, the scattering of the merry gang allows Dickens — through Charlie Bates — to reenact the entrepreneurial myth of the self-made man and so justify and universalize this middle-class ideal.[22]

II

In his 1841 preface, Dickens defends Nancy and asserts: "It is useless to discuss whether the conduct and character of the girl seems natural or unnatural, probable or improbable, right or wrong. IT IS TRUE" (xxviii). The capitalization of "IT IS TRUE" highlights Dickens's awareness that Thackeray, among others, criticized his sentimental, saintly characterization of "'Biss Dadsy'"[23] as "unnatural" and "improbable." While Nancy's loyalty to Oliver and Sikes may, in fact, be "true," the illustrations encode a different kind of physical truth in a reactionary way. Cruikshank undermines Dickens's intention that readers perceive Nancy and Rose to be "Two Sister-Women," as Dickens calls them in an early heading for Chapter XL,[24] just as Cruikshank distinguishes Fagin firmly from his ironic complement in Brownlow.

Cruikshank conveys a contemptuous attitude toward the prostitute and the "receiver of stolen goods" (xxv) that the text represses in its characterization of Nancy and Fagin, initially. In "Oliver Introduced to the Respectable Old Gentleman" (fig. 22), Cruikshank drains Fagin's den of Dickens's reassuring middle-class notions of community and emotional warmth. From the start, Cruikshank, more than Dickens, distorts Fagin's world by using the technique of chiaroscuro to exaggerate the possibility for malevolence. The ramshackle quality of the decrepit room and the billowing smoke from the boys' clay pipes darken the glimmer of gaiety in the criminal circle. Creating a backdrop behind the figure of Fagin, the silk handkerchiefs speak loudly of the criminal occupation Fagin teaches his "hopeful pupils" (53). The boys, whom Dickens describes as having "the air of middle-aged men" (50), actually have the receding hairlines of middle-aged men. The "merry old gentleman" (53) stands by the fire with a "toasting-fork in hand" (50), as the text describes, but Fagin's three-pronged toasting-fork, positioned close to the flames, resembles a devil's pitchfork. Thus, from Fagin's first appearance, Cruikshank visualizes the repeated but vague references Dickens makes between Fagin and the devil and firmly declares his character subversive.[25]

Oliver's reception in Mr. Brownlow's middle-class home in "Oliver Recovering from a Fever" (fig. 23) severs Fagin's world from bourgeois conventionality.[26] Cruikshank exploits the power of clothes to make marked social distinctions for reader-viewers in a class-conscious society. Both Fagin and Brownlow wear dressing gowns in these hearthside illustrations, but Fagin's greasy, shapeless flannel gown starkly contrasts with Brownlow's richly patterned, full-bodied fabric gown with stylized lapels. Brownlow, who "thrust his hands behind the skirts of his dressing-gown to take a good long look at Oliver" (71), has a more maternal air, magnified

Figure 22.
George Cruikshank, "Oliver Introduced to the Respectable Old
Gentleman," from Charles Dickens, "Oliver Twist," in
Bentley's Miscellany, etching, May 1837,
courtesy of Hannah M. Adler Collection, Skidmore College.

Figure 23.
George Cruikshank, "Oliver Recovering from a Fever,"
from Charles Dickens, "Oliver Twist,"
in *Bentley's Miscellany*, etching, August 1837,
courtesy of Hannah M. Adler Collection, Skidmore College.

through the width and fullness of his dressing-gown "skirts," which rival Mrs. Bedwin's.

Cruikshank's interiors here and in his serial plates *The Bottle* (1847) and its sequel *The Drunkard's Children* (1848) adhere to the Hogarthian tradition of graphic satire and caricature by using portraiture and interior decoration to comment upon character. In "Oliver Recovering from a Fever" and "Oliver Introduced to the Respectable Old Gentleman," portraiture further differentiates Oliver's potential father figures along class lines. A portrait of the ministering Good Samaritan rests above Brownlow's mantel, which also contains flowers and Oliver's medicine. Offering Oliver the very nourishment he craves in "Oliver Asking for More," Brownlow provides Oliver with a bowl of broth in "Oliver Recovering from a Fever" that is, in this case, far bigger than his spoon. The parable of the Good Samaritan, not mentioned in the text, accentuates Mr. Brownlow's goodness in bringing the orphan Oliver, wrongfully accused of robbing him, into his middle-class home and nursing him back to health. More importantly, the portrait also foreshadows Brownlow's adoption of Oliver at the close of the tale. In this plate, positioned relatively early in the novel, Oliver sits below the portrait of a woman, who — we learn later in the text — is actually his real mother. Thus, Cruikshank shows us that Oliver's "likeness" hangs in the home of a gentleman.[27]

In contrast, in "Oliver Introduced," a broadside of three thieves being "scragged" is pinned to the wall above Fagin's dark fireplace on whose mantel rests a lone liquor bottle. Brownlow's and Fagin's mantels as well as the images on the walls of their abodes declare class differences and elevate or defile their inhabitants, accordingly. Cruikshank's graphic inclusion of the hanging, preceding Dickens's introduction of this theme, drains Fagin's fireside of the potential for domestic insularity and well-being by declaring the occupation and destiny of its inhabitants. The inclusion of the broadside also foreshadows Fagin's eventual death "To be hanged by the neck, till he was dead" (343), which Cruikshank shows him vividly contemplating alone in "Fagin in the Condemned Cell" (fig. 24).

This depiction of Fagin's final hours remains one of the most compelling and famous of Cruikshank's etchings and arguably of Victorian book illustration.[28] It derives its power in part from the delineation of psychological terror: now deranged — pursued by his own demons — Fagin crouches as he gnaws his hand and gazes with terror into his solitary cell, made of cold stone. The furnishing is bare, giving prominence to the one doubly-barred window. Fagin's positioning seems as essential as the setting and his melodramatic pose. The grinning Fagin who greets Oliver warmly by his glowing hearth, the prying Fagin who boldly peers into Oliver's room in the Maylies' home, and the cocksure Fagin who gestures he is "in the know" to Noah Claypole, simply put, is cornered and, for the first time, alone. The starkness of the plate — atypical of Cruikshank's richly detailed illustrative style — magnifies his terror. The order for Fagin's execution, posted behind him, is the only telling interior decoration Cruikshank uses in "Fagin in the Condemned Cell" to comment on Fagin's character. The stippled effect on the cell walls — forming circles nearly the exact size of Fagin's eyes — forces us to return time and again to Fagin's circular, glazed eyes, locking him in a moment of intense fright as he contemplates his fate by hanging.[29]

Fagin's character in the novel grows darker as he consorts with Monks, who, from his first appearance in Chapter XXVI, appears decidedly murky. Described as having a face "much distorted and discoloured" (237), Monks slips mysteriously in and out of the shadows of the plot; his motivation for revenge is revealed only near novel's end when Dickens discloses Monks's devious plan to make his stepbrother one of Fagin's thieves in order to violate the conditions set by their father's will.

[131]

Figure 24.
George Cruikshank, "Fagin in the Condemned Cell," from Charles
Dickens, "Oliver Twist," in *Bentley's Miscellany*, etching, March 1839,
courtesy of Hannah M. Adler Collection, Skidmore College.

"The Evidence Destroyed," Monks's first appearance, focuses on the darker plot — the destruction of the only evidence that could prove Oliver's rightful heritage. However, in this plate Cruikshank conveys Monks's shadiness by placing him in shadows above a trap door, leading to the turbid Thames below. "Monks and the Jew" (fig. 25), where Monks appears alongside Fagin, is arguably one of the most powerful of the *Twist* plates because of its juxtaposition of menace and calm. The dark figures of Fagin, here referred to as "the Jew," and Oliver's wicked stepbrother, Monks, jar with the decidedly angelic Oliver and the pastoral surroundings, ironically framing the two men who peer through the latticed window and intrude on Oliver's daydreams. Here, again, we see Cruikshank exerting his artistic autonomy in vilifying Fagin in this image even more than the shady Monks: Fagin's visage appears darker than Monks's and clearly demonic.

Cruikshank's Fagin deservedly swings from the rope. Dickens's later characterization of Fagin concurs. Dickens describes in detail the "bloodless face" and "unwashed flesh, [which] crackled with the fever that burnt him up," eyes shining "with a terrible light" (344). He moves us into the mind of "the Jew," whose terrifying thoughts during his last night alive in Newgate Prison become almost mantra-like: "To be hanged by the neck, till he was dead — that was the end. To be hanged by the neck till he was dead" (343). But why, we might logically question, must Fagin "be hanged by the neck, till he was dead" to pay for his crimes? He is not guilty of a capital offense, though he certainly has committed countless crimes: he has trained young boys to be pickpockets, amassed stolen goods in his den, been an accessory to the Maylies' housebreaking, had Nancy followed, and, worse, incited Sikes to murder Nancy; these are all points John Sutherland provocatively ponders in his exploration of literary puzzles entitled *Can Jane Eyre Be Happy?*[30] Sutherland's reading entitled "Why is Fagin

Figure 25.
George Cruikshank, "Monks and the Jew," from Charles Dickens,
"Oliver Twist," in *Bentley's Miscellany*, etching, June 1838,
courtesy of Hannah M. Adler Collection, Skidmore College.

hanged and why isn't Pip prosecuted?" concludes that Pip goes free because he is a gentleman, and Fagin is hanged because he is not, despite, I might add, Dickens's initial insistence that Fagin is a gentleman.

Sutherland focuses on Dickens's later contempt for Fagin, which has bearing on my argument that Dickens oscillates between two middle-class attitudes toward the lower class — the first of mistaken self-projection; the latter of contempt, an attitude Sutherland documents well. Fagin has not committed murder, which, according to the laws of the 1830s when the novel was set, was virtually the only crime to justify the death penalty. To explore Fagin's fate from the perspective of new historicism reveals that a lengthy prison term or transportation for life — the fate of Dickens's Magwitch of *Great Expectations* (1861) and the actual fate of Fagin's prototype, Ikey Solomon, in 1831 — seem more plausible Victorian sentences than hanging. From this vantage point, Fagin's piercing cry, "'What right have they to butcher me?'" (346), seems leveled more at his betraying creator — who mistakenly construed him initially to be more middle class — than the turnkey, who overhears the remark, and the populace, who respond enthusiastically to Fagin's death sentence with "a peal of joy" (340).

Dickens's decision to "butcher" the "receiver of stolen goods" (xxv), whom he decidedly refers to as "the Jew" in his final hours, reveals Dickens's (and his contemporaries') ethnic and class biases: as the novel progressed, Dickens perceived Fagin as danger-ously "different." Since Fagin's character could not, ultimately, "serve the purpose of a moral," his filth, villainy, and racial other-ness needed to be contained. These very qualities that Dickens offsets in the opening chapters are present, nonetheless: even on first meeting, all the while Dickens calls him the "merry old gen-tleman" (53), Fagin looks "greasy," "shrivelled," and "repulsive"

[135]

(50). As the novel continues, Dickens's rhetoric ultimately builds, for Fagin, "the black stage, the cross-beam, the rope, and all the hideous apparatus of death" (347) and joins Cruikshank's depictions to condemn this element of lower-class life.

Dickens's regard for the saintly prostitute — who seemingly assuaged his middle-class readers through her loyalty and love for a middle-class child — did not wane, however. In a November 1837 letter to John Forster, Dickens confides his hope "'to do great things with Nancy.'"[31] But as Dickens was working through the idea of making Rose Maylie Nancy's saintly counterpart, he was already saddled with Cruikshank's unsatisfactory depiction of Nancy.[32] The original chapter heading of "Two Sister-Women" makes explicit their relative status of sister to each other and Oliver. In "Oliver Claimed by His Affectionate Friends" (fig. 26), Nancy blends in with Sikes, the tavern keeper, the butcher boy, and the other lower-class London "types."[33] Though Nancy's speech can rise in class affiliation just like Oliver's,[34] her sly expression, "dishevelled hair," and figure make her unsympathetic, common, and inconsistent with Dickens's sentimental "truth." Although Cruikshank elected not to illustrate the first interview between Nancy and Rose (a depiction which might have even more forcefully undermined the connection Dickens suggests), the two women appear together in "The Meeting" (fig. 27). This dramatic plate shows, in shadows, Noah Claypole (then Morris Bolter), who, at Fagin's bidding, follows Nancy to London Bridge where she meets with Rose Maylie and Mr. Brownlow and risks her life to save Oliver. Both women are positioned in profile, wear bonnets and shawls, and have compassion in their eyes. But these very likenesses call more attention to their readily apparent differences.

It is well-known that Cruikshank could not successfully draw an attractive woman, but my criticisms extend beyond that. In "The Meeting," a refined-featured, respectable, and neatly dressed

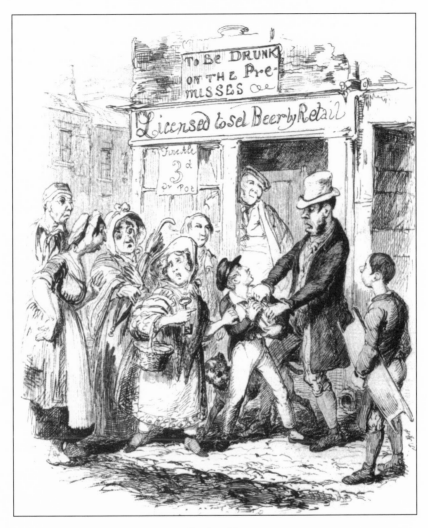

Figure 26.
George Cruikshank, "Oliver Claimed by His Affectionate Friends,"
from Charles Dickens, "Oliver Twist," in *Bentley's Miscellany*,
etching, September 1837,
courtesy of Hannah M. Adler Collection, Skidmore College.

Figure 27.
George Cruikshank, "The Meeting," from Charles Dickens,
"Oliver Twist," in *Bentley's Miscellany*,
etching, December 1838,
courtesy of Hannah M. Adler Collection, Skidmore College.

Rose gazes toward a squat, common, prematurely old Nancy. Nancy's dark frumpy bonnet, ragged shawl, and mid-length dress contrast to Rose's pert bonnet, neat shawl, and full-length gown. Their clothing alone confirms their differences in class and respectability in a text where Dickens declares the power of dress from the opening chapter:

> What an excellent example of the power of dress, young Oliver Twist was! Wrapped in the blanket which had hitherto formed his only covering, he might have been the child of a nobleman or a beggar; . . . But now that he was enveloped in the old calico robes which had grown yellow in the same service, he was badged and ticketed, and fell into his place at once — a parish child — the orphan of a workhouse — the humble half-starved drudge — to be cuffed and buffeted through the world — despised by all, and pitied by none. (3)

Illustrations of Oliver standing next to either "sister" sharpen the contrast between the "Two Sister-Women." In "Oliver Claimed," a broad-nosed, wide-mouthed, squat-faced though younger-looking Nancy grabs Oliver by the arm, much as the roughian Sikes does. But in "Rose Maylie and Oliver" (fig. 28), a dignified, slender, and well-bred Rose rests her willowy hand gently on Oliver's shoulder. Her refined features resemble Oliver's and Agnes's as indicated through portraiture. Although the image disappoints — Rose and Oliver seem too old, their posture too rigid — they share a "likeness," accentuated through their profiles, that makes them look like siblings and too different from Nancy even to be distant relatives. Dickens explains that Nancy carries "a little basket and a street-door key in her hand" (93) to look respectable enough to pose as Oliver's sister, but these and her

Figure 28.
George Cruikshank, "Rose Maylie and Oliver," from Charles Dickens,
"Oliver Twist," in *Bentley's Miscellany,* etching, April 1839,
courtesy of Hannah M. Adler Collection, Skidmore College.

clean white apron in the illustration "Oliver Claimed" become costume props accentuating her dishonesty in attempting to assume a higher station. Despite her supposed garb of respectability, Nancy blends in easily with the street folk, although Oliver does not. Perhaps Cruikshank is again exerting his autonomy in creating his own rendition of Dickens's character, described in the text as "not exactly pretty, perhaps" but "hearty," with "a great deal of colour" in her face and "remarkably free and agreeable" manners (57). The artist depicts Nancy in a manner that undermines the text's capacity to show Nancy to be like Rose: a worthy character who acts in a conscientious and private way, no doubt reassuring to Dickens's middle-class readers. While Dickens seduces us into believing that Nancy might have lived the life of a Rose Maylie had a kind Mrs. Maylie befriended her, Cruikshank, in his depictions of Nancy, dashes any such romantic conception of Nancy's character, intensified through her martyred demise. Through Cruikshank's eyes, we cannot see "something of the woman's original nature left in her still" (254), as Dickens insists. Not shown to be remotely angelic, as Oliver is depicted, or even a "very nice girl[ ]" (57), as Oliver perceives her to be, Cruikshank's slovenly, common Nancy, reassuringly, does not look worth caring about.

The images of Nancy and Fagin subvert Dickens's attempt to misconstrue some members of the dominated class just as they reinforce Dickens's increasing condemnation of the criminal element and fix Oliver's now famous request, "'Please, sir, I want some more'" (10). The occasional opposition between text and illustration in *Oliver Twist* no doubt stems from the individualistic personalities of an author who wanted the upper hand with his illustrators and an artist who increasingly demanded autonomy as the illustrated novel progressed and became a commercial success. Regardless of its source, the Cruikshank/Dickens opposition in the "original" work is noteworthy for the textual tension it signals. Cruikshank wrinkles Dickens's portraits of "nice" Nancy and an early maternal Fagin both literally and metaphorically. In his book illustrations, Cruikshank calls attention to Dickens's oscillation between an older attitude toward the lower class and a newly emerging attitude that does not seem firmly embedded in the novel but precariously applied to the preface and text of *Oliver Twist*.

Notes

1. George Du Maurier, "The Illustrating of Books from the Serious Artist's Point of View." *Magazine of Art* (August-September 1890): 350.
2. Many editions that retain illustrations do so only sporadically. For example, following Dickens's own later selection of illustrations, the Oxford edition of *Oliver Twist* (1982) prints only eight of Cruikshank's original illustrations. "Fagin in the Condemned Cell" and "Oliver Asking for More" are retained; however, other less memorable images, such as "Sikes Attempting to Destroy His Dog," are included rather than, for instance, "The Last Chance" or "Mr. Bumble and Mrs. Corney Taking Tea."
3. In the 1966 Oxford edition, editor Kathleen Tillotson includes a "twenty-fifth" illustration that Dickens rejected, known as the "Fireside" plate; see Tillotson's introduction to *Oliver Twist*, The Clarendon Dickens, ed. Kathleen Tillotson (Oxford: Oxford University Press, 1966), opposite xxiv.
4. See Henry James, *A Small Boy and Others* (New York: Charles Scribner's Sons, 1914), 120.
5. J. Hillis Miller, *Charles Dickens and George Cruikshank* (Los Angeles: William Andrews Clark Memorial Library, University of California, Los Angeles, 1971), 44.
6. See "The Work of Art in the Age of Mechanical Reproduction," in *Illuminations*, edited with an introduction by Hannah Arendt and

translated by Harry Zohn (New York: Schocken Books, 1976), 217-
51. Subsequent references to this work are cited parenthetically
within the text.

7. The essay focuses on the book version of *Oliver Twist*; however, the
illustrations included in this essay are photographed from its first
publication in *Bentley's Miscellany* (London: Richard Bentley, 1837-
39).

8. See Chapter 27, "Oliver Twist and the 'Apples of Discord'" in
Robert L. Patten's *George Cruikshank's Life, Times, and Art*, Volume
2: 1835-1878 (New Brunswick, N.J.: Rutgers University Press,
1996), 50-94.

9. Charles Dickens, *Oliver Twist*, edited with an introduction and notes
by Kathleen Tillotson (Oxford: Oxford University Press, 1982), 3.
All further references to *Oliver Twist* and Dickens's 1841 preface are
taken from this edition and cited parenthetically within the text
unless otherwise noted.

10. See, for example, Alexander Welsh's discussion of "City as a Problem" in *City of Dickens* (Oxford: Clarendon Press, 1971), 30-31; also,
see Richard A. Vogler, *Graphic Works of George Cruikshank* (New
York: Dover Publications, Inc, 1979), 160.

11. This oscillation occurs within the verbal characterizations of the
Artful Dodger as well as Fagin. The text's approval of the Artful
Dodger, who befriends the jolly green Oliver, also swings to con-
tempt; he is charged and "'booked for a passage out'" (277) to the
New World, where Monks is also sent at novel's close.

12. Welsh discusses Dickens's uncertain attitude toward charity in *City
of Dickens*, 86-100. Dickens's ideas on charity feature significantly in
other works like *Our Mutual Friend* (1865), particularly through
Betty Higden's tale.

13. Although not illustrated by Cruikshank, Dickens satirizes Mrs.
Mann's misappropriation of the branch-workhouse by describing
how "she appropriated the greater part of the weekly stipend to her
own use, and consigned the rising parochial generation to even a
shorter allowance than was originally provided for them" (4).

14. Mark Spilka, "On the Enrichment of Poor Monkeys By Myth and Dream; or, How Dickens Rousseauisticized and Pre-Freudianized Victorian Views of Childhood," in *Sexuality and Victorian Literature*, ed. Don Richard Cox (Knoxville, Tenn.: The University of Tennessee Press, 1984), 169.

15. Steven Marcus suggests that Oliver's speech serves as "Dickens's way of showing that grace has descended upon him"; see *Dickens: From Pickwick to Dombey* (London: Chatto and Windus, 1965), 80.

16. George Cruikshank's letter to the *Times* is quoted in Patten's *George Cruikshank's Life, Times, and Art*, 2: 56.

17. As Robert L. Patten observes in *George Cruikshank's Life, Times, and Art* (Vol. 2), "Dickens may all along have intended this development, so that Cruikshank's recommendations merely confirmed rather than initiated his own plans" (56). Cruikshank's claim for authorship long clouded any analysis of the cooperation between their arts. Cruikshank presents his full grievance with Dickens in *The Artist and the Author* (1870). For a concise discussion of the controversy over the authorship of such works as *Oliver Twist*, see John Buchanan-Brown, *The Book Illustrations of George Cruikshank* (London, Newton Abbott: David & Charles; Rutland, Vermont: Charles E. Tuttle, 1980), 27-32.

18. See Mario Praz quoted in Patten, *George Cruikshank's Life, Times, and Art*, 2: 56.

19. For more discussion of John Stuart Mill's "theory of self-dependence" and the ideal of the "self-made man," see Harold Perkin, *The Origins of Modern English Society 1780-1880* (London: Routledge & Kegan Paul, 1969), 224-25, and, in general, the chapters on "The Struggle Between the Ideals," "The Triumph of the Entrepreneurial Ideal," and "The Rise of a Viable Class Society."

20. As Patten notes in *George Cruikshank's Life, Times, and Art* (2: 82), "The interview between Rose and Nancy" was on a list of possible subjects Dickens gave to Cruikshank; Cruikshank crossed it out, electing to illustrate their second interview, a more dramatic scene in which Morris Bolter overhears Nancy.

21. For further discussion of Nancy's characterization and the fictional use of the prostitute, see Nancy Armstrong, *Desire and Domestic Fiction* (Oxford: Oxford University Press, 1987), 182-86. Her reading of Nancy informs this discussion.

22. In Chapter LIII, "And Last," Dickens tells how Charlie Bates reforms his character and remakes himself, realizing the entrepreneurial ideal of the self-made man. Dickens explains that "He [Charlie] struggled hard, and suffered much, for some time; but having a contented disposition, and a good purpose, succeeded in the end; and, from being a farmer's drudge, and a carrier's lad, is now the merriest young grazier in all Northamptonshire" (349).

23. Thackeray qtd. in Kathleen Tillotson's introduction to *Oliver Twist*, Oxford University Press edition (1982), xiii.

24. *Oliver Twist*, introduction to The Clarendon Dickens, xxxvi. Tillotson notes that the first of the descriptive headlines for Chapter XL read as "Two Sister-Women."

25. For further discussion of Fagin's visual association to the devil through the pitchfork toasting-fork, see Vogler, 150.

26. "Oliver Introduced" and "Oliver Recovering" are similarly structured compositions. Mrs. Bedwin mediates the triumvirate as Artful does in "Oliver Introduced," but she is positioned midway between the two characters whereas Artful is positioned close to Fagin only.

27. Cruikshank's original final plate, which Dickens rejected, returns Oliver to a similar fireside in the bourgeois interior of the Maylie's home. Cruikshank's use of the Good Samaritan picture has been noted in such sources as Robert L. Patten's review of the Clarendon edition of *Oliver Twist*, *Dickens Studies* III (1967): 165; Jane R. Cohen, "'All-of-a-Twist': The Relationship of George Cruikshank and Charles Dickens," *Harvard Library Bulletin* 17 (April 1969): 169-94 and (July 1969): 320-42. A picture on the wall and decorative objects on the mantelpiece recur in various transformations in Cruikshank's serial *The Bottle* to reveal the gradual dissolution of the family resulting from their first sip from "the bottle."

28. Likewise, Patten states, "It is arguably the most celebrated etching Cruikshank ever made and among the most famous book illustrations of all times." See Patten, *George Cruikshank's Life, Times, and Art*, 2: 88-89.

29. In his analysis of the *Twist* illustrations, Patten points out that the five previous depictions show Fagin "in some commanding pose — greeting Oliver while holding a toasting fork, or bowing before him with mock humility, spying on him as he dozes, recovering Nancy or appreciating Noah's low cunning." See Patten, *George Cruikshank's Life, Times, and Art*, 2: 90.

30. See John Sutherland's chapter "Why is Fagin hanged and why isn't Pip prosecuted" in *Can Jane Eyre Be Happy?* (Oxford: Oxford University Press, 1997), 52-60. It informs my argument.

31. Dickens's letter of 1837 qtd. in *Oliver Twist*, introduction to The Clarendon Dickens, xxxv.

32. Tillotson suggests Dickens would doubtlessly have criticized Cruikshank's portrayal of Nancy had he conceived the women as a pair sooner in *Charles Dickens*, introduction to The Clarendon Dickens, xxxvi.

33. Cruikshank often drew not from what he saw but what he recollected from earlier times and artists, which contributed to his class misrepresentation. For more discussion of Cruikshank's depiction of street characters and low life, see Vogler, 140 and John Buchanan-Brown, 43. For more discussion of Cruikshank's artistic style, see Jane R. Cohen, *Charles Dickens and His Original Illustrators* (Columbus, Ohio: Ohio University Press, 1980), 15-38, and Patten's biography.

34. As he revised, Dickens refined Nancy's language, looks, and behavior. See Tillotson's comments in her introduction to *Oliver Twist*, The Clarendon Dickens, xxxvi.

Rossetti and the Art of the Book

Elizabeth K. Helsinger

M ost studies of Dante Gabriel Rossetti's art in this century take as their objects of study either the poems and prose or the paintings and drawings, with a few critics focusing on the "double art" of certain poems and pictures considered together.[1] Yet Rossetti thought not of images or texts but of framed pictures and printed books of poetry. He designed and carefully supervised the framing of his paintings and the printing, layout, illustration, and binding of his and others' books. During his lifetime Rossetti managed to control the forms in which readers and viewers encountered his art and that of his friends and family to a degree quite unusual then or now. His published work is not adequately described as an art of words or of images or even of the two together: it is an art of the book.

I am not the first to draw attention to Rossetti's designs for book bindings or picture frames.[2] Few literary critics or art historians, however, consider how Rossetti's concern for books and pictures as physical objects necessitates thinking differently about the texts and images he presented in these forms. Jerome McGann is a recent exception, arguing that the printed page and the framed picture are signifying structures, each including both linguistic and iconic features.[3] McGann's emphasis on Rossetti's intellectual project links him to modern and postmodern poets who experiment with the graphic design of the poem on a page as an essential component of its meaning. Yet this stress on the semantic aspects of design does not fully capture effects of the book or framed picture on readers and viewers, particularly as these go beyond "the extent to which the decorative features of a text can be made to function in conceptual ways" (McGann 127) .

What follows if we take seriously the suggestion that for Rossetti the work of art is a different, more inclusive, and yet heterogeneous physical object than a text or an image? First, we shall need to look for effects that belong to the material artifact, and consider the way these shape or alter the reception of poem or picture. In the second place, we need to remember that this is a statement about a late-nineteenth-century poet-painter in London. Unlike that relatively disembodied abstraction, the image or the text, the object enters into everyday life; it is the historical form of the image or text and so is often deeply embedded in the sensory epistemology of a particular place and time. Finally, if we consider the book or the framed picture, we must expand our conception of the work of art. *Work* is a verb as well as a noun: a social and economic practice, or better, a set of practices, engaging artists or writers and their dealers or publishers, their buyers and collectors, their viewers and readers. This work is not easily encompassed within the restrictive definitions of creativity that have come to distinguish the fine from the decorative arts, art from craft or manufacture, or poetic composition from editing and printing. My focus on the physical forms Rossetti and others of his circle gave to books and pictures is meant to allow us to attend more closely to their work of making art and to their and their clients' habits of consuming art. Such a focus will unsettle distinctions between culturally prestigious "fine" art or literature and decorative arts or crafts, distinctions on which both aesthetic and economic value have come to depend — but then, these distinctions were much less clear in mid-Victorian Britain.

For middle-class Victorians in the 1850s and 60s, the object forms of art and literature were a focus of consuming interest. New technologies and materials helped make decorative covers and illustrated books widely available and much less expensive.[4] Many ordinary trade books were accordingly published in decorative formats. Good-quality prints from popular paintings, or small-scale reproductions of sculpture in new materials, became similarly easier and cheaper to produce and distribute in large numbers.[5] They fueled the interest in contemporary original art even among those who could not afford an original piece. As the interest in contemporary British art increased, and exhibitions became crowded social events for a broader range of Victorian society, the number of artists also grew.[6] Most of these were not singled out by critics and promoted by dealers into financially lucrative careers, but they might hope to make respectable livings by catering to the rapidly expanding appetite for decorative furnishings in even modest middle-class homes. The exhibitions were increasingly filled with small, often inexpensive works suitable for a middle-class family parlor. Subjects tended to reflect, in more or less realistic style, Victorian middle-class life or its imagined others (the Scottish Highlands, the exotic East, a costume-drama from British history or literature, an ordinary green English countryside inviting the urban visitor). Together with other commodities marketed as luxuries and objects of art — goods whose decorative qualities clearly exceeded functional demands — books that could adorn a drawing-room table and pictures that could hang on its walls aroused acquisitive desires in those with even a little extra money to spend.[7]

Rossetti shared his concern to control the design of the objects in which pictures and poems were sold with other artists in Pre-Raphaelite circles, including Holman Hunt, Ford Madox Brown, and William Morris. The Pre-Raphaelites were alert to the possibilities of an expanding market for objects to embellish domestic spaces. Indeed, they were themselves avid consumers. This is one of the most striking aspects of successive generations of Pre-Raphaelite artists: their close and informed engagement with the business of art and their participation in contemporary habits of buying and using it. Rossetti's art may appear to answer solely to the impulses of the solitary imagination — a myth to which Rossetti himself was eager to contribute. Yet he was acutely aware that the material forms of pictures and poems substantially affect how they are acquired and used. He bent his energies to assure that these crucial aspects of the work of art were not left to chance or the decisions of others.

I

Rossetti's opportunities to design books from cover to cover did not come until the 1860s, but his fascination with the decorative possibilities of objects and the walls and rooms where they might be arranged dates well back into the 1850s. The distinctive spaces Rossetti created, through rhythmic arrangements of the things he found or designed, first appear as settings for the Virgin Mary, Dante, Hamlet and Ophelia, or Mary Magdalene in paintings and drawings anchored by the stories to which they allude.[8] In Rossetti's striking small watercolors of the mid- and late-fifties, character and narrative are increasingly absorbed into the spaces they inhabit. Walls, niches, furniture, and objects take on their own life through the play of curious shape and flat surface patterning,

[150]

Figure 29.
Dante Gabriel Rossetti, *The Tune of the Seven Towers*, 1857, courtesy of
Tate Gallery/Art Resource, NY.

rendered in startlingly rich color. These seem to provide the *raison
d'être* for the figures rather than the other way around, as even the
titles indicate: *The Blue Closet, The Tune of the Seven Towers* (both
1857; fig. 29). By the late 1850s, Rossetti was not only picturing
but painting and arranging distinctive spaces for himself or his
friends — real or imagined personalities who, like the figures in
the watercolors (or in his illustrations for the Moxon Tennyson),
would come to seem inseparable from the decorative settings in
which they played a part.[9] Rossetti's work of the 1860s — books,

pictures, and the rooms in whose design they might participate as decorative objects — represents a more ambitious attempt to exploit the defining possibilities of decoration and design.

I am not arguing that the primary interest of Rossetti's designs is their symbolic or semantic content. A language distinguishing "meaning" from "appearance" or "depth" from "surface" is inadequate to describe his work because the two continually collapse into one another. Just as the viewer is thrust back to the surface of the shallow picture space (when, for example, a hand reaches in the window at the back of the room in *The Tune of the Seven Towers*, or the pattern of the picture is echoed in the design on the frame), so attempts to "read" the iconic significance of objects or their visual components are countered by the extent to which these are embedded in patterns that refuse to privilege the readable or symbolic elements — even when Rossetti himself, in the sonnets he wrote for his first exhibited painting, *The Girlhood of Mary Virgin*, calls attention to "the symbols" he has strategically scattered in the picture space. Nor can *The Blue Closet* or *The Tune of the Seven Towers* be fully explained as the representation of an emotional mood or idea, though that is certainly part of what they do. Decorative effect — the impact felt along the senses of patterns painted on and formed with objects — exceeds and may even distract us from the narrative future toward which the "symbols" point or the imagined emotional tone of the scenes depicted in the watercolors. Is this simply ineptitude? I think not: these lapses in strict linguistic or iconic economy force us back to the presence of *things* at their least profound. The role of text or image as object, as Rossetti's decorative arts remind us, can be a means of controlling the effect of a room or poem or a picture, and hence of constructing a distinctive look or persona for both the art object and its maker that is no less powerful for distracting us from interpretation — for returning us to surfaces, to rhythmic repetition and pattern, to "mere" decoration.

When Rossetti begins, very early in his work as poet and painter, to exploit the effects of patterned surfaces, he shares with his contemporaries a heightened desire to decorate with objects. Their desire was stimulated by the overwhelming displays at the annual Royal Academy Exhibitions or — in 1851 — in the vast spaces of the Crystal Palace. There mid-century Britain showed off its arts and middle-class Victorians acquired the tastes that furnished their homes. These two venues exercised enormous influence in the cultural memories of those who sought to participate as artists or consumers in the excited interest in contemporary arts that were to mark the next several decades. The great glass greenhouse dubbed the Crystal Palace housed the first international exhibition, in London during the summer of 1851, of what were called the industrial or manufacturing arts.[10] The Royal Academy annually sponsored the most important show of contemporary fine art. Neither Rossetti, nor, at least by some accounts, William Morris, seems to have actually entered the original Crystal Palace.[11] But with the help of copious coverage in the press, in both words and images, even those who did not attend these vast social rituals could construct a vision of what they were like. For several generations of Pre-Raphaelites, appalled by both the arts on display and the way they were presented, the Crystal Palace and the Royal Academy exhibitions were twin spurs to their ambitions to reform Victorian art.

Neither the goods themselves nor the ways in which they were publicly displayed were intended primarily to guide domestic consumption. At the Crystal Palace, every form of design in industrial or hand-manufacture was welcomed, especially those using unusual materials or new technologies. Critics complained that excellence of design was too often equated with novelty, ingenuity, and fantastical elaboration of surfaces: decoration defied the limitations of its material and the common sense of everyday

[153]

use.[12] Especially among the luxury goods, the pieces on display were virtuoso performances. This was, in effect, a display where the decorative packaging not only outshone but might completely obscure the objects. It is not surprising that book bindings and picture frames could be exhibited while books, like paintings, could not. At the Royal Academy exhibitions, on the other hand, the emphasis was on the paintings. The chance to see so many pictures for oneself was exciting and subtly flattering. As in the Crystal Palace, the sheer abundance of national production was impressive, as were the wealth of materials and styles and the evident amount of labor invested. But visitors found it difficult to single out from the chaotic accumulation of goods on display a successful individual piece, much less to detect an original national school or character. The pictures were hung floor to ceiling and frame to frame, competing with each other and with the crowds who attended. Too often they were doomed to disappear into the undifferentiated blur of wall-to-wall images. Where visitors were dependent on the placement of pictures (those "on the line" at eye level were agreed to have the best chance of being noticed) and the attention of reviewers to help them sort out what they would look at, it was not easy for prospective purchasers to exercise discrimination.[13]

Pre-Raphaelite experiments in designing objects, beginning in the 1850s and intensifying in the 1860s, sought solutions to the problems of making and marketing artful objects suited to domestic consumption: art to live with. The crowds at the Crystal Palace and the Academy exhibitions were mute testimony to the eagerness of Victorians to do exactly that. In both cases exhibition spurred consumption, even if the objects on display were not for sale (at the Crystal Palace) or the most desirable pictures were already sold to dealers or out of reach of a visitor's purse (at the Academy). Yet as we have seen, those exhibitions seemed designed to frustrate efforts to select and integrate, in any coherent way, art objects into Victorian homes. Pre-Raphaelite design experiments begin with the decoration of the Oxford Union Debating Hall in the summer of 1857, proceed to the furnishing of Morris's new home, Red House, in 1860, and culminate in the production of furnishings and interior designs as a commercial business. In their work for "The Firm" in the 1860s, '70s, and '80s, Morris, Rossetti, Edward Burne-Jones, and Philip Webb tried to achieve harmonious overall effects in particular spaces as well as to improve the design of individual objects. Meanwhile Rossetti, the charismatic figure whose enthusiasms often catalyzed these collective activities, turned in 1862 to the task that was to absorb much of his time and money for the rest of the decade: furnishing and decorating the large house he leased for twenty years in Chelsea. His book designs, like most of his picture frames, were made at the time when he was also constructing interiors for himself and his friends and clients. I shall return to Rossetti's Tudor House.

His illustrations for books in the 1850s, however, already suggest a strong interest in decorative effect. These early illustrations were visually brilliant and innovative interpretations of the poems for which they were produced, as others have amply noted.[14] Critical attention has been less concerned with their decorative effects, however, taking its cue from Rossetti's own comments. Rossetti was anxious to defend his status as a creative artist even when working for a commercial publisher and a popular audience to sell other poets' poems. (The myth of the artist's detachment from commerce was itself not without important market value, an irony with which artists since at least the beginning of the nineteenth century had been struggling.) He was certainly not thinking of himself primarily as a decorator or an illustrator, identities which commanded neither the social and cultural power nor the potential financial rewards open to the painter in the 1860s. In

[155]

Figure 30.
Dante Gabriel Rossetti, *The Maids of Elfen-mere*,
engraved by the Dalziel Brothers for William Allingham,
The Music Master, 1855.

the disjunctions between the illustrations Rossetti produced in the 1850s and what he wrote about them, we can see the problems faced by the artist professionally interested in distinguishing fine from decorative art who was, nonetheless, fascinated by the decorative possibilities of art's object forms.

Rossetti's published work for books begins with the single, stunning engraving, *The Maids of Elfen-mere* (fig. 30) for his friend William Allingham's collection of poetry, *The Music Master* (1855). Burne-Jones, then an Oxford undergraduate, singled out Rossetti's illustration in an article for Morris's *Oxford and Cambridge Magazine*:

> It is I think the most beautiful drawing for an illustration I have ever seen, the weird faces of the maids of Elfinmere [sic], the musical timed movement of their arms together as they sing, the face of the man, above all, are such as only a great artist could conceive.[15]

The Maids of Elfen-mere, and the five designs Rossetti contributed two years later to the illustrated edition of Tennyson's early poetry published by Edward Moxon, suggested to artists wholly new conceptual and visual possibilities for book illustration. Dispensing with the distancing effect of the vignette and the sketchy fine lines of much contemporary work, these images focus on a few large figures, rendered with strong contrasts of black and white, who bring the emotional intensity of apparently static scenes startlingly close to the viewer. This insistence on immediate, even intimate engagement in the world of the poem is joined to a disconcerting sense of estrangement: the apparently fraught relations between the figures are not easy to explain as ordinary human experiences or emotions. Especially in *The Lady of Shalott* (fig. 31), the closeness and strangeness is raised to an almost claustrophobic

Figure 31.
Dante Gabriel Rossetti, *The Lady of Shalott*,
engraved by the Dalziel Brothers,
Moxon edition of Tennyson's *Poems*, 1857.

pitch by the crowding of every inch of the small picture space (about three inches square). The setting is, in both images, itself mysterious and unfamiliar. In *The Lady* one might almost say that the space itself is alien to the three-dimensional world of Euclid or Alberti.

The disconcerting spaces and faces are "weird," as Burne-Jones notes, yet the drawing strikes him as supremely "beautiful." His perceptions are a useful guide. The pleasure of aesthetic order present in both drawings derives at least in part from repetition or patterning: "the musical timed movement" of arms that Burne-Jones notices in *The Maids*. In *The Lady*, the patterned fabrics on the figures and the rhythmic ordering of motifs in adjacent areas (for example, the torches fixed to the hood of the boat) blend figures and space into a heavily patterned single surface, almost like a patchwork quilt. Although Burne-Jones clearly responds strongly to the patterning in Rossetti's illustration, neither he nor Rossetti defends these as decorative images.

As illustrations, *The Maids of Elfen-mere* and, more markedly, *The Lady of Shalott*, are not at all modest, particularly when read through Rossetti's comments on what he wanted to do, as they usually are. According to Rossetti, he is not content simply to picture a scene as it is described in a text so as to make it more "real" for the reader ("realization," in this sense, was a Victorian synonym for illustration, as Martin Meisel has shown).[16] He wants, instead, to capture a tone or mood or idea representative of the whole poem, inventing decor and details to produce a highly condensed, replete image *of* the text, not simply a rendition of a scene *from* it. Such an act of condensation and representation is not, he says, a repetition in a different medium of the representations already present in the poem, but a separate intellectual and imaginative act. The artist's aim is to "embody [the work's] ideas," as Rossetti wrote Allingham — and inevitably to embody its ideas is also to interpret them.[17] Alternatively, writing of his designs for Tennyson's "The Palace of Art," he notes that he chooses passages which leave something to the imagination, in effect (though he wishes to avoid "killing, for oneself and everyone, a distinct idea of the poet's") choosing passages where he can find the germ of a different poem of which he will be the author (*Letters* 1.239). Tennyson's allegory describes the soul who builds herself a palace furnished with pictures, tapestries, and statuary; the poem is itself lavishly furnished with brief evocations of a series of such subjects. Rossetti takes two of these and creates them as works of art: Saint Cecilia and the death of Arthur. Here (in Rossetti's much-quoted words, again to Allingham) he has chosen passages "where one can allegorize on one's own hook" (*Letters* 1.239). Rossetti's comments assume the creative authority associated with the Romantic artist. Whether he describes illustration as the condensed embodiment of the poem, as in *The Maids* and *The Lady*, or as allegorical pictures on subjects named in the poem, as in the two illustrations for "The Palace of Art," Rossetti makes the strong claim that his designs are themselves works of art.

These attitudes toward illustration do not take into account the effect of poems and pictures as parts of a book. In the Moxon Tennyson, particularly, the lavish number of illustrations by many different artists made for a visually discordant volume.[18] To be fair, Rossetti had no say in the overall design of either *The Music Master* or the Moxon Tennyson; he was only a minor contributor. It remains an open question whether, given an entire volume, the artist who insisted that his pictures should go their own way might have moved beyond the uneasy conjunction of the single image with text to consider the different problems of creating a coherent book. Two projects tantalize with the promise of what might have been. As early as 1848 he described plans to etch twelve of his designs to be published with his own translation of Dante's *Vita*

Nuova. And in 1854, after again announcing the Vita Nuova plan, he proposed that he and Lizzie Siddal should illustrate a volume of Scottish ballads that Allingham was editing.[19]

Yet there is other evidence that Rossetti was already thinking about the image as one part of a more complex process of producing a work of art. Though few of the frames he designed in the 1850s survive, it was evidently his practice carefully to oversee the making of frames for his pictures throughout his career, either when they were exhibited (which was rare after 1850) or, more commonly, when they were sent to a purchaser. For the exhibition of his first two paintings in 1849 and 1850, he designed special frames on which texts were attached or inscribed — his own sonnets for The Girlhood of Mary Virgin and Latin religious texts for the Ecce Ancilla Domini, an Annunciation. The texts, together with the arched top of the frame he gave to the first picture, would have suggested early Italian religious art and drawn attention to the symbolism of many decorative elements in the pictures, thus setting the terms in which the pictures would be understood and strongly suggesting the attitudes with which they should be approached.[20]

In all his designs, Rossetti balanced the several functions of frames differently from most of his contemporaries. His frames do, of course, help to entice the eye and to make the images stand out from the backgrounds against which they may be seen. They also serve as signs that these are objects of special value — marking them as works of art and, in early examples, religious icons. But Rossetti's frames are relatively modest by contemporary standards; the materials are not expensive nor very elaborately worked.[21] The frame used frequently by Rossetti for small heads or half-figures in the1860s, for example, is typical in its use of a simple broad flat, bordered on both the inside and outside edges with small carved, shallow squares and roundels set into the narrow bands of

Figure 32.
Dante Gabriel Rossetti, *Water Willow*, 1871;
partial view of frame designed by Rossetti,
courtesy of Samuel and Mary R. Bancroft Collection,
Delaware Art Museum.

reeds to mark the corners and sides (fig. 32). A more formal version uses a similarly broad flat of gilded wood, interrupted by slightly larger raised and carved medallions (fig. 33). Versions of this frame were used not only by Rossetti but also by Ford Madox Brown and William Holman Hunt. It gives something of the effect of a plain wide mat, especially with the rather simple decorative or textual markings preferred by Rossetti and Brown.[22]

Unlike many heavier, inward-sloping contemporary frames, these Pre-Raphaelite frames do not suggest a window or a proscenium opening to a view or scene. They do not prepare the eye to seek deep recession into the illusionistic space of the image. Rossetti's and Brown's frames encourage viewers instead to recognize the picture as a flat surface, an idea reinforced by the quite shallow spaces, sometimes cut off by patterned backgrounds, depicted in the images themselves. Two things we noted in Rossetti's book illustrations work together with the flat frames to make these pictures seem on the verge of discarding spatial illusion: the repleteness of the image (there are few empty spaces; pattern and detail proliferate) and the use of relatively large figures that reach to the borders or are even cramped within the picture space. The minimal linear designs on the frames echo elements of flat patterning within the image. Arranged to emphasize the verticals and horizontals of the frame, these linear designs repeat similar verticals and horizontals within the image, again suggesting continuity between the planar surfaces of frame and canvas. The cumulative effect of these devices is to create a unified decorative object, minimizing the distinction between frame and image by setting up a play of design elements across the more or less continuous surface of both.

Alastair Grieve's astute observations drew attention to several of these effects some time ago, but we can press his observations further. First, it appears that Rossetti considered the frame as an

Figure 33.
Dante Gabriel Rossetti, *Lady Lilith*, 1864-68
(repainted 1872-73); frame designed by Rossetti,
courtesy of Samuel and Mary R. Bancroft Collection,
Delaware Art Museum.

integral part of the pictorial object that would vary from one version of the image to another or require alteration when he took back previously completed pictures to rework and reframe them. The pictorial object so conceived is a historically changing form for a pictorial idea. And second, these variations and alterations take into account the viewing context — the way the client will use the pictures, the kind of space in which they will be hung, and the part they play in the client's collection or in the artist's own oeuvre. For example, Rossetti later reframed *The Girlhood of Mary Virgin*, changing the nature of the pictorial object to accord with his own changing ideas about the art object and perhaps also with the tastes of a new owner. The new frame still included his sonnets, but dispensed with the arched shape, bringing this early work into conformity with the secular and much more obviously decorative works Rossetti was then painting. In other cases Rossetti executed replicas of his pictures or different versions of the same idea, often in a different medium; here, too, there are examples of his making new frames to designate the difference in the pictorial object, its owner, and its relation to its setting. Thus, in one particularly complicated example, *The Salutation of Beatrice* was first realized as a watercolor drawing bought by his artist friend George Boyce in 1854 and framed with textual references by Rossetti either then or in the early 1860s when he borrowed the drawing back from Boyce. The nearly square frame, with a broad flat, had roundels with schematic suns in the four corners and smaller roundels with stars along the four sides, with a brief quotation from Dante at the bottom and the textual reference at the top. But Rossetti also painted a very similar scene as one of a pair of panels illustrating Beatrice denying her salutation to Dante on earth and awarding it to him in heaven. The two scenes, separated by an emblematic figure of Love, were painted on the doors of a cabinet installed in Morris's Red House in 1860. In its original

[165]

Red House setting, the cabinet had been part of a highly architectural piece of furniture designed by Morris and Webb: a bench overhung with shelves and cabinet and topped with a platform to which stairs ascended from the back, creating a balcony for musical performance within Morris's sitting room.[23] The painted panels on the cabinet doors, otherwise unframed and without explanatory texts, helped fit this furniture to the rest of the room, whose walls and ceilings were extensively painted to create a rich interplay of colorfully patterned and painted surfaces. When the panels were later removed, Rossetti put them in a double frame, different from that on the single Boyce picture, for sale to the dealer Ernest Gambart. For this frame Rossetti used another version of the emblematic figure of Love on the frame to join the two panels and added a design of squared rosettes filling the corners, with texts inscribed under each panel and a double title in the center, making a single free-standing pictorial object. It is possible that the unusually detailed symbolism and the proliferation of texts on the frame respond to the problem of selling through a dealer, where Rossetti would have no other opportunity to influence the way a future purchaser would understand the images and could not consider the particular setting in which the picture would be placed.

As this example indicates, Rossetti's designs for pictorial objects attend when possible to their effect within the larger scheme of a room or a collection. Particularly for collectors who owned multiple examples of his work (and this was often the case, since he tended to work for a very few clients with whom he cultivated ongoing relationships), the repetition of the same or similar frames could enhance the cumulative impact of his pictures and powerfully influence the way in which they would be seen, as in the drawing room of one of Rossetti's best patrons, Frederick Leyland. (It was Leyland for whom James Abbott McNeill Whistler created his Peacock Dining Room, now in the Freer Gallery in Washington, D.C.) We know from the correspondence between the two men that the effect of the Rossetti paintings that line the walls of this room was achieved by protracted negotiation.[24] Leyland attempted to specify exactly the dimensions of each picture to fit "my scheme of decoration" (Fennell 37) while Rossetti insisted on his right to let his own conception determine the size and shape of the pictures and constantly substituted different pictures for those he initially offered. The framing of each picture was apparently up to Rossetti, who took into account his own interests in creating coherent decorative objects and setting off his work from that of others. But he was also sensitive to the importance of establishing the heightened atmosphere of intense yet languid aestheticism Leyland required. Rossetti had already advised Leyland in the furnishing and decoration of other houses. He also knew the emotional and visual needs that had drawn the meticulous, austere, and ruthless businessman to Pre-Raphaelite art and the circle of artists and collectors Rossetti entertained at Tudor House.[25] A contemporary photograph shows Rossetti's pictures arranged in Leyland's drawing room so that the eye follows a rhythmic path — Leyland thought of his pictures in musical terms, as sounding the notes of musical composition — moving from one large yet spiritually distant female face and figure (for example, his *Lady Lilith*, fig. 33) to another around an otherwise formally and richly furnished room.[26] Slight variations in pose as well as size and framing help introduce lyrical movement into a rather stiff decor.

A quite different aesthetic shaped the sitting room of Rossetti's own house, where he put together a motley, eclectic assortment of objects to achieve that impression of a special and distinctive taste to which visitors attested.[27] The catalogue from the sales of his furnishings after his death lists, among other items in this

room, Chinese lacquered cabinets, Dutch tiles, mirrors in elaborate Jacobean or simple circular frames, pictures in Rossetti's own
flat frames, an early Italian madonna in a Gothic frame, vernacular and eighteenth-century English chairs, Oriental rugs, a stuffed
owl, and a sofa painted by Rossetti.[28] A watercolor drawing by his
studio assistant, Henry Treffy Dunn (*Sitting Room at 16 Cheyne
Walk*, 1882, National Portrait Gallery, London), shows this heterogeneous collection assembled into a whole that is far more unified than any list can suggest, in part by echoing linear patterns
picked out in gold from carpet to furniture to tiles, lacquer work,
and mirrors, set against the harmonizing green tones of walls and
sofa cushions and floor covering, all multiplied in the many mirrors. The means struck visitors as odd, but they found the effect
created strangely compelling. Sidney Colvin, remembering the
experience nearly forty years after Rossetti's death (" . . . the dark-
green sparsely picked out with red and lighted here and there by a
round convex mirror; the shelves and cupboards laden with brass-
ware and old blue Nankin china"), breaks off suddenly to evoke
instead the watercolors of the 1850s: "their harmonies, their passionate intensities of expression and their rare originality and
often, though not always, their beauty of group-composition and
pattern" (Colvin 75). Linking the "rare originality" of the watercolors to the equal intensities achieved by Rossetti in his sitting
room, Colvin goes on to associate both with the distinctive voice
of the poet reading his poems aloud:

the readings . . . were among the marking events . . . of my
life. . . . Rossetti's way was not dramatic in any ordinary
sense of the word. It was rather a chant, a monotone; but
somehow he was able with little variation of pitch or
inflection to express a wonderful range and richness of
emotion. His voice was magical in its mellow beauty of

[168]

timbre and quality and in its power to convey the sense of a whole world of brooding passion and mystery, both human and elemental, behind the words. (Colvin 76)

Colvin's recollections evoke a ghostly scene: the voice of the poet reaches beyond and "behind the words" to affect the hearer in a way apparently inaccessible to those who encounter the poem on the page.

II

Rossetti's designs for books in the 1860s attempt to embody in the bound and printed book something of the "magical" effect Colvin heard when the poems were read aloud. Unlike most authors, who left book design to illustrators, cover designers, engravers, binders, and the publishers, printers, and engraving firms who commissioned their work, Rossetti never underestimated the physical forms of books as a medium of expression for the author or, increasingly, the purchaser. Many consumers expected books to be not only attractive objects in their own right but also potential elements in the decoration of their homes. Advice books routinely instructed late-Victorian readers to consider home decoration, after clothing, as crucial to constructing a social profile with personal inflections.[29] And in countless contemporary drawings and photographs commissioned to record the success of such domestic decor, elaborately bound books are prominently displayed.[30] The books whose physical forms Rossetti took such pains with in the 1860s assert the claims of the book and its contents against the ambitions of purchasers who would press them into their own designs. His books give to a body of written work something like what contemporaries registered as the compelling *presence* of his early watercolors, his rooms in Chelsea, or his poems read aloud in his own voice. While Rossetti himself

— or at least a romantic figure by that name — may be for some readers always the imagined presence lending power to the things he has made, such presence is also constructed as the property of the objects themselves — they are so made as to impose or compel attention just as the physical presence of a strong personality might. The particulars of the presentation are crucial to the work of Rossetti's art, whether as picture, room, or book.

Rossetti uses his book designs, moreover, as the distinguishing mark not of a single author but of a family of writers and the broader social and artistic circles to which they belonged. There is, indeed, an unresolvable tension between autonomy and collectivity in Rossetti's artistic ambitions. The work of creating the particular presence of a book as he pursued it — or of creating the look of a room or a framed picture — was never an individual enterprise. Though the product might be both immediately distinctive and unusually coherent, it is the result of multiple and often conflicting social practices, a situation Rossetti actively solicited. His books are the material forms of a sometimes uneasily shared work of art.

Rossetti helped to make at least eight books in the ten-year period between 1861 and 1871. He designed bindings for his 1861 volume of translations, *The Early Italian Poets;* for two volumes of Algernon Charles Swinburne's poetry, *Atalanta in Calydon* (1865) and *Songs before Sunrise* (1871); for his brother William Michael's translation of Dante's *Inferno* (1865) and his sister Maria's commentary on Dante (1871); for his sister Christina's two collections, *Goblin Market and Other Poems* (1862, with a slightly altered edition in 1865) and *The Prince's Progress and Other Poems* (1866); and for his own first volume of original poetry, *Poems* (1870). He did his most extensive work for *Goblin Market, The Prince's Progress,* and *Poems,* the books that I shall examine most closely.

[170]

Rossetti's work for these three books in the 1860s, by contrast with his illustrations of the 1850s, considers the volume in its entirety from the selection and arrangement of its contents to binding, endpapers, title pages, and illustration. Few of his contemporaries involved themselves in so many aspects of a book's production. Only Morris among his wide circle of acquaintances shared his approach to the book as a total work of art, combining the disparate labors of writing, editing, illustrating, printing, binding, publishing, marketing, buying, displaying, and reading. Rossetti's own activities did not extend quite so far — unlike Morris, he never designed a new typeface, sought out special inks and paper, or became his own printer and publisher. But Morris did not begin to realize his ideas until he began the Kelmscott Press in the 1890s. Working thirty years earlier with commercial printers, binders, and publishers, Rossetti had already begun to integrate physical form with literary content. His practices unsettle a number of our — and perhaps his — ideas about the work of art.

The design of binding and illustrations is only one part of the more extensive process of shaping books that engaged Rossetti. The literary work of editing and assembling occupied an increasingly important place. For Christina's volumes, the printer sent proofs to both Christina and Gabriel. While Christina had the ultimate say, her brother did not hesitate to recommend changes of every sort from words to titles to the omission of some poems or the composition of new ones. Their long correspondence over the evolving volume of *The Prince's Progress* is a vigorous exchange.[31] Both had their own ideas about the crafting of Christina's collection, but the give and take was evidently stimulating as well as, on occasion, provoking to the ostensible author. Rossetti's close involvement with the literary construction of the book should be kept in mind when considering the illustrations he produced.

He sought the same help when it came to his own volume. Between August 1869 and April 1870 not only Christina but brother William Michael, Swinburne, and William Bell Scott read the constantly changing versions of the collection as it shuttled back and forth among the author, the printer, and the friends and family called in to contribute to its production. At least the later stages of composition were social, not solitary. Though Rossetti certainly exercised tight control over that process, he understood the task of composing and printing a book to be the work of many hands. Neither the author nor the designer works alone; the result will never be exactly what was first envisioned in the mind's eye — a consequence Rossetti endlessly denounced (the stupidity of engravers and printers who will not follow his directions is a constant theme) yet just as consistently invited.

In the extended process by which these volumes were shaped, the line between poetic composition of a verbally satisfying work and the crafting of the book as a physical object is blurred in a fascinating way. Both turn out to be, in a double sense, collective activities, for the book and even its component parts are not only the product of many hands but also collections of separate poems and sometimes pictures. Composition extends to the selection and arrangement of these elements into larger collective forms. This is particularly evident if we look more closely at the major work in *Poems* (1870), the unfinished sonnet sequence entitled "The House of Life." The structuring trope of the title is both spatial and temporal: the sonnets are reified moments ("A sonnet is a moment's monument," begins the sonnet on sonnets placed at the opening of the sequence in the 1881 version). The sonnet-moment is invoked as a precious artifact ("Carve it in ivory or ebony . . . and let Time see/ Its flowering crest impearled and orient") or a painting ("let this my lady's picture glow/ Under my hand . . . Lo! It is done. . . . Her face is made her shrine . . . .").

Pictures and artful objects fill the rooms of the poem's "House" to contain the emotional experience of a lifetime.[32] (The Italian "stanza" is, literally, a room.)

Selection and ordering are crucial to the display of this collection, as they were to those in Tudor House or Leyland's drawing rooms. The sonnets do not appear in the order in which they were first written; Rossetti constantly rearranged them. He began to work with a printer long before he was ready to make the fair copy that the printer ordinarily expected: indeed, for Rossetti there is never a fair copy.[33] He had very unfinished manuscript drafts set up in type, one poem to a sheet, so that he could see them in that form; from there he continued not only to rewrite words and lines and to add whole new passages and poems — periodically sending revised sheets back to the printer to be set up afresh — but also to play with the order of poems, reshuffling pages, and with the composition of type as it appeared on the pages: the size and spacing, font and capitalization. The crafting of "The House of Life" as a collective form, a single long poem, continues intermittently from the fall of 1869 until its second publication in 1881, just before Rossetti's death. The poem published in 1870 is a momentary arrest in the ongoing process of expanding and rearranging a growing collection. For Rossetti, then, it is impossible to separate writing, revision, editorial selection and arrangement, and even the design and setting in type of the page: they proceed simultaneously, each change modifying and modified by others, in an extended compositional process. If we draw out the implications of Rossetti's practice to a more general definition of art, it would be difficult to speak of an "original" creative act, distinct in kind and quality, to be claimed as the exclusive prerogative of the poet or the artist and invoked to separate the work of art from those of collecting, editing, decorating, crafting, or even manufacturing. Rossetti's practice, in other

[173]

words, threatens distinctions which determine economic as well as aesthetic value.

Late in the process of putting together a book, Rossetti designed the binding. He worked on the form of the book as it was issued by a commercial publisher — that is, his book designs were not simply created for the private libraries of individual clients. All his designs used the most common form of binding for a moderately priced book, stiffened cloth on paper boards, with title and decorative design pressed into the cloth (by a brass block cut to the artist's design) and filled with gold leaf.[34] Rossetti drew the designs and specified the size and proportions of the boards, the relationship of lines to edges, the thickness of the lines, the color and texture of the cloth, and the color and, for *Poems*, a pattern for the endpapers. He also designed the illustrated title page and facing frontispiece for *Goblin Market* and *The Prince's Progress*. He specified the wood engraver (W. J. Linton) he preferred. Moreover he checked and corrected the work of both the binder and the engraver.

Victorian decorated cloth bindings usually focused on two areas of the book as separate problems of design: the spine, visible when the book is shelved with other volumes and identifying the volume by title and author; and the front cover (the back cover was not always decorated, and then usually in a simpler version of the front design). The front or top cover would be displayed when the book was laid out on a table as part of the decorative furnishing of a room. For this reason it normally received the most elaborate treatment. The whole cover was apt to be used for an elaborate design symmetrical on two axes, covering the visible face of the book on display with a framed medallion composed of a complex network of geometrical or curling lines — most commonly stamped in gold on cloth, but occasionally, especially in the late 1840s and early 1850s, constructed of molded papier-mâché, as in the volume visible on the table in Holman Hunt's 1854 painting, *The Awakening Conscience* — where, as Ruskin explained, it is a sign of a vulgar and nouveau taste, part of the "fatal newness" of the furniture in the overdecorated parlor of a kept woman.[35]

Rossetti's bindings show two striking differences from this contemporary practice: first, the decoration is extremely restrained. On the top cover for the 1862 *Goblin Market* (fig. 34), a simple arrangement of a few interlaced vertical and horizontal gold lines emphasizes the tall, slim proportions of the volume.[36] The triangular groups of tiny circles in opposing angles and the doubled line next to the spine create an asymmetrical but balanced pattern of lines and rectangular spaces, recalling the interest of Rossetti and his friend Whistler in Japanese design in the 1860s. The spare use of gold enhances without obscuring the contrasting color and texture of the dark cloth. For the covers of Swinburne's two books, Rossetti has enlarged the tiny circles to roundels and filled them with stylized motifs linked to the subject matter of the volume — patterns suggesting those on Greek vase bases for *Atalanta in Calydon*, and moon, stars, and a rising sun for *Songs before Sunrise*. The widely spaced motifs define an open field and focus attention on the adjacent spine, where the central roundel is repeated.

As these examples already suggest, Rossetti's designs depart sharply from contemporary practice in a second way: they treat the different faces of the binding together as the connected parts of a single unit. The top and bottom lines of the *Goblin Market* cover are continuous with those on the spine, with the three-circle motif repeated under the label; the roundels of *Songs before Sunrise* also continue across the spine. *Poems* (fig. 35) goes further: the fine gold grill, with its grace notes of stylized flowering plants, extends right across the spine and onto the back cover. The spine forms the central vertical panel or hinge for a pattern that is symmetrical when the covers of the volume are spread but asymmetrical when the top

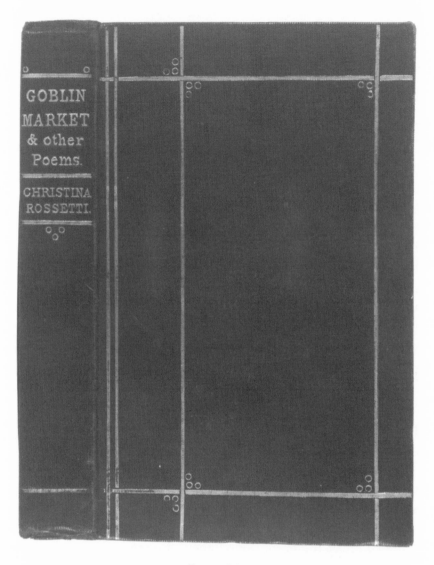

Figure 34.
Dante Gabriel Rossetti, cover, *Goblin Market*,
first edition, 1862,
courtesy of Special Collections Department,
University of Virginia.

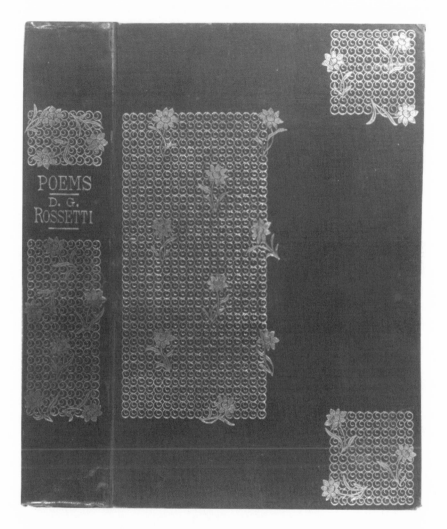

Figure 35.
Dante Gabriel Rossetti, cover, *Poems*, 1870,
courtesy of Special Collections Department,
University of Virginia.

[177]

cover is viewed alone. Opened flat, the cover would resemble the double frame of Rossetti's *Salutation of Beatrice* (two large panels, set in a rectangular frame with large squares at each corner, and joined by a thin vertical strip inscribed with identifying texts and figure). But this is not the way one would — or at least should — ordinarily display the book. As a book cover, the continuous design *wraps around* three sides of a volume, both defining it as a three-dimensional object and indicating that the fourth or unwrapped side will open. *The Prince's Progress*, a similarly continuous design, evokes the clasps of a medieval book or chest: this is the cover as container, a book to be picked up and read.

Opening *The Prince's Progress* shows the care that connects spine to covers again at work to create a harmonious sequence as the pages are turned. Inside the apple-green cloth cover of *The Prince's Progress*, the color shifts to a complementary red-brown. For *The Early Italian Poets*, black cloth with gold opens to endpapers in the same dark chocolate or mulberry red-brown; the cover of *Poems* is a deep, dull blue-green overlaid with its grill or trellis in gold, followed by very light blue-green endpapers printed with a variation of the cover grill and flowers in a slightly darker shade. The color of the binding for *Poems* was also used for Swinburne's *Songs before Sunrise* and for Morris's two volumes from the same period, 1870-73; all were published by Rossetti's friend F. S. Ellis. The uniform color and related designs are probably the result of Rossetti's active interest in using bindings, like frames, to give a distinctive identity to works by himself and his family and friends, much as he had once urged the uniform use of the identifying initials PRB on early Pre-Raphaelite paintings.

Beyond covers and endpapers lie the double-page spreads of frontispiece and title page that Rossetti provided for *Goblin Market* and *The Prince's Progress* (figs. 36-39). Unlike his illustrations for books in the 1850s, these designs are fitted to the poem they

Figure 36.
Dante Gabriel Rossetti, frontispiece, *The Prince's Progress and Other Poems*, by Christina Rossetti, 1866, courtesy of Special Collections Department, University of Chicago.

[179]

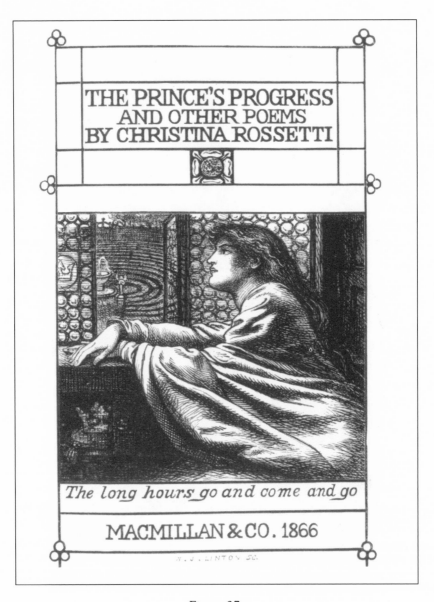

THE PRINCE'S PROGRESS
AND OTHER POEMS
BY CHRISTINA ROSSETTI

The long hours go and come and go

MACMILLAN & CO. 1866

Figure 37.
Dante Gabriel Rossetti, title page, *The Prince's Progress and
Other Poems,* by Christina Rossetti, 1866,
courtesy of Special Collections Department, University of Chicago.

illustrate, the collection they head, and the bound volume in which they are found. The title-page design for *The Prince's Progress* recalls Rossetti's usual vocabulary for frames and bindings: squares and rectangles, lines and tiny circles grouped in triplets, but with just the suggestion here that the lines extend to curl into the triplets, as the lines of the cover extend to curl into a spiral (the decorative clasps that enclose *The Prince's Progress*). The image incorporated into the design repeats motifs from that design: the concentric circles of the pool around the fountain, the pattern of the window glass. It refers forward to the title poem, from which its text is taken, but also provides, with a wit fully attuned to Christina's, a figure for the expectant reader of the volume (like the princess of the poem, the reader is presumably trying to envision the progress of the prince; possibly, like the princess, the reader will also find that progress growing tiresomely slow). Finally, as illustration to the title poem, the image on the title page is designed to work with that on the facing page to capture the intertwined stories of the dis-tractable prince and the princess condemned (or perhaps too con-tent) to await his dilatory progress to claim her hand.[37] The images can be read together from either direction. Starting from the title page, the controlling point of view is that of the princess as "The long hours go and come and go" and the prince does not appear. From left to right, however, they suggest the perspective of the prince, who has finally arrived to discover the princess has grown old and died while he dallied along the way. Viewed through his eyes, the intently longing princess depicted on the title page will be the image that haunts his remorseful memory, reproaching him more effectively than the words and looks of her maidens: "You should have wept her yesterday."[38]

The component parts of *Goblin Market* are similarly finely integrated. The deep-blue linen of the cover opens first to the chocolate-brown endpapers, then to the double-page spread of

frontispiece and title page. These two images have been often discussed separately as interpretations of the poem: in both, the sensuous bodies of the two girls bring out the sexual undercurrents Rossetti found in this poem of temptation couched in the deceptive form of a nursery rhyme.[39] Encountered together at the front of the book, however, they incorporate the reader as yet another subject of the poet's and the illustrator's critical play with the temptations and pitfalls of looking, buying, and consuming. In the frontispiece, the rounded forms of the fruit and the girl are open to the leers of the goblins and invite the knowing look of the adult reader: an invitation prepared by the rich feast of color on the preceding pages. If we look at the title page, however, the sisters' ripe

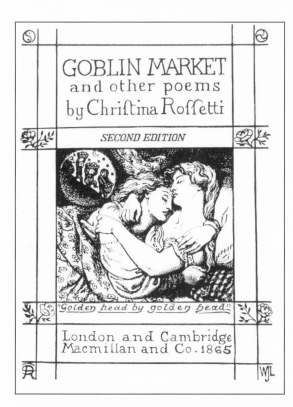

Figure 39.
Dante Gabriel
Rossetti, title page,
*Goblin Market and
Other Poems,* by
Christina Rossetti,
second edition,
1865.

bodies and their — or our — suspect dreams are firmly set within framing lines decorated with wild roses, recalling the austere lines of the cover. Rossetti's grotesque goblins swarm and grin most unpleasantly in the frontispiece, threatening the girl but also holding up an unattractive mirror to any leering reader. But in the title-page design they have been shrunk to diminutive size, contained in the circular inset, more comically whimsical than actively frightening. (These goblins are strongly akin to Maurice Sendak's "wild things" — not accidentally, since Sendak borrows frequently from nineteenth-century children's book illustrators.) The two pages offer and then apparently retract an unsettling message to adult readers, with Christina's sly wit. Lest we should find this reading too reassuring, however, consider another way that the two pages can be read together. The diagonal line of a hill divides the frontispiece from top left to bottom right. Down this hill goblins have descended to offer magic fruit that one of the poem's two sisters is about to buy with a lock of her hair; the other sister, refusing to be tempted, ascends the hill, though with one backward glance over her shoulder. The descending hill, dark against a light sky, is repeated in the circled inset at the top left of the image on the facing page. A diagonal line dividing this image would begin with the line of the hill; the bedclothes would fall on one side, the heads of the sleeping sisters on the other, with the two halves of the picture knit together by their interlaced arms. As the right-hand illustration is smaller and begins lower on the page, the diagonal from the left page leads right into that of the title-page illustration: the fruit-bearing goblins are, as the inset suggests, marching straight into the sisters' dreams. But we can also reverse the reading: even the innocent dreams of the girls in the nursery may lead us to the not-so-innocent consuming pleasures of the market and the leer of the goblins, our doubles, once again.

Rossetti's design for *Goblin Market,* read through the illustrations that form a part of that design, work with Christina's poem to remind the reader that poems and pictures, like girls and goblin fruits, have physical bodies whose attractions powerfully influence our responses to them. The aesthetic of the literary text inheres in the real as well as imagined sensory experience of it. Possessive desires are at play not only in Covent Garden or other markets where fruit or women's bodies are sold but also at the Crystal Palace and the Royal Academy, as well as at the gallery, museum shop, art fair, department store — or the book store.

Such a reading accords well with Rossetti's artistic practice in the 1860s, which, as I have argued, unsettles the distinctions we and he would like to make between the work of "fine" or "high" art, that purified conception of the poem or the picture and its solitary maker, and those other decorative objects more obviously the products of many hands and competing interests, reproduced commercially for sale and domestic use. Rossetti's art of the book does not allow us to make these distinctions. It forces us to expand our ideas of what constitutes the work of art by embodying poems and pictures in material, historical forms that are the product of an extended social process. His books are collections in which he combines and oversees the work of poet, editor, designer, printer, and publisher. Yet at the same time Rossetti's books do not submit easily to the purposes of others. Perhaps because Rossetti himself loved too well to "allegorize on his own hook," he designed books or framed pictures or assembled rooms that convey a distinctive sense of presence, compelling attention and producing effects that exceed the linguistic or iconic aspects of text and image. Working already well within an age of mechanical reproduction, Rossetti finds a way to imbue his poetic objects with the kind of aura that neither craft nor commercial manufacture — and his books participate in aspects of both — is supposed to allow.[40] There is much more to be said on this subject, which may help us to reassess the disputed place of Pre-Raphaelitism as both a deeply historicizing movement and the first avant-garde of British modernism.

Notes

1. The phrase is from Maryan Wynn Ainsworth, *Dante Gabriel Rossetti and the Double Work of Art* (New Haven: Yale University Art Gallery, 1976). On Rossetti's poems for his own pictures, see also, besides the essays in Ainsworth's volume, the useful survey by Wolfgang Lottes, "'Take Out the Picture and Frame the Sonnet': Rossetti's Sonnets and Verses for His Own Works of Art," *Anglia* 96 (1978): 108-33.

[185]

2. See Alastair Grieve's important articles, "The Applied Art of D.G. Rossetti — 1: His Picture Frames," *Burlington Magazine* 115 (January 1973): 16-24 and "Rossetti's Applied Art — 2: Book Bindings," *Burlington Magazine* 115 (February 1973): 79-84; see also William E. Fredeman, "'Woodman, Spare that Block': Published and Unpublished Illustrations and Book Designs of Dante Gabriel Rossetti," *Journal of Pre-Raphaelite Studies* 5 (Spring 1996): 7-41. More specialized discussions of Rossetti's frames and bindings in the context of other Victorian examples can be found in: Lynn Roberts, "Nineteenth Century English Picture Frames I: The Pre-Raphaelites," *The International Journal of Museum Management and Curatorship* 4 (1985): 155-72; Giles Barber, "Rossetti, Ricketts, and Some English Publishers' Bindings of the Nineties," *The Library*, 5th series, 25 (1970): 314-30; and Douglas Ball, *Victorian Publishers' Bindings* (London: The Library Association, 1985), 37, 56, 59, 67, and 159-62.

3. Jerome J. McGann, "Rossetti's Iconic Page," in *The Iconic Page in Manuscript, Print, and Digital Culture,* ed. George Bornstein and Theresa Tinkle (Ann Arbor: University of Michigan Press, 1998), 123-40.

4. See Ball, *Victorian Publishers' Bindings;* among many studies of the illustrated books, Paul Goldman gives an especially good account of publishing and buying in *Victorian Illustrated Books, 1850-1870: The Heyday of Wood-Engraving* (Boston: David R. Godine, 1994). Ruari Maclean's *Victorian Book Design* (1963) is especially useful among older studies.

5. See Lyndel Saunders King, *The Industrialization of Taste: Victorian England and the Art Union of London* (Ann Arbor: UMI Research Press, 1985).

6. On the explosion of interest in picture-viewing and buying (particularly of contemporary British art) and the concomitant multiplication of the number of artists in Victorian Britain, see Gerald Reitlinger, *The Economics of Taste,* vol. 1: *The Rise and Fall of Picture Prices, 1760-1960* (London: Barrie and Rockliff, 1961), 143-73; Paula Gillett, *The Victorian Painter's World* (Gloucester: Alan Sutton, 1990); and, as *Worlds of Art: Painters in Victorian Society* (New

Brunswick: Rutgers University Press, 1990); Jeremy Maas, *Gambart: Prince of the Victorian Art World* (London: Barrie & Jenkins, 1975); and Dianne Sachko Macleod, *Art and the Victorian Middle Class: Money and the Making of Cultural Identity* (Cambridge: Cambridge University Press, 1996).

7. Gerald Reitlinger, *The Economics of Taste*, vol 2: *The Rise and Fall of Objets D'Art Prices Since 1750* (London: Barrie and Rockliff, 1963) is helpful for contextualizing picture-buying with other art-object-buying.

8. In, for example, *The Girlhood of Mary Virgin*, 1849, Tate Gallery; *The First Anniversary of the Death of Beatrice* (Dante Drawing the Angel), pen and ink, 1849, Fitzwilliam Museum, Cambridge; watercolor, 1853, Ashmolean Museum, Oxford; *Hamlet and Ophelia*, pen and ink, 1858, British Museum; and *Mary Magdalene at the Door of Simon the Pharisee*, 1858, pen and Indian ink, Fitzwilliam Museum, Cambridge. See also *Sir Launcelot in the Queen's Chamber*, 1857, pen and ink, Birmingham City Museum and Art Gallery, *The Wedding of St. George and the Princess Sabra*, 1857, watercolor, Tate Gallery, and *A Christmas Carol*, 1857-58, watercolor, Fogg Museum, Harvard University — though the latter two are closer to works like *The Blue Closet* and *The Tune of Seven Towers*, described below. All exhibit carefully worked interiors and curiously designed objects, furnishings, and costumes, where the figures increasingly threaten to disappear beneath the flat patterning of their clothing and the walls and furnishings surrounding them, turning the picture into another object covered in surface decoration.

9. Thus the Oxford Union Debating Hall is transformed to a space where Rossetti's (and Morris's and Burne-Jones's) favorite literary characters of this period, Arthur, Lancelot, Guinevere, Galahad, mingle with their real-life counterparts: Morris and Jane Burden and Rossetti, painted and written into the roles they begin to live in the Debating Hall over the summer and fall of 1857. Rossetti enters enthusiastically into designs for the walls and furnishings of his expanded flat in Blackfriars, when he marries Lizzie Siddal in 1860. The whole circle participates in the decoration of Morris and Jane Burden's new home, Red House, in 1860-61, and in the costumes

and games and creative projects acted out within that defining decorative space. And Rossetti continues to attend carefully to the interdependent creation of domestic decor and artistic persona in the decoration of his own house, from 1862, and the advice he gave to friends and clients throughout the 1860s.

10. The Great Exhibition was officially titled the "Exhibition of Industry of All Nations." Its contents, and those of other exhibitions held in preceding and succeeding decades, were variously referred to as "industrial arts" or "manufacturing arts," though they also included, on occasion, sections devoted to "fine arts." The boundaries between the former and the latter were, however, sometimes difficult to discern: the Great Exhibition, for example, included in its "Fine Arts" hall sculpture but not painting, while extending to a variety of decorative objects exhibiting new inventions or technical processes, such as wax flowers, carved egg shells, dolls, toys, models, lithographs, and color wood engravings.

11. Though Morris is often described as reduced to tears by the Great Exhibition, Fiona Macarthy notes that the seventeen-year-old schoolboy "refused to enter the Crystal Palace . . . with his family, remaining sulking outside on a seat," *William Morris: A Life for Our Time* (New York: Alfred A. Knopf, 1995), 121. Rossetti makes no reference to the Exhibition in his published correspondence, nor do the accounts of his brother or friends mention his presence there.

12. See, for example, Ralph Nicholas Wornum, "The Exhibition as a Lesson in Taste," the prize essay in a competition sponsored by the *Art-Journal* and printed in a special issue republished as an illustrated catalogue, *The Crystal Palace Exhibition* (1851; New York: Dover Publications, 1970).

13. There is a long history to complaints about viewing conditions at the Royal Academy, dating back to the beginning of the century. Note the difficulties of Rossetti's fictional character in his prose-tale fragment, "St. Agnes of Intercession," composed around 1850 and first published in William Michael Rossetti, ed., *The Collected Works of Dante Gabriel Rossetti* (London: Ellis and Scrutton, 1886), 403-04.

14. For example, Paul Goldman, *Victorian Illustration: The Pre-Raphaelites, the Idyllic School, and the High Victorians* (1996) 1-2; and William Vaughan, "Incongruous Disciples: The Pre- Raphaelites and the Moxon Tennyson," *Imagination on a Long Rein*, ed. Joachim Moller (Berlin: Jonas Verlag, 1988), 149-60.

15. [Edward Burne-Jones], "Essay on *The Newcomes*," *Oxford and Cambridge Magazine* 1 (January 1856).

16. Martin Meisel, *Realizations: Narrative, Pictorial, and Theatrical Arts in Nineteenth-Century England* (Princeton: Princeton University Press, 1983), 29-37.

17. Rossetti to William Allingham, 23 July 1854, in *Letters of Dante Gabriel Rossetti*, ed. Oswald Doughty and John Robert Wahl, vol. 1 (Oxford: Clarendon Press, 1965), 208. See also letter of 19 September 1854 discussing his pen-and-ink drawing of *Hamlet and Ophelia* "so treated as I think to embody and symbolize the play" (1.223).

18. Richard Stein discusses the discordance between the Pre-Raphaelite and other illustrations and the differences as well as the common ground among the designs by Millais, Hunt, and Rossetti. This discordance contributed to what many critics (and most collectors of illustrated books) have agreed is the unsatisfactory effect of the volume as a whole. See Richard L. Stein, "The Pre-Raphaelite Tennyson," *Victorian Studies* 24 (1981): 279-301; and Percy Muir, *Victorian Illustrated Books* (New York: Praeger Publishers, 1971), 130-32.

19. It is not surprising that Rossetti did not rush to carry out either project. Quite apart from his chronic difficulties executing the ideas he could produce so easily, these ambitious projects with multiple illustrations would probably not have persuaded a commercial publisher. Though anthologies of popular poetry or new editions of already popular poets did appear multiply illustrated, a collection of Scottish ballads or a new translation of the *Vita Nuova* by an author with no proven popularity was a risky investment. When Allingham did eventually publish the collection he had edited, it had only a single title-page vignette. Rossetti's volume of translations was published in 1861 without illustration — as it was, the publication had to be subsidized

by John Ruskin. For Rossetti's plans for an illustrated edition of the *Vita Nuova*, see his letter to Charles Lyell (his godfather) of 14 November 1848, *Letters* 1. 49, and to Francis MacCracken, 14 May 1854, *Letters* 1.197. For the proposed project of an illustrated collection of ballads, Rossetti to Ford Madox Brown, 23 May 1854, *Letters* 1.200, and various letters to Allingham, 1.189, 191, 194, 202, 208, 209. There were also other, more short-lived illustrated-book ideas, including Rossetti's proposal that Lizzie Siddal should illustrate a volume of Christina's poetry (Letter to Allingham, 28 March 1854, 1.183).

20. Though the frame does not survive, Holman Hunt possessed a daguerreotype showing the picture in its original frame and inscribed "December 1853," reproduced in his W. Holman Hunt, *PreRaphaelitism and the PreRaphaelite Brotherhood*, vol. 1 (New York: Macmillan, 1905), opposite 363.

21. On Rossetti's (and other Pre-Raphaelite) frames, and their relation to more conventional Victorian frames, see the Roberts and Grieve articles cited in note 1. Nicholas Penny's Pocket Guide, *Frames* (London: National Gallery Publications, 1997) is also useful and has a short bibliography.

22. Rossetti and Brown worked together on frames in the mid-60s and possibly much earlier; Rossetti was Brown's pupil in 1848-49. Holman Hunt, by contrast, put much more elaborately worked symbolic and textual designs on his frames, as in *The Finding of the Saviour in the Temple*, 1854-60, Birmingham Museums and Art Gallery.

23. Webb's piece was actually a remodeled version of a settle originally made (1856) after Morris's design for the rooms he shared with Burne-Jones in Red Lion Square (never installed because it proved too large). Rossetti painted the cabinet doors in 1859-60 for the Red House piece. See *William Morris*, ed. Linda Parry (London: Philip Wilson Publishers in association with the Victoria and Albert Museum, 1996), 155-56. The cabinet settle, now painted white and with Rossetti's panels removed, is still at Red House; see illustration 9 in Edward Hollamby, *Red House. Philip Webb* (London: Phaidon Press, 1991), n.p.

24. See *The Rossetti-Leyland Letters: The Correspondence of an Artist and his Patron*, ed. Francis L. Fennell Jr. (Athens, Ohio: Ohio University Press, 1978), 8, 11, 15-16, and 23ff.
25. See the discussion of Leyland's interest in the Pre-Raphaelites in Macleod, *Art and the Victorian Middle Class*, 284-89; Fennell, *Rossetti-Leyland Letters*, xvi, also notes the psychological needs Leyland met in his visits to Rossetti and his Pre-Raphaelite-hung sitting rooms.
26. The photograph, by H. Bedford Lemere, is reproduced from the original negative at the National Monuments Record in *The Opulent Eye. Late Victorian and Edwardian Taste in Interior Design*, Nicholas Cooper (London: The Architectural Press Ltd., 1976), plate 40. See also Macleod, *Art and the Victorian Middle Class*, plate 52. Leyland, a dedicated amateur musician, preferred pictures from Rossetti on musical themes or with musical instruments (e.g., *Veronica Veronese*, *A Sea Spell*). Leyland suggested to Whistler the use of musical analogies for the titles of his pictures. Rossetti's paintings for Leyland similarly are often studies in a narrow range of color harmonies, a fact to which he draws Leyland's attention in several letters (Fennell xxv-xxvi and 43-45). Hence the arrangement of the pictures might be thought of as itself a more extended musical composition in more than one respect.
27. For example, Henry Treffy Dunn's *Recollections of Dante Gabriel Rossetti & his Circle, or, Cheyne Walk Life*, ed. Rosalie Mander (Westerham: Dalrymple Press, 1984), 14. After Rossetti's death there many published accounts of visits to his house at 16 Cheyne Walk, Chelsea, which register the strong effect of Rossetti's unusual rooms and the compelling attractions of the company he gathered there, including Sidney Colvin, "Some Personal Reflections," *Scribner's Magazine* 67 (January 1920): 74-77; Gordon T. Hake, *Memories of Eight Years* (London: Bentley, 1892), chs. 55-7; Valentine C. Prinsep, "A Chapter from a Painter's Reminiscence. II. Dante Gabriel Rossetti," *Magazine of Art* 27 (1904): 167-72 and 281-86; and J. Comyns Carr, "With Rossetti in Cheyne Walk," *Coasting Bohemia* (London: Macmillan, 1914), 42-55.

28. T. G. Wharton, Martin, and Co., Auctioneers, *Contents of 16 Cheyne Walk, Chelsea*, July 5- 7, 1882.

29. For example, the books of Mary Eliza Joy Haweis, several republished in 1878 under the collective title of *The Art of Beauty*.

30. The work of H. Bedford Lemere, a photographer who specialized in photographing houses and interiors, provides many examples; see Cooper, *The Opulent Eye*, but also the evidence of paintings such as Holman Hunt's *The Awakening Conscience*, 1854, Tate Gallery, where an elaborately bound book is prominently displayed on a table in the newly furnished apartment of a kept woman.

31. See *The Rossetti-Macmillan Letters*, ed. Lona Mosk Packer (Berkeley: University of California Press, 1963).

32. Quotations from the prefatory sonnet and sonnet 10, "The Portrait," from "The House of Life," in W. M. Rossetti, ed., *Collected Works* (1886).

33. On the exceedingly complex relations among manuscripts and the pages printed at various stages between August 1869 and April 1870, see Roger C. Lewis, *Thomas James Wise and the Trial Book Fallacy* (Aldershot, England: Scolar Press, 1995).

34. See Ball, *Victorian Publishers' Bindings*.

35. John Ruskin, Letter to *The Times*, 1854, in *The Works of John Ruskin*, eds. E. T. Cook and Alexander Wedderburn, vol. 12 (London: George Allen, 1903-12), 334.

36. See Grieve's article on Rossetti's bindings, cited in note 1, for a number of acute observations from which my own descriptions have benefitted.

37. Diane D'Amico plausibly suggests that Christina intended an implicit criticism of the princess's too-willing acceptance of her handmaids' advice to wait and sleep. See her *Christina Rossetti: Faith, Gender and Time* (Baton Rouge, Louisiana: Louisiana State University Press, 1999), 83-88.

38. I can't help wondering if the horned projections to the spirals that I called "clasps" on the binding aren't meant to be appropriately suggestive of snails. Christina, who shared with her brother an interest in the smaller forms of animal life, would have appreciated the joke.

39. Besides Goldman, *Victorian Illustration*, see, for example, Gail Lynn Goldberg, "Dante Gabriel Rossetti's 'Revising Hand': His Illustrations for Christina Rossetti's Poems," *Victorian Poetry* 20 (Autumn-Winter 1982): 144-59.

40. See Walter Benjamin's much-cited essay, "The Work of Art in the Age of Technological Reproducibility," better known as "The Work of Art in the Age of Mechanical Reproduction" from its inclusion under that title in *Illuminations*, edited with an introduction by Hannah Arendt and translated by Harry Zohn (New York: Schocken Books, 1969), 217-51.

Love, Death, and Grotesquerie:
Beardsley's Illustrations of
Wilde and Pope

James A. W. Heffernan

"If I am not grotesque I am nothing."
— Aubrey Beardsley

Aubrey Beardsley came of age some seventy years after English publishers had started producing illustrated books. According to Martin Meisel, they originated largely in the 1820s, when technological innovation made it possible to print a book with pictures that illustrated the text.[1] Meisel usefully distinguishes the nineteenth-century meanings of "illustration" and "realization." Realization was the faithful re-creation of a verbal description or a painting *on the stage* — "a translation into a more real, that is more vivid, visual, physically present medium" in three dimensions; illustration meant "enrichment and embellishment" on the page, with the artist's imagination freely at work in two dimensions (Meisel 30). Yet for all the freedom of the illustration, the nineteenth-century illustrated novel is a work of collaboration: artist and writer working together to tell a story. While

[195]

Dickens early on established the primacy of the text as both con-
ceptually and chronologically prior to illustrations, artists did not
simply offer arrested moments of stopped time to punctuate the
moving line of a narrative. They found ways to tell what Meisel
calls "a moment's story," and conversely, novelists drew word-pictures of their own to complement the movement of their narratives (Meisel 17, 56). The illustrated novel thus presented itself as
something to be experienced both visually and sequentially as a
series of actions and scenes.

In the illustrated books of the eighteen-nineties, however, the
artist took full command of the pictures. Instead of producing a
book by means of continuing collaboration, the illustrator —
writes Lorraine Kooistra — "typically . . . received the completed
manuscript of poetry, drama, or fiction direct from the publisher
and produced the illustrations with little or no connection to the
writer, who was sometimes surprised by the final product."[2] In a
sense, therefore, the artist stood outside the text as its "first public
reader," its first interpreter and critic (Kooistra 3-4). Aubrey
Beardsley exemplifies this kind of independence. In his illustrations for Oscar Wilde's *Salome* and Alexander Pope's *The Rape of
the Lock*, as we shall see, he reads not only the text but the life of
its author: something unprecedented, so far as I know, in illustrated books before the nineties.

Beardsley's illustrations for the first English edition of Wilde's
Salome, which appeared in 1894, also radically revised the conventions of "realization." *Salome* was a play, something written to be
realized on a stage. But in February 1893, some three years before it
was first staged, the play was published in French, and its publication instantly prompted the twenty-one-year-old Beardsley to produce a sensational picture depicting a moment in the play that
could never be visually "realized" on stage because it is too
grotesque to be seen; the stage directions call for total darkness. In

spite of or perhaps because of its grotesquerie, the picture led Wilde to commission Beardsley to illustrate the English edition of *Salome* — with pictures that Wilde found hardly suitable for his play.[3]

Beardsley's illustrations to Wilde's play, then, are clearly not the work of a collaborator but of a precociously gifted artist with a style uniquely his own: a style that seems not so much to serve the text as to appropriate it for its own idiosyncratic ends. Yet Beardsley's illustrations to *Salome* are considerably more than an exercise in graphic self-indulgence; they constitute a provocative reading of the play. Furthermore, when studied along with Beardsley's illustrations for Pope's *Rape of the Lock*, which appeared two years after *Salome*, they allow us to see the threads of grotesquerie that permeate both of these works. Beardsley views the *Rape* from an unmistakably fin-de-siècle perspective; Pope's figures play out their parts in an Art Nouveau world of riotous ornamentation. Ultimately, however, this ornamentation manages to reach the very core of Pope's poem.

Pope's poem seems at first no kin to *Salome*. What can the pampered, delicate, decorous Belinda share with the savagely sensual dancer who not only takes the head of a prophet but also kisses the very lips that have denounced her? What could link the sparkling, sprightly wit of Pope's Augustan mock-epic to the ghastly decadence of Wilde's late-nineteenth-century play? Beardsley's art points the way to an answer. The simple fact that he illustrated both the play and the poem may lead us to see what common ground underlies their obvious differences. If Salome's frustrated lust for John leads her to demand his head so that she may fetishize it, the Baron's lust for Belinda drives him to cut a lock of her hair so that he may fetishize that. If Salome's necrophilia is grotesque, so is the Cave of Spleen to which a distraught Belinda flies when she loses her lock. If Belinda's hair entrances the Baron, John's hair entrances Salome, and various kinds of extravagant coiffeurs permeate Beardsley's illustrations for both works. To view them side by side through Beardsley's eyes is to see not only what specific features they share but also how each of them represents the ambivalence of its heroine and the kinds of destruction generated by desire.

I

To fully understand what Beardsley contributed to the first English edition of Wilde's play, we must begin with Beardsley's sensational debut. In April 1893, the inaugural issue of a London magazine called *The Studio* featured his work and formally intro-duced him in an article by Joseph Pennell, "A New Illustrator: Aubrey Beardsley."[4] The nine drawings Beardsley furnished for this issue included one which, according to Kenneth Clark, "aroused more horror and indignation than any graphic work hith-erto produced in England."[5] This was Beardsley's illustration of the moment just after Salome kisses the severed and bleeding head of John the Baptist at the end of Wilde's *Salome* (fig. 40). In slightly altered form, the picture would reappear one year later in the first English edition of Wilde's play (fig. 41). But since the play had just been published and would not be staged for another three years, as noted above, Beardsley's "Salome with St. John's Head" set before the eyes of the public for the very first time what Wilde had simply suggested by the words that he wrote for his necrophil-iac heroine — the very last words she speaks in the play: "J'ai baisé ta bouche, Iokanaan, j'ai baisé ta bouche" ("I have kissed your mouth, Jokannan, I have kissed your mouth").[6]

The stage directions tell us that Salome speaks these words on a set first darkened by the passing of a great cloud across the moon and then suddenly lit by a shaft of moonlight that exposes her to Herod, who promptly orders her killed (lines 1063-65, 1069-70).

Figure 40.
Aubrey Beardsley, "Salome with St. John's Head," from *The Studio* 1.1, April 1893, courtesy of Dartmouth College Library.

It is this moment of ghastly revelation that Beardsley depicts. At upper left, a thick cluster of white rimmed disks in various sizes suggests moons — or possibly suns — in eclipse. At upper right, Salome gazes entranced at the face of the severed and dripping head of John the Baptist, which she holds in both her hands immediately before her face. With the edge of a quarter-segment of moon behind them cutting directly under their chins like the blade of a rounded axe, she kneels humpbacked as if in adoration of the man whose head she has demanded on a platter. Their two heads nearly meet and in some ways match. While her open eyes and grinning lips confront John's closed lids and downturned mouth, both display Medusan hair. Her thick black locks writhe up and down like snakes; his snaky locks fall whitely over her hands, and beneath his neck a slender, broken

[199]

Figure 41.
Aubrey Beardsley, "The Climax," from Oscar Wilde, *Salome* (London: Elkin Mathews & John Lane, 1894), courtesy of Dartmouth College Library.

stream of white widens to the shape of a cobra at the bottom of the picture, where a white lily stands in black water. At left are blocked the words J'AI BAISÉ TA BOUCHE IOKANNEN J'AI BAISÉ TA BOUCHE. Because these words appear just above a snakelike white tendril rising sinuously from a narrow, white-rimmed, vaginal oval of black, they seem almost to be spoken by a snake.

The serpentine form of the tendril as well of John's hair and blood reflect Beardsley's careful reading of Wilde's play, which fascinated him.[7] Having tried in vain the fortress of his virtue, having sought in vain to kiss him when alive, Wilde's Salome imputes to John the serpentine nature traditionally used to signify the treacherous charm of women, beginning with Eve.[8] Shortly after the fall in John Milton's *Paradise Lost*, for instance, Adam explicitly denounces Eve as a serpent. Calling her just as "false" as Satan, he says she needs only his serpentine shape and color to "show / [Her] inward fraud" and thus to warn all other creatures away from her (10.867-71). Salome herself is traditionally snakelike; Ewa Kuryluk notes that on the eleventh-century bronze door of Verona's San Zeno, the sinuous line of the dancing princess is distinctly serpentine.[9] But Wilde's Salome sees herself quite differently. Knowing full well that John thinks her a harlot like her mother Herodias (1022), she nonetheless charges him with taking her virginity (1046-47) and casts *him* as a serpentine tempter. She is captivated first by his body, which she ambivalently calls both lily white and repulsively leprous (304-17), and then by his hair, which she finds both lustrously black and horrible, "like a crown of thorns" and "like a knot of serpents coiled around thy neck" (334-35), evoking both Christ and Medusa. Finally she longs for his superlatively red mouth, which for her is "like a pomegranate cut in twain with a knife of ivory" (336-37) and which she finally determines not only to kiss but to bite "as one bites ripe fruit" (1010-11). Thus John's very lips become for her the apple of temptation.

His lips excite her precisely because they are forbidden fruit. By the mere act of speaking to the living John, she defies the command of Herod, who forbade anyone to speak with him (181-83), and in kissing the lips of the dead John, she does what the living John would "never" allow (353-54). In life, as Kuryluk observes (220), the lips of Wilde's John the Baptist echo the curses of John the Revelationist, for just as the Revelationist denounces the whore of Babylon and predicts the apocalyptic destruction of the world (Rev. 6:12-13), Wilde's John denounces Salome as a daughter of Sodom and Babylon (291, 621) and predicts — in the very words of the Revelationist — that

> the sun shall become black like sackcloth of hair, and the moon shall become like blood, and the stars of the heaven shall fall upon the earth like unripe figs that fall from the fig-tree, and the kings of the earth shall be afraid. (652-55)

Salome's murderous passion for John is mirrored, as Kuryluk suggests, by the ruthlessness of the curses he hurls at her (Kuryluk 220). John foretells the destruction of a corrupt world, and he most especially seeks the annihilation of Salome. To exemplify his banishment of "all wickedness from the earth," he prays that she be stoned, pierced, and crushed: "Let the people take stones and stone her. . . . Let the captains of the hosts pierce her with their swords, let them crush her beneath their shields" (623-26). The last part of John's wish is precisely fulfilled at the end of the play by Herod's soldiers, who "rush forward and crush [Salome] beneath their shields." Commanding them in the very last words of the play to "Kill that woman!" (1069), Herod unwittingly does the murderous bidding of John just as he had reluctantly done to John the murderous bidding of Salome. What enrages Herod is exactly what Beardsley's inaugural drawing depicts: the spectacle of Salome infatuated with a bleeding head.

To grasp the full impact of this picture, we should consider the precedents for it in literature and visual art as well as its immediate source in Wilde's play. The scriptural versions of the Salome story say nothing of her passion for John and identify her only as the daughter of Herodias, who tells her to ask for John's head after her dancing has moved Herod to offer her anything she wants (Matthew 14:3-12, Mark 6:17-28). Later versions of the story eroticize the motives of Herodias. While Mark tells us simply that she sought to punish John for criticizing the unlawfulness of her marriage to her husband's brother (Mark 6:18-19), nineteenth-century versions of the story — before Wilde — made her John's rejected lover. In Heinrich Heine's satirical poem *Atta Troll* (1847), a phantom Herodias riding a horse in a pageant of the dead on the night of St. John's Day holds the prophet's head and fervently kisses it (Kuryluk 200). Whether or not Wilde knew Heine's poem directly, he certainly knew another work which took this striking episode one step further. In 1888, four years before writing his play about Salome, Wilde reviewed J. C. Heywood's *Salome*, a dramatic poem in which a live Herodias kisses the prophet's head (Ellman 340).[10]

According to Richard Ellman, Wilde saw this striking detail — which apparently originated with Heine and Heywood — as the potential climax of his own work (340). But so far as I know, Wilde was the first to make Salome rather than Herodias the lover of John. This distinguishes his play not only from the work of Heine and Heywood but also from the treatment of Salome in Joris Huysman's *A Rebours* (1884), which Ellman calls the "principal engenderer" of Wilde's play (340). In Huysman's description of a painting by Gustave Moreau we might indeed see the genesis of Wilde's Salome: "the symbolic incarnation of undying lust, . . . the monstrous Beast, indifferent, irresponsible, insensible, poisoning, like the Helen of ancient myth, everything that she touches" (qtd. Ellman 340). But Huysman's words describe Moreau's painting of Salome dancing for Herod. In Moreau's painting of Salome presented with the Baptist's head, she manifests not lust but horror (Ellman 340) — the antithesis of what Wilde's Salome displays.

For Salome's infatuation with the head of John, therefore, we might consider two other precedents in nineteenth-century literature and art. One is John Keats's *Isabella*, whose "passionate humanity" Wilde had come to admire by the age of twenty (Ellman 42).[11] Near the end of this Gothic romance in verse, the heroine unearths the head of her lover, who has been murdered by her brothers, and kisses it. Putting it into a garden pot and covering it with soil, she then plants basil over it. Isabella's lugubrious tending of her basil plant, "ever fed . . . with [her] thin tears" (line 425), is depicted by William Holman Hunt in *Isabella and the Pot of Basil* (1867) (fig. 42), a painting that both Wilde and Beardsley could have known.[12] This is a study in genteel necrophilia. Dressed in a thin white chemise with a geometrically patterned blue shawl falling about her waist, Isabella stands leaning over a large painted majolica pot that sprouts a thick clump of basil and rests on a richly embroidered cloth adorning a prie-dieu inlaid with ivory and precious stones. With her left leg bent and her left foot perched on the ledge of the prie-dieu, she seems half kneeling at the shrine of the pot, which she holds in both her hands while gazing intently upon it and letting her long black hair flow over it — as if it were the hair of Lorenzo himself. The only sign of the head within the pot is the little bald skull on the handle nearly touched by the ends of Isabella's tresses.

From the Isabella of Keats and Hunt to the Salome of Wilde and Beardsley is not so wild a leap as may at first appear. For all its domestic decor and decorum, the mingling of the sacred and the

Figure 42.
William Holman Hunt, *Isabella and the Pot of Basil*, 1867,
Tyne and Wear Museums, Newcastle Upon Tyne, England,
photograph from Jan Marsh, *Pre-Raphaelite Women*
(London: Weidenfeld & Nicolson, 1987), plate 121.

[205]

erotic in this painting along with its accent on plant life and long wavy hair — a traditional sign of promiscuity — all subtly antici- pate, however unwittingly, the climactic scene that Wilde drama- tizes and Beardsley draws.[13] In Hunt's painting, a young, half-kneel- ing woman dressed in white and crowned with long black wavy hair gazes on and holds in both her hands a pot containing the buried head of her lover, and a leafy plant springs from the soil around his buried head just as flowers rise "like incarnations of the stars" from the buried corpse of Keats himself in Percy Bysshe Shelley's "Adon- ais" (line 174). In Beardsley's drawing, a kneeling, white-robed young woman crowned with long black wavy hair gazes on and holds in both her hands a head from which blood drips into a pool that begets a lily — the talisman of the Pre-Raphaelite Brotherhood and Wilde's iconic signature.[14] Wilde and Beardsley thus expose the grotesque eroticism latent in Hunt's sentimental tableau.

The other precedent for the climactic scene of Wilde's play appears in a book that Wilde read on his honeymoon in Paris in June of 1884: Stendhal's *Red and Black* (Ellman 250). Like Wilde's play, Stendhal's novel ends with a woman kissing the severed head of the man whom she has loved but who has finally rejected her.[15] Mathilde-Marguerite de la Mole, Stendhal's antiheroine, has long adored the audacity of her sixteenth-century namesake, Queen Marguerite of Navarre, who buried with her own hands the head of her executed lover, Boniface de la Mole.[16] Theatrically passion- ate as well as proudly aristocratic, Mathilde despises conventional squeamishness. "What woman alive today," she asks, "would not be too horrified to touch the head of her decapitated lover?" (Stendhal 246). On the very last page of the novel Mathilde dra- matically answers this rhetorical question. Finding the severed head and body of the newly executed Julien Sorel on the floor of the room occupied by his friend Fouquet, who has managed to buy Julien's corpse, she picks up the head, sets it on a little marble table, and kisses its forehead; then she carries it to the cave where Julien asks to be buried and puts it in the ground with her own hands (Stendhal 408).

To these precedents for the dramatization and depiction of a Salome infatuated with the bleeding head of John may be added a small cluster of etchings that date from an earlier fin de siècle — the 1790s. In 1793, a French artist named Villeneuve published two etchings of heads severed by the guillotine and dripping blood from the neck: Louis XVI and the Comte de Custine, a general of the revolutionary army who had been executed for conspiring with the British against the new Republic.[17] Each held aloft by the hand of an unseen executioner, these severed heads are meant to show the triumph of liberty over tyranny and treachery ("sang impure," the impure blood). But they also signify acts of desecration, for as Ronald Paulson notes, the severing of powerful heads — above all that of the king himself — subjected living persons to "the iconoclastic treatment dealt out to religious images in churches."[18] Salome's desecration of John's severed head thus recalls the iconoclastic implications of beheading. It likewise recalls the way Thomas Rowlandson represents French Liberty in an etching entitled "The Contrast" (1792), where a Medusa-headed woman brandishes the head of a man on the central prong of a trident and thus usurps — as Neil Hertz notes — the pose of Cellini's Perseus holding the severed head of Medusa.[19] Beardsley not only shows a Medusa-headed woman holding the severed head of a man; he also puts serpentine locks on the man, as we have seen, thus implying that Salome has the power to turn John's head into the image and likeness of her own.[20] If anything, her set lips and lantern jaw make her face more masculine than that of John, whose drooping mouth and delicate chin suggest effeminacy.

Latent or overt in all of these images is the assault of the secular and erotic upon the sacred. When we read the final lines of

Wilde's play and view Beardsley's illustration of them in light of what earlier writers and artists had done with severed heads, we can see that desecration and fetishism go hand in hand. As Kury-luk shows, Beardsley consummates a tradition of the grotesque that began with the Renaissance discovery of monstrous frescoes in ancient Roman "grottoes" and became a subculture bent on subverting "official Christian culture with inappropriate forms and shocking iconography."[21]

The shocking iconography of Beardsley's illustrations for the English edition of *Salome*, which first appeared in 1894, begin with its title page. In the original (and later bowdlerized) version, a horned, garlanded, armless, nude, and flagrantly hermaphroditic Pan herm gazes grinningly down on a winged nude boy kneeling with his half-raised phallus on display.[22] The figures suggest a par-ody of the crucifixion, with Christ supplanted by a demonically grinning Pan set between would-be sacred candles and the mourner at the foot of the cross replaced by a pseudo-angel who looks not worshipfully up at the god but leeringly out at us.[23] Beardsley's design not only mocks Christian iconography. In fea-turing a monumental hermaphrodite, it also flaunts what Chris Snodgrass calls a sign of self-enclosed sterility, an "emblem of solipsistic, unfulfilled desire — particularly homosexuality, onanism, and that *vice supreme* cerebral lechery, all of which char-acterized to Victorians decadent disillusionment and withdrawal from practical life" (Snodgrass 60).

The title page thus begins to show how far Beardsley's illustra-tions for *Salome* swerve from Wilde. While Beardsley's hermaphro-dite vaguely prefigures the androgynous features of Salome, the double-sexed figure points less to Wilde's heroine than to the bisexual life of Wilde himself. Several of Beardsley's other illustra-tions allude to that life, for Wilde's own features appear in the feminized moon watched by the Young Syrian and the Page of

[208]

Herodias ("The Woman in the Moon"), in the face of Herod ("Eyes of Herod"), and also in the face of the owl-capped jester presenting the queen in "Enter Herodias." Whatever he thought of these particular caricatures, Wilde found Beardsley's illustrations for *Salome* generally unpalatable. Though "Salome with St. John's Head" had instantly won his admiration, he reportedly complained that the "Japanese" style of Beardsley's illustrations did not fit his "Byzantine" play and that they resembled the "naughty scribbles" of a "precocious schoolboy."[24]

Up to the 1970s, critics seconded this judgment. From Arthur Symons on, they generally agreed that Beardsley had simply made his own way, ignoring Wilde's text and spawning irrelevant images.[25] Recent critics have disagreed. Elliott Gilbert calls the 1894 *Salome* "one of the most successful collaborations of poet and illustrator in history"; Linda Zatlin finds playwright and artist each revealing the triumph of male authority over the rebelliousness of female power; and Ian Fletcher rightly notes that "the principal images of the play certainly appear in the drawings."[26] But no one theme binds text and image in this so-called collaboration. As Robert Schweik has recently shown, the illustrations and the play both conjoin "strikingly incongruous elements."[27] Wilde's Salome, for instance, is first virginal and withdrawn, then suddenly filled with lust for John; Beardsley's Salome is aggressively Medusan in "The Climax" and erotically feminine in the "Tail Piece" (fig. 43), which shows a masked Pierrot and satyr gently lowering her slender nude body into a box designed to hold the large powder puff poised beside it.[28]

When it appeared with Wilde's *Salome*, Beardsley's drawing of Salome kissing John's severed head (fig, 41) could be called "The Climax" (rather than "Salome with St. John's Head") because the text of the play itself made further words unnecessary. Beardsley also cut the words that had appeared in the *Studio* picture (J'AI

Figure 43.
Aubrey Beardsley, "The Tail Piece," from Oscar Wilde, *Salome*, 1894,
courtesy of the Dartmouth College Library.

BAISÉ TA BOUCHE . . .) and several other elements: the spidery, filigreed figures just above Salome's ankle and behind her head; the long black lock hanging down below Salome's arms; the slender pair of wings just above the lily; the black bar running just under the two heads at upper right; and the fringes adorning the edges of John's locks as well as of Salome's locks and of her feet. The result is a simpler, starker, more concentrated depiction of Salome's necrophilia. At the same time, Salome herself is made more feminine. Her nose, chin, and feet are all smaller, and her hair is ornamented with stippled swirls. For all its Medusan menace, then, "The Climax" subtly prefigures the powder puff eroticism of "The Tail Piece," where Salome's tightly curled hair in turn recalls the eclipsed moons of "The Climax."

The salience of a powder puff in the very last illustration for *Salome* not only exemplifies Beardsley's way of re-creating the incongruity of Wilde's play. It also links *Salome* — or more precisely Beardsley's illustrations for *Salome* — to his illustrations for *The Rape of the Lock*, which first appeared with them in 1896.[29] As Beardsley helps us to see, both works incongruously mingle the social and domestic rituals of civilized life — applying makeup, formal dining, dancing, card-playing, tea-drinking, gossiping, flirting — with acts of brutal barbarity: rape and decapitation. While the "rape" of Pope's poem is ostensibly just a metaphor for the cutting of a lock of hair, the act of cutting hair is an assault on the head — a form of decapitation — and a pair of scissors may be used as a weapon of assault, a kind of sword. Well before he started work on his designs for *The Rape*, Beardsley subtly drew this connection in his revised version of "The Toilette of Salome" (fig. 44).

Both versions of this picture, which depict an episode that cannot be found in the play, show Salome seated in her dressing room and attended by a masked Pierrot; both versions also include one or more domestic objects that will re-appear in the illustrations for *The Rape*: books, vases, teacups, and a powder puff conspicuously waved by the Pierrot.[30] But while the second version removes three of the figures and many of the props (such as the double bass and the vase of flowers to be found in the first), it adds two pairs of scissors — one tucked into the pocket of Pierrot's apron and the other on the top tier of the *étagère* at right. The context makes the scissors ominous. With her previously seminude figure now anachronistically sheathed in a sleek and sweeping costume of the

Figure 44.
Aubrey Beardsley, "The Toilette of Salome," from Oscar Wilde,
Salome, 1894, courtesy of the Dartmouth College Library.

[212]

1890s, Salome wears a great oval black Ascot hat that covers her head nowhere else in these illustrations and that serves a purely symbolic purpose in this one. Though wholly impractical (it can only impede the dressing of her hair), the black hat prefigures the great oval platter on which John's head will be served to her in "The Dancer's Reward" as well as the black moons (or black suns) that fill the background to Salome's necrophilic kiss in "The Climax." But if the hat prefigures the platter on which Salome gets the head she has demanded, the masked clown's scissors may well convey — as Milly Heyd says — "a hinted threat to the heroine's head, insinuating that revenge is soon to follow" (133).

Superficially innocent and domestic but also potentially sinister and even deadly, scissors play a major part in Pope's *Rape of the Lock*. On the front cover of the edition he illustrated, Beardsley presents them as the central icon of the poem (fig. 45). Holding in all twenty unlit candles, two rococo candelabra support between them an oval frame enclosing a pair of richly ornamented open scissors whose points in turn enclose a floating lock of hair. The oval frame prefigures the mirror described in the passage on Belinda at her dressing table — a mirror shown as oval in Beardsley's "The Toilet" (fig. 46), where a pair of plain black scissors appears on the dressing table. Furthermore, the candles depicted on the binding cover stand on what looks like an altar, which is what Belinda's dressing table is called in Pope's poem (1.127). Outlined in white against a black background, the thin vertical lines of the candles as well as the other white verticals suggest what Pope calls "Slight Lines of Hair" (2.26). But in any case, the framing of the scissors and the lock reveals the ambiguity of both.

Consider first the scissors. As an instrument of beautification, they may look light, beautiful, richly ornamented, and even adorable, which is how they appear in Beardsley's cover; on the other hand, they may look plain, black, and functional, which is

Figure 45.
Aubrey Beardsley, front cover from Alexander Pope, *The Rape of the Lock*
(London: L. Smithers, 1896), courtesy of Dartmouth College Library.

[214]

Figure 46.
Aubrey Beardsley, "The Toilet," from Alexander Pope, *The Rape of the Lock*, 1896, courtesy of Dartmouth College Library.

[215]

the way they appear in Beardsley's "Toilet," where they rest unobtrusively on the altar of her dressing table between the ornamented candlestand and the fancy bow tied at the corner. Though scissors are surely crucial to the art of hairdressing, they are not mentioned among the beauty aids that Pope identifies on Belinda's dressing table in the poem (gems, combs, pins, puffs, powders, and patches), and in Beardsley's illustration as in Pope's poem, Belinda is too busy adoring (or admiring) her own heavenly reflection to notice anything so trivial as a pair of scissors. In the poem, furthermore, the sylphs responsible for her hair seem to be charged with everything *but* cutting it: setting and separating ("divid[ing]") its strands (1.146), curling them (2.97), and tending Belinda's favorite lock (2.115). Yet in telling us that some of the busy sylphs attending Belinda "divide the Hair" (1.146), Pope may ambiguously refer to either separating or cutting it. In any case, Beardsley's hieratic elevation of the scissors and the lock on his cover makes strikingly visible what may well rise up before the mind's eye of the Baron in Canto 2. Hours before dawn and Belinda's awakening, he builds an altar of "vast *French* Romances" to love, lights the pyre with billets-doux, "and begs with ardent Eyes/ Soon to obtain, and long possess the Prize" (2.43-44).[31] While Belinda ignores the scissors on her dressing table, the Baron could be adoring the means to his prize as well as the lock itself.

Beardsley's cover likewise exploits the erotic ambiguities of the lock and its taking. Robert Halsband suggests that the sinuous shape drawn between the scissors' ends on Beardsley's cover hovers between signifying a lock of hair and a spermatozoon. If Halsband is right, the wavy form furnishes something like an objective correlative for the ambiguity of Pope's titular trope.[32] In Pope's title, a word that literally means the forcible abduction or sexual invasion of a woman is figuratively used to mean the cutting and taking of a woman's hair — a trivial prank. Yet throughout the

poem, literal and figurative meanings change places with disarm-
ing frequency. In so doing, they radically destabilize the opposition
between the trivial and the grave. Mighty contests rise from trivial
things in this poem because trivial things can turn momentous just
as harmlessly figurative meanings can turn dangerously literal. The
gossip at Hampton Court is said to be killing — figuratively, of
course: "At ev'ry Word a Reputation dies" (3.15). But half a dozen
lines later, hungry judges sign a sentence of real death, "And
Wretches hang that Jury-men may dine" (3.21). In the mock-bat-
tle of the final canto, mock death fells beau and witling alike:
"One dy'd in *Metaphor*, and one in *Song*" (5.59). But when the
Baron — menaced by the "fierce *Belinda*" — seeks "no more than
on his Foe to die" (78), we are slyly reminded that from at least
the time of Donne in the early seventeenth century, "die" could
mean "ejaculate." Ridiculous as this battle may be, it is driven by
real passion and real desire. If Belinda can demand her lock more
loudly than Othello roared for his handkerchief (5.103-106), the
line between comedy and tragedy seems hardly thicker than a hair,
which is what "Beauty draws us with" (2.27). The spermatozoic
lock of Beardsley's cover thus originates — or leaps up, one might
say — from the passion that animates Pope's poem and from the
sexual innuendoes of his language.

The sexual innuendoes of *The Rape*, I suspect, did just as much
as its would-be triviality to sink the poem in the estimate of later
Victorian critics. According to one anthologist, it was "pretty" but
also "trivial" (like Belinda herself, it would seem), and Matthew
Arnold predictably found it lacking in "high seriousness."[33] But
Edmund Gosse called it a "little masterpiece in Dresden china,"
and ironically enough, he urged Beardsley to illustrate it precisely
because he thought this precocious young artist had been wasting
his talent on fluff — "doing so much illustrating work of a trivial
kind."[34] Fortunately, however, Gosse also urged Beardsley to treat

[217]

this masterpiece "in his own spirit," which is fully alive to the rich combination of playfulness, artificiality, irony, and deep serious-ness (as distinct from high seriousness) that drives the poem.

In its own way, the poem seriously dramatizes the sexual mag-netism of hair even as it derides the idolatry that hair excites. To see more clearly why Victorian critics found the poem trivial, we must realize that it mock-heroically trivialized precisely what Vic-torian culture had glorified. In Canto 4, Thalestris fans the rage of the luckless — and now lockless — Belinda by imagining what the Baron will make of her precious ringlet:

> And shall this Prize, th'inestimable Prize,
> Expos'd thro' Crystal to the gazing Eyes,
> And heighten'd by the Diamond's circling Rays,
> On that Rapacious Hand forever blaze? (4.113-16)

Victorian readers might well find this passage sacrilegious. For in the 1840s and 1850s, jewelry made from plaited hair became an obsession. "Hair was powerful," writes Elizabeth Gitter,

> and the ubiquitous Victorian lock of hair, encased in a locket or ring or framed on the wall, became, through a Midas touch of imagination, something treasured, a totem, a token of attachment, intrinsically valuable, as precious as gold.[35]

Or as virginity. For to read Elizabeth Barrett's response to Robert Browning's request for a lock of her hair is — as Gitter notes — to see that she considers such a request second only to asking for her sexual surrender:

> I never gave away what you ask me to give *you*, to a human being, except my nearest relatives & once or twice or thrice to female friends, . . . never, though reproached for it, — and it is just three weeks since I said last to an

asker that I was "too great a prude for such a thing"! . . . and prude or not, I could not — I never could — *something* would not let me.[36]

Belinda would readily understand. For her, too, a lock of hair is an intimate possession as well as a mark of beauty and a sign of sexual magnetism. From its title onwards, the poem repeatedly identifies the taking of the hair with sexual conquest even as it pretends to separate the two. Ostensibly it mocks the practice of confusing appearance with reality, social gaffes with moral lapses. To be equally frightened, as Ariel is, that a nymph may "stain her Honour, or her new Brocade" (1.107) is to show oneself fundamentally — and ridiculously — lacking in a sense of moral proportion. But just what does "Honour" mean in this poem? Fearing that the Baron may publically display Belinda's lock in a diamond ring, Thalestris cries, "*Honour* forbid! at whose unrival'd Shrine / Ease, Pleasure, Virtue, All, our Sex resign" (4.105-6). If "Honour" demands the sacrifice of virtue as well as of pleasure and ease, can it be anything more than reputation, which is of course based on the appearance of virtue, so that figuratively staining one's honor is morally indistinguishable from literally staining one's brocade? Falstaff famously calls honor nothing but "Air" (*Henry IV* 5.1.1), but this poem makes it inhere in precisely what is visible, above all in whatever hair is visible. Hence the supreme irony of Belinda's cry after the Baron takes her lock: "O hadst thou, Cruel! been content to sieze / Hairs less in sight, or any Hairs but these!" (4.175-76). To save the hairs of her head, the hairs which publically signify her "Honour," she would presumably have been willing to sacrifice the hairs of her maidenhead. Thus would "Virtue" have knelt at "Honour"'s shrine.[37]

To be sure, it is the Baron who genuflects to the Goddess of Love as he prays for her blessing on his quest (2.35-46). But in his illustrations of Belinda at her toilet (fig. 46) and the Baron at his

Figure 47.
Aubrey Beardsley, "The Baron's Prayer," from Alexander Pope, *The Rape of the Lock*, 1896, courtesy of Dartmouth College Library.

[220]

altar (fig. 47), Beardsley shows each in profile and wearing a dressing gown, with the kneeling form and praying hands of the Baron figuratively mirroring the seated form and slightly extended right hand of Belinda as she literally gazes into her own mirror. Placed in elegantly furnished boudoirs, both figures appear against a *trompe l'oeil* backdrop of nature at its most artificial. What seems at first a set of windows overlooking foliage behind Belinda proves instead to be a three-paneled screen stippled with the orderly trees and round temple of a formal garden, and in the Baron's room, the would-be window is a large tapestry stippled with twin clumps of trees flanking a distant house. Stippled on the wall beneath the Baron's tapestry are bouquets linked by hanging garlands, just as garlands hang over the tops of the panels of Belinda's screen and decorate her elaborate coif. Finally, both rooms are conspicuously occupied by what Pope's account of them never mentions: candles. Two slim candles rise above Belinda's head from the sculpted candlesticks on either side of her table; a three-branched candelabra stands on a table just behind the Baron; and before him, standing up over the curving flames of the billet-doux that he has just lighted atop his pyre of books, a burning candle rising from a filigreed floor-based candlestick looms well above his head.

If the Baron's burning candle may be taken to signify his priapic excitement, as Zatlin suggests, the unlit candles on Belinda's dressing table may likewise suggest her latent desire to be ravished, which is revealed both by the language of Pope's first canto and the puff-skirted courtier peering through the garlanded curtains of Belinda's bed in "The Dream," Beardsley's frontispiece to the poem.[38] Beardsley's courtier has all the ambiguity of Pope's. With his long black curls, his skirt garlanded in flowers, and his delicate profile almost identical to that of Belinda in "The Toilet," this androgynous figure personifies what Pope's Belinda conjures in her dream: "A Youth more glittering than a *Birth-night Beau*" (1.23).

[221]

But his long, thin, star-topped baton prefigures the burning candle of the Baron's boudoir and likewise implies a priapic excitement that is explicitly represented by another drawing Beardsley made a few months after "The Dream." Drawn to illustrate a passage in Juvenal's sixth satire, "The Impatient Adulterer" shows a man bending forward to peer through a set of bedcurtains just like the courtier — except that he is naked from the waist down and fingering his half-erect penis (repr. Halsband, fig. 46). To see how closely his long black curls and his leaning, peering stance resemble those of the well-padded courtier, to see the link between the adulterer's hand on his naked phallus and the courtier's pointing forefinger, is to see how well Beardsley captures the fundamental ambiguity of the youth's moral posture in Pope's poem.

This sylph, who calls himself Ariel and who claims to be Belinda's protector, actually behaves very much like Milton's Satan. Satan first tempts Eve by whispering to her ear as she sleeps (*Paradise Lost* 5.35-37), and he begins by telling her that all Nature is ravished by her beauty (1.43-46). Ariel does likewise. Summoned by Belinda's unnamed guardian sylph, he whispers to the ear of the sleeping Belinda, calls her "Fairest of mortals," and urges her to know her "own Importance" (1. 27, 35). Ariel, therefore, is just as seductive as the men he is supposedly guarding Belinda's purity against. Even while warning her against "the whisper in the dark," he is whispering to her in the early morning light.[39] Even while later commanding his troops to guard Belinda closely from male advances, he also reminds them of their duty to keep her as lovely and fragrant as possible (2.91-100) — in other words, to keep her supremely desirable. And even while urging Belinda herself to beware of man, he tells her that any woman who rejects mankind is "embrac'd" by a sylph, by one of those who easily "Assume what Sexes and what Shapes they please" (1.68-70). Pope thus writes the recipe for Beardsley's androgynous

[222]

courtier, an exquisitely equivocal amalgam of delicacy, would-be solicitude, and lust.

In Beardsley's illustrations as in Pope's poem, Belinda subtly reveals a lust of her own. "The Billet-Doux" shows her sitting up in bed propped against a huge pillow, backed by a rococo headboard and flowered wallpaper. Wearing a bonnet tied around her chin and an elaborately frilled bedjacket, she seems at first glance fully protected. But the angle at which she holds the Baron's note makes it lead the viewer's eye directly to her exposed left breast. Beardsley thus depicts the sudden impact of the Baron's fervent words upon a newly awakened Belinda. Though Ariel in her dream has just been warning her to beware of "some dread Event" and above all to "beware of Man!" (1.109, 113), the billet-doux makes her instantly forget these warnings: "Wounds, Charms, and Ardors, were no sooner read / But all the Vision vanish'd from thy Head" (1.119-20).

Combining as it does the pampered innocence of a children's book heroine with the sensuality of a courtesan, Beardsley's drawing aptly expresses the sexual ambiguity of Pope's Belinda.[40] When "awful Beauty puts on all its Arms" in the dressing table scene, Belinda is not arming herself against sexual overtures but doing everything possible to attract them. The "purer Blush" she paints on her cheeks with rouge (1.143) is cosmetically more delicate than the natural reddening of embarrassment would be. But while the latter suggests moral purity, or at least a virginal spontaneity, the cosmetically purer blush is morally tainted, the work of artifice, the sign of the courtesan.

A comparable ambiguity marks the scissors, the "little Engine" of Belinda's downfall (3.132). By showing a pair of scissors on Belinda's dressing table, Beardsley reminds us — as I have noted — that scissors are often used to trim and beautify a woman's hair. In the drawing called "Rape of the Lock" (fig. 48), Beardsley's picture

Figure 48.
Aubrey Beardsley, "The Rape of the Lock," from Alexander Pope, *The Rape of the Lock*, 1896, courtesy of Dartmouth College Library.

of the moment just before the lock is cut, the sumptuously frilled and bountifully bewigged figure holding a pair of open scissors by the frozen cascade of Belinda's coiffeur (which is all we see of her head) could be a hairdresser giving her a final trim. But the wink of the dwarf in the foreground tells us that the Baron is bent on amorous theft even as the dwarf himself — who typically signifies lust in Beardsley's iconography — slyly pilfers a cup of coffee.[41] As a sardonic observer of the action rather than a would-be guardian angel of the heroine, the dwarf is Beardsley's antithetical answer to Pope's sylphs, whom he does not depict at all.[42] The dwarf's full-skirted coat and high-heeled shoes make him a miniature parody of the Baron, and the sheer intricacy of pattern in the men's embroidered coats, the women's figured dresses, and the extravagantly curled wigs may well suggest the "mystick Mazes" (1.92) into which Belinda's conflicting desires lead her.

In the poem, her response to the Baron's advances is anything but straightforward. At the very moment when Ariel tries to warn her of the scissors, he is balked by her own passion for the Baron:

As on the Nosegay in her Breast reclin'd
He watch'd th' Ideas rising in her Mind;
Sudden he view'd in spite of all her Art
An Earthly Lover lurking at her Heart.
Amaz'd, confus'd, he found his Pow'r expir'd,
Resign'd to Fate, and with a Sigh retir'd. (3.141-46)

In the text these lines are immediately followed by the passage on the cutting of the lock, where the scissors' blades "the sacred Hair dissever / From the fair Head, for ever and for ever!" (3.153-54). Subliminally implying the severance of the head itself, Pope constructs a mock-heroic version of decapitation. Heyd even suggests that the dwarf's knowing wink at the scissors in Beardsley's illustration intimates the artist's own "passionate desire to cut off a woman's head" (82). In Beardsley's second version of "The Toilette" for *Salome*, as we have seen, the princess's would-be hairdresser is a masked Pierrot — a demonic clown — who encircles her head with his right arm and waves a powder puff before her eyes while pointing with his sharp left elbow to a pair of black scissors stuck in the pocket of his white apron. If scissors can signify the revenge finally taken on the heroine's head in *Salome*, they may help to explain Belinda's alarm at the assault on her hair.

The cutting of the lock in *The Rape*, however, is followed not by any literal decapitation but by Umbriel's descent to the Cave of Spleen in a passage that led Beardsley to the most intricate, grotesque, and claustral of his illustrations for the poem. To this point, Beardsley has given us ornately furnished interiors. His picture of Belinda on the barge in "The Barge" includes not even a glimpse of Pope's "Silver *Thames*" (2.4), and the glorious sun of Pope's passage appears on the lavishly decorated side of the boat only as a set of little round sunbursting faces with "phallic and testicular forms" (Halsband 100) hanging from their mouths. The outdoor world appears just once, in the background of the picture of the Baron wielding his scissors (*Rape of the Lock*), where a large window frames a double row of trees so nicely that this "natural" scene could be yet another picture — like the tapestry on the wall of the Baron's boudoir.

In "The Cave of Spleen" (fig.. 49), Beardsley takes this interiority to its claustral extreme. Illustrating the line that "Men prove with Child, as pow'rful Fancy works" (4.53), stippled embryos nestle in the swollen belly of a man at lower left and the thigh of the man beside him. Images of enclosure and entrapment abound. At lower right, one woman sits in a closed jar, and just above the peacock-winged female nude appears the bust of a man in a cage of diagonal crosses. Directly above him a tiny bare-breasted woman

Figure 49.
Aubrey Beardsley, "The Cave of Spleen," from Alexander Pope, *The Rape of the Lock*, 1896, courtesy of Dartmouth College Library.

with the round face of a mop-haired child peers out at us through a veil. Since she perches over the reclining figure of Spleen, she may be Affectation, one of Spleen's two handmaids, for the frowning old frump just above clutching a set of books and scrolls to her chest is clearly Pope's "*Ill-nature* like an *ancient Maid*" (4.27). But just as Beardsley puts spectacles on this ancient maid, he adds a veil to the face of Affectation. In what Halsband aptly calls this "grotto of hair" (103), virtually all the figures are caught up in hair or hair-like forms, in a swirling profusion of curls, netting, plumes, peacock feathers, and wigs. In the midst of this bizarre world sits the half-profiled figure of Pope himself in a pose borrowed from Godfrey Kneller's portrait of him (Halsband 106). With sunken cheek and narrowed eyes under his turban-like morning cap, he gazes out at us warily, holding on his lap what seems an embryo made of curled hair — an emblem of the poem he has begotten.

Beardsley likewise works his own variations on Pope's theme of metamorphosis, of "Bodies chang'd to various forms by *Spleen*" (4.48). Taking his cue from Pope's lines on anthropomorphic teapots and impregnated men (4.49-53), Beardsley presents not only a bird-woman and several teapot-shaped men but also — looming large on the left — a conspicuously feminized Umbriel, who is male in Pope's text but here displays the hourglass figure of a tightly corseted woman with stupendously plumed turban, richly ornamented sleeves, and thighs draped in what appear to be stippled pearls. Subtly recalling the hermaphroditic nude on the suppressed title page for *Salome*, Umbriel epitomizes the gender-crossing that permeates Pope's poem from the first canto, where the glittering youth displays an effeminacy that is plainly caught — as we have already noted — in Beardsley's illustration of Belinda's dream. At the same time, this effeminate figure assumes the boldly erect stance and assertive manner of a man about to fight. Holding up sceptre and spleenwort with his left hand as he points with his right, he seems precisely the kind of warrior that Belinda aimed to be when she set out to challenge and conquer at Ombre "two adventurous Knights" (3.26). For if men can look and act like women in this poem, women can behave like men.

Belinda does so plainly in the last of Beardsley's full-scale illustrations for the poem, "Battle of the Beaux and Belles" (fig. 50). Superficially, this picture replaces dark confusion with the appearance of decorum and light. Misshapen hybrids give way to well-dressed men and women gathered in a drawing room; the windowless wall of the cave is supplanted by a pair of windows; and in place of Umbriel's tight black bodysuit, Belinda wears a billowing, delicately stippled dress that forms a triangle of light with the décolletage of the white-plumed woman just behind her (presumably Thalestris). But the overturned chair and the kneeling Baron and the cast-down walking stick signal confusion, and for all its light, the picture is framed and freighted by darkness: by the dark curtains at the top, by the broad strip of nearly black carpet below, and by thick dark wigs quite as large as any of those to be found in the cave — especially on the head of Belinda herself. Just as importantly, her frowning face and the forward thrust of her upper body repeat the bellicose stance of Umbriel, and the single curly lock resting on her right shoulder repeats the lock dangling from the headdress of the Goddess of Spleen. Belinda thus combines the grace of a lavishly dressed young woman with the aggressiveness of a warrior.

To compare this picture with the earliest illustration of the battle scene, however, is to see that Beardsley stops well short of turning Belinda into the "fierce Virago" that Thalestris becomes when she issues the call to arms (5.37). In a 1714 engraving of Canto 5 of *The Rape*, Louis Du Guernier shows a simply clothed Belinda leaning over the almost supine figure of the Baron and thrusting the point of a bodkin into his chest while he tries with

Figure 50.
Aubrey Beardsley, "Battle of the Beaux and Belles," from Alexander
Pope, *The Rape of the Lock*, 1896, courtesy of Dartmouth College Library.

his right hand to push her forearm away (repr. Halsband 15). The foreground of this illustration may have led Beardsley to put an overturned chair in his picture of the battle, as Halsband notes.[43] But Beardsley treats the confrontation between Belinda and the Baron altogether differently than Du Guernier does. Resplendent in towering wig and elaborately ruffled dress, Belinda faces down the Baron without touching him, sternly clutching her fan at her side rather than striking him with it.[44] Equally self-possessed, the Baron kneels erectly before her in thickly curled wig, finely stippled ruff, and richly embroidered coat. With his hand on his chest and his head held firmly up, he strikes a pose somewhere between abashment and defiance. He could well be signifying, in fact, what he says when Sir Plume demands the return of the lock in Canto 4:

> . . . by this Lock, this sacred Lock I swear,
>
> . . . .
>
> That while my Nostrils draw the vital Air,
> This Hand, which won it, shall for ever wear. (4.137-38)

Besides composing a balance of antithetical elements — abjection and self-assertion, grace and fury, confusion and decorum, light and dark — Beardsley puts in the very center of this picture a figure who has by now come to serve as a detached, amused observer: the page-boy dwarf. Heyd identifies this figure with Beardsley himself. Through him, she says, Beardsley expresses "the little man's fear of the large woman" even as he plays the clever fool, sharing with us his amusement at the antics of the others (80-81). But if the dwarf signifies Beardsley himself, he also signifies Beardsley's alliance with Pope, for his position in the center of "Battle" corresponds precisely to that of the poet in the center of "The Cave." Their expressions and posture are different, of course; while Pope sits pensively staring out at us, the dwarf stands

[231]

between the two chief antagonists — Belinda and the Baron — with a look of complacence if not amusement. But the dwarf's turban resembles Pope's soft round hat, and the dwarf's head is cocked to the right just as Pope's is cocked to the left. Beardsley's implicit linking of the two reminds us that Pope was only four and a half feet tall and sometimes called himself a dwarf, as Halsband notes.[45] All three figures are at once outside the action and yet central to the creation of its meaning for the observer — whether reader, viewer, or both.

Beardsley's tailpiece for *The Rape* ("The New Star") includes neither a dwarf nor anything like the satyr and Pierrot figures interring the princess in the tailpiece for *Salome*. After the flagrant grotesquerie of the "Cave of Spleen" and the embroidered confusion of the battle in the drawing room, the tailpiece offers a compact vision of sweetness and light. Plumed, wigged, and sashed, a man in the carnival costume of the court of Louis XIV holds delicately in his thumb and forefinger the "sudden Star" that Belinda's stolen lock becomes as it finally shoots into the sky and thereby prompts the star-gazing John Partridge to predict the fall of Louis (5.127-28, 139-40). Yet the tidy symmetry of the star is offset by the Baroque extravagance of the courtier's plume and wig, which evokes all the riotous profusion of hair and plumage that we have seen throughout these illustrations, especially in "The Cave of Spleen." Grotesquerie is an eruption of buried energies. True to its etymological roots in the *grotta* (cave), the grotesque evinces — in the words of Chris Snodgrass — "not only something playful and carelessly fantastic but also something ominous and sinister, the discovery of a totally different 'underground' world in which the realms of the animate and the inanimate are no longer separate and the 'normal' laws of symmetry and proportion are no longer valid."[46]

In his illustrations for both *Salome* and *The Rape of the Lock*, Beardsley's elegantly grotesque art surely reveals the ominous powers of an underground world typically buried by the rituals of the civilized life. But it also continually shows the interplay between these two worlds. If the openly lustful and bloodthirsty Salome can don a modish dress and hat, accept the ministrations of a hairdresser, and offer her cheek to a powder puff, the delicate and virginal Belinda can just as readily feel the stirrings of desire, the lust to conquer, and the deforming effects of rage. Beardsley's fin-de-siècle illustrations for the 1894 edition of Wilde's play and the 1896 edition of Pope's poem enable us to see that we can never escape the grotesque. "Not merely the human personality," writes Snodgrass, "but the very nature of the world is grotesque, in the sense that we can at any point and without provocation be the targets of malicious forces, the most familiar elements of everyday life suddenly becoming strange and evil."[47]

* * * *

In the monograph from which I quoted at the beginning of this study, Lorraine Kooistra argues that illustrated books are always "books of conversations" (247). Through pictures, she contends, the artist enters by various means into dialogue with the writer.[48] For the most part, however, the author answers the artist and his reading of the text only insofar as the text itself talks back, confirming or contesting what the artist graphically says of it. Beadsley's illustrations of Wilde and Pope generate a series of conversations. Responding at first to the text of *Salome* with a drawing that prompted Wilde to commission a suite of illustrations for it, Beardsley then draws a set of pictures that relentlessly explore and expose what the play dramatizes: the conversation between the grotesque and the beautiful. When these graphic "readings" of Wilde's play are themselves read in conjunction with his illustrations of Pope's poem, they generate a further conversation between the play and the poem, between the savagery of the one and the delicacy of the other. The pictures reveal the grotesquerie of both.

Notes

1. Martin Meisel, *Realizations: Narrative, Pictorial, and Theatrical Arts in Nineteenth-Century England* (Princeton: Princeton University Press, 1983), 30.
2. Lorraine Janzen Kooistra, *The Artist as Critic: Bitextuality in Fin-de-Siècle Illustrated Books* (Aldershot, England: Scolar Press, 1995), 3.
3. Richard Ellman, *Oscar Wilde* (New York: Alfred A. Knopf, 1988), 376.
4. Mark Samuels Lasner, *A Selective Checklist of the Published Work of Aubrey Beardsley* (Boston: Thomas G. Boss, 1995), 12.
5. Kenneth Clark, *The Best of Aubrey Beardsley* (New York: Doubleday, 1978), 70.
6. Oscar Wilde, *Salome*, lines 1067-68, in *Lady Windermere's Fan, Salome, A Woman of No Importance, An Ideal Husband, The Importance of Being Earnest*, ed. Peter Raby (Oxford: Clarendon Press, 1995), 91. Hereafter I cite line numbers from the English translation of the play (Raby 65-91) made by Lord Aldred Douglas with considerable help from Wilde and possibly others (Lanfer 32).
7. See Chris Snodgrass, *Aubrey Beardsley: Dandy of the Grotesque* (New York: Oxford University Press, 1995), 52. As D. J. Gordon notes, most of Beardsley's drawings originate from works of literature ["Aubrey Beardsley at the V. & A.," *Encounter* 27.4 (Oct. 1966): 14]. He read voraciously, thought of himself as a man of letters even after making his name as an artist, wrote an unfinished novel (*Under the Hill*), and planned to write a good deal more, including — at the time of his death — a critical introduction to Ben Jonson's *Volpone* (Snodgrass 105).

8. In Thomas Hardy's *Tess of the d'Urbervilles* (1891), published just the year before Wilde wrote his play, the Satanically seductive Alec d'Urberville likewise accuses the guileless Tess of having tempted him away from his life as a preacher: "And why then have you tempted me? I was firm as a man could be till I saw those eyes and that mouth again — surely there never was such maddening mouth since Eve's . . . . You temptress, Tess; you damned witch of Babylon. . . ." *Tess of the d'Urbervilles*, ed. Scott Elledge, 3rd ed. (New York: Norton, 1991), 254. Even the would-be virtuous Angel finds Tess serpentine — before their fateful wedding night. Though he takes her to be a virgin during their courtship at Talbothays, he sees at one point "the red interior of her [yawning] mouth as if it had been a snake's" (Hardy 133).

9. Ewa Kuryluk, *Salome and Judas in the Cave of Sex. The Grotesque: Origins, Iconography, Techniques* (Evanston: Northwestern University Press, 1987), 196.

10. Ellman, *Oscar Wilde*, 340.

11. Ibid., 42. In addition, Beardsley's voracious reading must have included the poetry of Keats, since he attended the unveiling of a bust of the poet at Hampstead in the summer of 1894. (Haldane MacFall, *Aubrey Beardsley: The Man and His Work* [London: John Lane, Bodley Head, 1928], 17.) Like Keats, Beardsley died of tuberculosis at the age of twenty-five, living just two months longer than the poet.

12. From his student days at Oxford Wilde admired the Pre-Raphaelites (Ellman 31) and staunchly defended them in his very first American lecture of 9 January 1881 (Ellman 164-65). On Beardsley's admiration for the Pre-Raphaelites, especially Dante Gabriel Rossetti and Edward Burne-Jones, see Ian Fletcher, *Aubrey Beardsley* (Boston: Twayne, 1987), 5, 30-31.

13. On wavy hair, note Milton's account of Eve's "disheveled" tresses "in wanton ringlets waved / As the vine curls her tendrils, which implied / Subjection, but required with gentle sway" (*Paradise Lost* 4.305-308). On the morning after Eve is tempted by Satan in a

dream, Adam awakens to find her "With tresses discomposed, and glowing cheek / As through unquiet rest" (5.9-10).

14. See Ellman, *Oscar Wilde*, 45, 87, 115, 117, 206.
15. But while John rejects both sensual love and Salome consistently, Julien rejects Mathilde only after having an affair with her and then emotionally returning to his original mistress, Mme de Renal.
16. *Red and Black*, trans. and ed. Robert Adams (New York: Norton, 1969), 243-44.
17. [James Cuno], *French Caricature and the French Revolution* (Los Angeles: Grunwald Center for the Graphic Arts, University of California, 1988), 194 and plates 89-90.
18. "The Severed Head: The Impact of French Revolutionary Caricatures on England" in Cuno, 58.
19. Cuno, 64, fig. 16, and Neil Hertz, "Medusa's Head," in *The End of the Line: Essays on Psychoanalysis and the Sublime* (New York: Columbia University Press, 1985), 162.
20. In *The Dancer's Reward*, which shows Salome receiving John's head on a platter and gripping his forelock, his hair is wavy and black — just like that of Salome herself in *Salome with St. John's Head*.
21. Kuryluk, *Salome and Judas*, 3, 7. Kuryluk also suggests that the gradual ossification of Christianity in the twentieth century makes the end of the nineteenth century "the last period in European history when the sacrosanct mattered enough to provoke sacrilegious attacks" (6). In light of the stir generated by recent works such as Andres Serrano's *Piss Christ* (a crucifix immersed in what the artist claims to be his own urine), Kuryluk overstates her point somewhat.
22. After deleting the genitalia at the request of his publisher, Beardsley composed a bit of verse:
    Because one figure was undressed
    This little drawing was suppressed.
    It was unkind, but never mind,
    Perhaps it was for the best. (qtd. Lanfer 32)
23. See Snodgrass, 57-58; Karl Beckson, "The Artist as Transcendental Phallus: Aubrey Beardsley and the Ritual of Defense" in *Reconsider-*

ing Aubrey Beardsley, ed. Robert Langenfeld (Ann Arbor, MI: UMI Research Press, 1989), 214; and Milly Heyd, *Aubrey Beardsley: Symbol, Mask, and Self-Irony* (New York: Peter Lang, 1986), 160-61.

24. Sir William Rothenstein, *Men and Manners* (London: Faber and Faber, 1931), 183-84. On the other hand, Beardsley's picture of Salome with the head of John had prompted Wilde to commission from him the illustrations for the English edition of the play (Ellman 376) and to send him (in March 1893, even before the picture was published) a copy of the Paris edition inscribed, "For Aubrey: for the only artist who, besides myself, knows what the dance of the seven veils is, and can see that invisible dance. Oscar." From the copy in the Sterling Library, University of London, qtd. Rupert Hart-Davis, ed. *The Letters of Oscar Wilde* (London, 1962), 348n.

25. See Ian Fletcher's review of criticism ranging from Arthur Symons' *Aubrey Beardsley* (1898) to Malcolm Easton's *Aubrey and the Dying Lady* (1972) in *Aubrey Beardsley* (Boston: Twaye, 1987), 57-59.

26. Elliott Gilbert, "'Tumult of Images': Wilde, Beardsley, and *Salome*," *Victorian Studies* 28 (Winter 1983): 159; Linda Zatlin, *Aubrey Beardsley and Victorian Sexual Politics* (Oxford: Clarendon, 1990), 94-95; Fletcher, *Aubrey Beardsley*, 64.

27. "Congruous Incongruities: The Wilde-Beardsley 'Collaboration,'" *English Literature in Transition, 1880-1920* 37 (1994): 9-26.

28. As Chris Snodgrass notes, the perfectly unmarked body of Salome in this picture shows no sign of having been crushed to death by the shields of Herod's soldiers, which is what is said to happen at the end of the play (Snodgrass, 147; *Salome*, 1070-71).

29. *The Rape of the Lock . . . Embroidered with Nine Drawings by Aubrey Beardsley* (London: Leonard Smithers, 1896).

30. Snodgrass finds in the original (expurgated) version of "The Toilet" "a surfeit of cunningly disguised sexual 'perversions'"; four of its five figures, he says, are covertly masturbating (65). While only two of the five could actually be masturbating (the hands of the other three are all otherwise engaged), the picture does mingle domestic implements with signs of lust and potential castration: the phallic spout of

the teapot pointing at Salome, the bladelike shelf pointing directly to the naked genitals of the boy at right (Snodgrass 65).

31. Unless otherwise noted, the italics in lines quoted from *The Rape* are in the original.

32. For Halsband's suggestion see *The Rape of the Lock and its Illustrations 1714-1896* (Oxford: Clarendon, 1980), 91.

33. *The English Poets*, ed. T. H. Ward (1880; rpt. 1891) 3:59, qtd. Halsband, 86; *English Literature and Irish Politics*, ed. R. H. Super (Ann Arbor, Michigan 1971), 180.

34. Gosse to A. E. Gallatine, 19 June 1902, MS in Princeton University Library, qtd. Halsband 87n.

35. Elizabeth G. Gitter, "The Power of Women's Hair in the Victorian Imagination." *PMLA* 99 (1984): 942-43.

36. *The Letters of Robert Browning and Elizabeth Barrett Browning: 1845-46* (Cambridge: Harvard University Press, 1969), 288-89, qtd. Gitter, 943.

37. Linda Zatlin construes Belinda's final cry as evidence that she finds the Baron impotent because of his "inability to cut her pubic hairs" (51, 189). But in my view, we may far more plausibly infer that Belinda unwittingly refers to being quite literally raped or ravished, sexually "sieze[d]."

38. Overstating her point, however, Zatlin sees the whole configuration of candle and altar in Beardsley's illustration as a giant phallus, with the books forming a scrotum and the flames pubic hair (51).

39. Even apart from the allusions to Milton's Satan in this passage, any portrayal of a "sleepwatching" man — a man gazing on a sleeping woman — implies the possibility of rape. See Leo Steinberg, *Other Criteria* (London: Oxford University Press, 1972), 99.

40. In Beardsley's frontispiece for Aristophanes' *Lysistrata* (1896), which appeared just a few months after the illustrated *Rape*, an openly sensual Lysistrata stands fingering her crotch (she is ostensibly "Shielding Her Coynte") and tickling a huge erect phallus with a leafy branch. Like Belinda in "The Billet-Doux," she wears a heavily ruffled dressing gown and bares one breast.

41. On the lasciviousness of Beardsley's dwarves, see Zaitlin, 188-89. Since Beardsley does not show Clarissa handing the scissors to the Baron, as she does in the poem (3.127-30), the dwarf is something like the Baron's co-conspirator.

42. "The dwarf's smile is a knowing one," writes Milly Heyd; he is aware of what is about to happen, since the illustration does not show the actual cutting off of the lock. The dwarf is conscious of the danger lurking in this seemingly idyllic situation, but he stands aside and does not take an active part in the action" (Heyd 812). Noting the similarities between Beardsley's illustrations for *The Rape* and Hogarth's *Marriage à la Mode* (such as the use of screens, coffee drinkers, and overturned chairs), Heyd reads Beardsley's dwarf as a variant of the black boy in plate 4 of Hogarth's *Marriage*, where the black boy kneeling at lower right grins and points to the horns of his toy Actaeon as a sign that his lady (in line with his pointing finger) will soon be cuckolding her lord (Heyd 81).

43. Halsband, 106. As Milly Heyd notes (81), there is also ample precedent for Beardsley's overturned chair in Hogarth — in pictures such as plate 2 of *Marriage à la Mode* (1745) and plate 6 of *The Rake's Progress* (1735); the latter shows not only a downed chair but a kneeling Tom Rakewell on the floor beside it, anticipating the kneeling Baron.

44. While far less violently aggressive than Du Guernier's Belinda, she is decidedly more hostile than in Thomas Stothard's watercolor of 1798, where Belinda looks down sweetly on the Baron as he kneels ardently before her.

45. Halsband, 109. Pope's consciousness of his physical deformity was likewise matched by Beardsley's. Though Beardsley's height (approximately 5'10") placed him well above the stature of a dwarf, he was extremely thin, with a "hatchet face" fringed by tortoiseshell-colored hair hanging to the eyebrows (David Cecil, *Max: Biography* [Boston: Houghton Mifflin], 95). "Beardsley," writes Heyd, "lived with the conviction that a physical deformation clung to him like a black silhouette and his self-image underwent parallel reductive transformations.

The flight from physical limitations and the capacity to rise above them is expressed in his art, which is drawn to metamorphosis" (83).

46. Snodgrass, 163, citing Wolfgang Kayser, *The Grotesque in Art and Literature*, trans. Ulrich Weisstein (New York: Columbia UP, 1957), 21, and Geoffrey Galt Harpham, *On the Grotesque: Startegies of Contradiction in Art and Literature* (Princeton, NJ: Princeton UP, 1982), 51.

47. Snodgrass, 164, drawing on Victor Hugo, "Preface to Cromwell" in *Dramas*. Vol. 3 of *The Works of Victor Hugo* (Boston: Little Brown, 1909), 8-23.

48. She examines "five dialogic relations" that I have space only to enumerate here: quotation, impression, parody, answering, and cross-dressing (249).

Dream Blocks:
American Women Illustrators
of the Golden Age, 1890-1920

Ruth Copans

At the turn of the twentieth century, illustration was at its peak. In 1895, writing in *Munsey's* and speaking of the American readership, Philip Rodney Pauling noted: "If we would find where in the world of art the artist is most sure of winning and keeping the heart of the people, we must turn to illustration. . . . We care less, as a people, for the lofty canvasses of some modern Raphael, than for the more tangible and useful excellences of beautiful books and handsome periodicals."[1] The climate was receptive; the audience, nurtured by the visual representations found in illustrated newspapers during the Civil War, had fully emerged.

The technology of illustration experienced rapid advance; together the economics of publishing, advertising, and selling created the conditions for a fertile market. By the turn of the century, illustrated books and periodicals had become something of a fad, with as many as 100,000 pictures published annually. This increase in published images was made possible by the invention of the

[241]

halftone process in 1881. Pictures could be broken down into tiny dots and printed on a high-speed press eventually using four-color halftone plates. In 1890, a halftone plate cost $20, where previously, illustrations were engraved by hand at a cost of $300 to $500 per woodblock.[2]

In 1900, no fewer than 5,500 different magazines existed for children and women, and thus arose a concomitant demand for illustrators of women's magazines and books. This development opened a niche for women artists just at the time when the role of women was changing and when the suffragette movement and the women's rights movement were creating a climate where women could envision alternatives to their more traditional domestic roles of wife and mother. Ironically, the changes in mechanical reproduction that Walter Benjamin laments in "The Work of Art in the Age of Mechanical Reproduction" actually enabled talented women artists to come forward, giving us access to the vision of the woman illustrator not otherwise possible. Although the work of women artists including Jessie Willcox Smith, Alice Barber Stephens, Charlotte Harding, Elizabeth Shippen Green, and Violet Oakley has been relegated to calendars, not museums, it merits reevaluation. By exploring the lives of these women artists through the extant letters and personal records, their professional achievements in the book arts, and their connection to Howard Pyle (who mentored many of them), we can begin to reclaim the voice of American women artists during what art historians concur was the "golden age of illustration."

Home, mother, family remained the best selling themes in women's books and magazines. Although the family and domestic life these publications portrayed rarely reflected the more advanced social changes of the latter part of the nineteenth century, who better to portray the ideal of the American housewife and mother than women? As commissions for book and magazine illustrations became available to women, they were most often assigned the subjects one might expect: fairy tales, romances, sentimental tales, and stories about domestic harmony. One must wonder if these were not, in fact, the preferred subjects for many of the women illustrators. Jessie Willcox Smith recounted in a short autobiographical piece how:

> [o]ne time I, fortunately or unfortunately, got the illustrating of an Indian book. I hated to do Indians and I struggled and plodded through the task and was delighted at last to complete the commission and dispatch it to the publisher. You imagine my surprise when, a few days later, the same publishers sent me another Indian story to illustrate. I received it with none too good grace, but in those days I was not declining any work, and I appreciated that my future hinged on how I fulfilled my early commissions. So, unpleasant though I found the work, I took infinite pains to make it both attractive and accurate in detail. When the third Indian story came in quick succession, I said to myself, 'This must cease'. And so I wrote to the publisher that I did not know much about Indians and that if they had just an every-day book about children, I thought I could do it better. I was immediately rewarded with one of Louisa M. Alcott's stories, and a letter saying they were glad to know I did other things as they had supposed Indians were my specialty.[3]

Illustration was now considered an acceptable career for women, and the fact that it could be done at home was an added incentive. Learning to sketch was often an integral part of a middle-class woman's education, along with music, embroidery, and other "feminine" arts. More liberal views that allowed, and even encouraged, women to earn money began to prevail at the end of the nineteenth century. The notion that illustration was compatible with family life begs closer examination, however, since many women were forced to interrupt or even abandon their careers if family responsibilities intervened. No one would dispute that the rival demands of motherhood and a career were straining; for every woman who successfully juggled the two with impressive results, there were others who retired from illustration out of fatigue and frustration. The professional lives of these women, successful as they were, demanded hard work and dedication. Almost all of them at some point or another were forced to take a break because of illness provoked by the intensity of their labors. Such realities are a far cry from the stereotypical, romantic portrait of a woman sketching.

It is important to remember how essential it was for a woman to be self-supporting if she were not independently wealthy or married. At the turn of the century, a growing number of middle- and upper-class women had to support themselves and their families when left vulnerable by the huge casualties of the Civil War. Concomitantly, an important need arose for vocational training of "surplus women," a brutal euphemism for spinsters, widows, and divorcées without support.[4] An average illustrator made $4,000 a year, enough for a house and servant. Popular illustrators earned between $10,000-$75,000 a year and thus counted among the wealthy. Eighty women illustrators were active during this period, earning adequate and in some cases extraordinary incomes for the time. In a 1908 article entitled "The Illustrator and His Income," Amos Stote stated that "Illustration has proven a remunerative calling for women as well as for men; and in their competition the women have two, at least, advantages — their industry and their facility." He goes on to admire the achievement of three of the women illustrators whom we will consider in these pages, attesting to their financial success: "Elizabeth Shippen Green, Jessie Will-cox Smith and Violet Oakley own a goodly mansion of colonial design, built of the cheques received from their publishers."[5]

While these women did indeed achieve financial success, they won it because of an artistic achievement that merits our atten-tion. Although most often admired for their "feminine" approach to illustration, an approach that exhibited a sensitivity and insight into a particular subject or theme, they were also acknowledged to be fine craftsmen and interpreters. This was a talented lot of illus-trators with a capacity to capture more than a stereotypical domes-tic setting, even in drawings that had the domestic as manifest content. If the subject matter they were assigned bound them to feminine themes and concerns, their artistic embellishments and expression placed them on an equal footing with their brother illustrators. Despite the inevitable (for the times) patronizing tone we hear in the contemporary critics who complemented these "ladies" for their "delicacy and insight,"[6] and their ability to add "a new perfume to our sentiment,"[7] the extraordinary quality of their drawing shows how capably they handled their commissions. Their work often captured harmonious scenes of daily life with the only discordant note between lovers or children, but their artistic skill rendered these seemingly mundane themes moving and pow-erful. Clever at interpreting the commercial demands of their day and in responding to the pragmatic requirements of self-suffi-ciency, many of these women, despite their financial and artistic success, have again sunk into obscurity.

Even in their time, recognition as artists was slow to come to women, but their acceptance into the profession of illustrator came early and was enthusiastic. In part, this acceptance can be explained by the fact that illustration has always been considered on a lower rung in the hierarchies of art. As Walt Reed suggests in his study of the American illustrator:

In recent years it has been fashionable for Art Critics to couple the word 'mere' with 'illustration' in dismissing pictures that tell any kind of a story. And, since illustration is usually commissioned, it has also been viewed as impure, commercial art when contrasted with the nobler motivation of the fine arts in which the artist is free to express his innermost feelings. . . .[8]

Jessie Willcox Smith, who achieved fame and fortune as an illustrator of domestic scenes, especially children, has been compared with Mary Cassatt, an accomplished painter whose work hangs in great museums all over the world. Yet, Smith's reputation has never really emerged from the eclipse occasioned by her lowly profession of illustrator; again, her work is more likely seen on calendars or greeting cards than in museums. Ironically, Jessie Willcox Smith was said to have had Mary Cassatt's drawings hanging on her walls. And, of course, our judgment of illustrative art depends largely on reproductions and not originals, most of which have been lost or destroyed.

Perhaps the most crucial issue for women artists at the turn of the century was that of education. While modest art training had for some time been considered a part of the "gentler sex's" education, the transition from amateur artist to professional illustrator could not happen until the second half of the nineteenth century. As Cheryl A. Jones has noted in her essay on American women illustrators: "(t)he rise of increased educational opportunities and the recognition of women as professionals led to the replacement of the image of the dilettante 'lady artist' (the image of the 'lady artist' was primarily a product of the late eighteenth and early nineteenth centuries)."[9] In this transitional era, Philadelphia became one of the centers for training women artists. The School of Design for Women, the Drexel Institute, and eventually the

Pennsylvania Academy of Fine Arts all offered classes in drawing for women by the end of the century.

Professional training for women, especially in the Philadelphia area, remains even now inseparable from Howard Pyle, brilliant illustrator, and more important, inspired teacher. Pyle not only taught some of the most famous male illustrators, such as N. C. Wyeth, Frank E. Schoonover, Stanley Arthurs, and Maxfield Parrish, but also some of the most successful women illustrators, Elizabeth Shippen Green, Jessie Willcox Smith, and Violet Oakley among them; he encouraged them to pursue professional careers, mentored them, found commissions for them, and took them seriously at a time when they were likely to be considered amateur dabblers rather than hard working professionals.

Howard Pyle was born in 1853 to a Quaker family in Wilmington, Delaware. The oldest of four children, he was an avid reader, who, as a boy, had a passion for the illustrated newspapers of his day and loved books with pictures. Pyle discovered with delight the illustrations of John Leech, John Tenniel, Dante Gabriel Rossetti, and Edward Burne-Jones, among others. A daydreamer, Pyle wasn't much of a student, and his realistic parents sent him at age sixteen to the closest art school, Van de Weilen's School in Philadelphia. Even as Pyle acquired technical skills, he deplored how the role of the imagination in illustration was ignored. Over the next few years Pyle worked in his father's leather business while continuing his experiments with drawing. Eventually, *Scribner's Monthly* accepted one of his pieces, and at twenty-three he went to work in New York City for *Harper's*. From 1883 to 1887 Pyle illustrated six books which exhibited two divergent tendencies: traditional and decorative inclinations, and impressionistic fascination with the transitory effects of movement and light. He had early on resolved that "(l)iterary ideas could be depicted convincingly if two elements were present: a total surrender to the

world of the imagination. . . and a firm commitment to realism. . . .
The two — romance and reality — were vital to every successful
picture."[10]

In 1894 Pyle taught his first class when he was already secure
in the field as an author-illustrator. He possessed an expansive,
generous character, great intensity and energy, and a remarkable
ability to do several things at once, traits which made him a particularly brilliant and inspiring teacher. The end of the century
saw a shortage of talented illustrators, and Pyle set out with an
almost missionary zeal to fill this need. He taught at the Drexel
Institute of Art until 1900 when he created his own school for
illustration. Impatient with the dilettantes he was obliged to
instruct at Drexel, he wanted a total commitment from his students. He stressed the importance of developing a pictorial sense
and built on students' latent imaginary powers. Pyle hand-picked
the candidates for his experimental school. He started out with
ten students, including two women. The school was more of a
colony, and students paid for only room and board and for sup-
plies; there was no tuition. The conditions, however, were Spartan.
The students worked six days a week from 8 A.M. to 5 or 6 P.M.
From this crucible emerged many of the greatest illustrators of the
period and indeed a specific genre of American illustration: the
Brandywine School. Pyle's school lasted until 1905. By then he
himself had written and illustrated 24 books, illustrated over 100
titles, and had his drawings published in every major magazine in
America. His students were among the most sought after illustrators in America. More important for our purposes here, by the
time of Pyle's death in 1910 at age fifty-eight, he had trained more
than sixty women illustrators.

Yet, even Pyle in 1904 seems to have turned on his female
constituency, and, curiously, he stopped accepting women as students. In a full-page article in Philadelphia's *The North American*

(Sunday, 19 June 1904) entitled "Why Art and Marriage Won't Mix," Pyle affirms: "(t)he pursuit of art interferes with a girl's social life and destroys her chances of getting married. Girls are, after all, at best, only qualified for sentimental work." There is a half-page illustration of a woman in a smock painting a picture of soldiers marching through an arched doorway (ironically, hardly a domestic or sentimental scene), and sitting behind her is an obviously ardent suitor. The article continues that Pyle "will have no more girl students. Love and practical art, from his point of view, are very likely to interfere. And he doesn't care to referee."[11] Several other reasons stated in the article for Pyle's rejection of women are given, supposedly tongue in cheek, but the fact that they reinforce the stereotypical excuses for not educating women is striking, especially from a man who for years had trained and encouraged some of the finest women illustrators of the period. Michele H. Bogart in her recently published book, *Artists, Advertising, and the Borders of Art*, asserts that Pyle was concerned with the feminization and, thus, the trivialization of the profession.[12]

In examining the work of women in the field of illustration during that period, one is struck by the myriad ways they enhanced and promoted the goals of Howard Pyle to both educate and entertain the reader. Contrary to Pyle's assertions about women and marriage, Alice Barber Stephens exemplifies the women who managed to have successful careers as illustrators alongside rich and satisfying family lives. Considered a pioneer among women, Stephens was one of the first female students to study at the Pennsylvania Academy of Fine Arts when, in 1876, it opened its doors to women. There she came under the influence of Thomas Eakins and later did the engraving of his illustrations for *Scribner's*. Eakins's influence can be seen in Stephens's realistic rendering of physical features and her obvious sympathy toward her sitter's character. Stephens was the eighth of nine children

[249]

and had trained as an engraver to earn money to ease her family's financial burden. In the mid-1880s she stopped engraving because of her health and started using pen and ink. Stephens taught at the Philadelphia School of Design from 1883 to 1893. She had married another teacher of drawing in 1890, took a year off when her son Daniel was born, and resumed her teaching in 1894. She had a continuous career as an illustrator, which lasted until 1926.

For years Stephens illustrated for *Harper's*, whose turn-of-the-century volumes are full of her elegant drawings, distinguished often by her realistic vignettes and figures with shining eyes. Contemporary newspaper articles attest to high public and critical appreciation for Stephens's work, as do the many letters from the writers whose stories and books she illustrated. As early as 1893, she was publicly praised in *Woman's Progress* as "one of the foremost women illustrators of the day, and one whose pictures have found their way into homes all over the land."[13] Over the next decades, numerous articles appeared concerning not just Stephens's artwork, but also her home, studio, garden, and artist-astronomer son.

More moving than the news and magazine articles are the letters from authors, many honored that Stephens would be illustrating their tale or book. In 1895, A. Conan Doyle, whose books and stories Stephens was to illustrate over several years, wrote to say that Stephens's picture of the four men illustrating "Stark Munro" "is the very best illustration I have had to any work of mine."[14] Edward Bok, an editor of the *Ladies Home Journal*, shared in a letter to Stephens what Mrs. Charles Terry Collins, an author, had said: "I cannot tell you how delighted I am with Mrs. Stephens' illustrations. Her people are as real as possible and 'Sister Green' is simply capital. It is an inspiration to better writing to have such support in an artist."[15] In 1908, Margaret Deland reiterated this view that good pictures could inspire good writing: "I am sure your pictures will go far to make up for the shortcomings of the story, although I hope that when I have worked over the proof I can improve it somewhat, and make it more worthy of your steel — so to speak."[16]

Meaningful praise for Stephens's art also comes in a letter from Howard Pyle dated 1897. Although Stephens had not studied with Pyle, they shared some of the same students. In sending a costume for Stephens to use for her illustrations, Pyle offers this prize compliment: "I hope you will always ask me for anything in which I can be of use to you. My return is very ample in the added perfection of your beautiful art."[17]

Stephens frequently drew mothers, lovers, and children, yet her dramatic scenes and illustrative vignettes were truly exceptional, charged with emotion, and always-respectful enhancements of the text. "Looking up into her mother's face expectantly" (fig. 51) from *Susanna and Sue* (1909) demonstrates Stephens's ability to capture and depict the intimate and affectionate relationship between a mother and her daughter. *Susanna and Sue*, written by Kate Douglas Wiggin, is the story of a mother who leaves behind a dissolute husband and self-absorbed son and takes refuge with her daughter in a Shaker community. In this illustration, Susanna has escaped to the second floor of the barn where she sits on "an old-fashioned, list-bottomed, straight-backed Shaker chair in front of the open window."[18] Here Susanna and her daughter Sue speak of their home and the Shaker community that has embraced them. Susanna recounts a Shaker story to her daughter as she struggles to determine whether their place is amongst the Shakers who have taken them in, or back in the world where maternal and wifely duties beckon. Their intent glances, their flowing skirts, and the peaceful intimacy of the moment bind the two characters. We see through the window, the world from which they've taken leave, a world which will eventually intrude upon them, calling Susanna

[251]

Figure 51.
Alice Barber Stephens, "Looking up into her
mother's face expectantly," from Kate Douglas Wiggin,
Susanna and Sue, 1909, courtesy of
Lyrical Ballad Bookstore Collection.

[252]

back by making her understand, through a dream based on the very story she's telling, the importance of her worldly responsibilities. Stephens beautifully captures the warmth and affection of the daughter leaning against her mother's knee, listening to her words, watching her mend. As with so many of the illustrations of the period, the viewer feels a nostalgic tug into a dreamy, rural, domestic world.

Stephens's status as an accomplished artist enabled her to establish not just her own place but that of other women artists "shoulder to shoulder with their brothers in art."[19] "As a 'pioneer,'" notes Anne Barton Brown, "Stephens did not aggressively lead the way for women to advance as artists, but, perceiving the new opportunities available, she readily took advantage of them. Her success set standards and paved the way for other women."[20] Stephens's commitment to furthering women artists in their careers is evidenced by her participation in the founding of the Plastic Club, the first and longest lasting art club for women, of which she was vice president from its inception in 1897 until 1912.

Stephens's training of other women artists brought her into contact with Charlotte Harding, a student of immense talent who would also study with Howard Pyle. Harding was the oldest of three children, born in 1873 in Newark, New Jersey, to English parents. In 1881 the family moved to Philadelphia, where in 1889, at age sixteen, Harding won a scholarship to the Philadelphia School of Design for Women. She finished four years of school in three. Her path led her to Alice Barber Stephens's "Life and Portrait" class in 1894, and Stephens was to remain a major influence on Harding's professional life. Although Stephens was fifteen years older, the women became close friends and colleagues, sharing a studio from 1899 until 1903. Charlotte Harding's distinctive style, with a broader, more casual hand, was in many ways more modern than Stephens's, but the older woman's influences can be found in

Harding's natural sympathy with her characters and her powerful depiction of emotion as well as action.

From 1894 to 1900, Harding took classes with Howard Pyle at Drexel and benefited from his encouragement and support. The Brandywine River Museum's extensive collection of correspondence from Pyle to Harding shows his admiration for her work and the lengths he would go to in support of a talented student. In 1897, Pyle procured work for Harding doing illustrations for Edward Bulwer-Lytton's novels; along with the commission came an invitation to come to the seashore where, as Pyle said, "I will let you have the use of my Studio in the mornings and will give you criticisms of a half hour a day. . . . For this I shall not charge you anything by way of tuition fee. . . ."[21] During these early years, Harding met with great success, regularly illustrating books and magazines, winning occasional awards for the high quality of her work. Her illustrations for Helen Hay Whitney's *Verses for Jock and Joan* (1905) are representative of her irresistible, somewhat impressionistic drawings of children. The illustration entitled "Algy" (fig. 52) from that book demonstrates her breezy, fluid style. The drawing emphasizes a warm intimacy between mother and son, accentuated by the textures of the wicker chair, shades, and dappled light that further contextualize the drawing. The small dog, Algy, "With *such* an angry face" loves to jump and "kiss" the boy, but the child asserts, "And if some one must kiss me, why/I'd rather have mamma."[22] It is noteworthy that the mother is at the same level as the child, physically embracing him. No longer engaged in the domestic tasks of home, the mother, instead, indulges in the leisure activity of reading. The informality of Harding's image without border and with nature at bay reflects the social changes in the lives of women as well as the new conventions of illustration where emotions can be so cleanly portrayed.

Figure 52.
Charlotte Harding, "Algy," from Helen Hay Whitney, *Verses for Jock and Joan*, 1905, courtesy of Hyde Collection Art Museum.

Charlotte Harding married James Adams Brown in 1905 but continued her work for some years even after the birth of her daughter in 1908. Gradually, however, deadlines were harder to meet, and the strain and demands of the work seem to have taken their toll. A letter from Harding's daughter sheds light on Charlotte Harding's personal dilemma trying to juggle the two demanding roles of mother and artist:

> My only recollection of my mother as an illustrator was when she was doing a rush job for some magazine. One room in the house was set aside for a studio with a screen folded horizontally as a barricade to keep me (four years old) out. Alas, the telephone rang; she went to answer it. I seized the opportunity to 'help' with the picture, stepped across the barricade and added spectacles in charcoal to all the figures. My mother did not spank me; she just sat down and cried. She got the drawing off by the deadline; but I guess that incident marked the beginning of the end of her professional career.[23]

By 1913 when she and her husband and daughter moved to Brooklyn, New York, Charlotte Harding's career had for all intents and purposes ended. No doubt far from the support and comradeship of her fellow artists, she found it harder to maintain the rigorous routines necessary to meet deadlines. In 1925 she wrote to fellow illustrator and Pyle student Thornton Oakley that " . . . a growing daughter precludes work — but in a year or so she will be in college — and I will be back at work!" This hope was never realized. In 1934, Harding donated several illustrations to the Library of Congress, and Leicester B. Holland, chief of the Division of Fine Arts, replied:

> Taste is a matter hard to describe but though I cannot say just why, I always took a particular pleasure in your work. There is a quality of freshness and coolness about it, that somehow gave me the sensation of a stream of running water. The impression hasn't died and your drawings give

me now exactly the same sensation of clear breeziness that they used to.[24]

In 1947, when Thornton Oakley requested some of her drawings for a collection of art by Pyle students, Harding wrote to say that ". . . outside of a few drawings I collected for Washington some years ago, everything else went into a bonfire. I had no reason to keep anything else for that phase of my life had ended years before."[25] Unlike Alice Barber Stephens, Charlotte Harding was unable to juggle the conflicting demands of work and motherhood, and here it must be acknowledged that women, like Stephens, who married artists seemed more likely to be able to continue their careers.

The importance of a supportive environment for one's art can be seen in the communal arrangement of the "Red Rose girls." In 1902, Elizabeth Shippen Green, Jessie Willcox Smith, and Violet Oakely, three up-and-coming illustrators, rented their first communal property, an old inn called the Red Rose, and they were celebrated by their contemporaries as the Red Rose girls. It has been suggested that part of the success of Green, Smith, and Oakley may be attributable to the fact that they created a communal and mutually supportive living situation in which their work could thrive. For fourteen years, 1897–1911, they lived and worked together. Green was the only one to marry; she remained childless. In her article, "A Rose by Any Other Name," Charlotte Herzog explains that "Their professional and financial success made them the idols of a whole generation of women artists. Based on mutual respect and interdependence, their network and community afforded them the time, freedom, money, and control over their lives necessary to succeed as professional artists."[26] Violet Oakley and Jessie Willcox Smith lived in close proximity to each other until Smith's death in 1935. Green moved permanently back to

[257]

the vicinity when widowed in 1951, although she and her husband had owned property in the area for some time before this date. All three women remained committed artists throughout their lives, producing a staggering quantity of work.

Elizabeth Shippen Green managed to sustain a long, successful career as an artist. By the time of her marriage in 1911, Green was forty and beyond child-bearing age for those times, and her reputation was firmly established as a successful illustrator. Green and her architect-administrator husband, Huger Elliott, were clearly comrades in art. Years of clever, witty, and elegantly designed Christmas cards, often with images of the couple nestled somewhere within the city or house where they currently resided, demonstrate a rare combination of domestic and professional intimacy.

Elizabeth Shippen Green was born in Philadelphia on 1 September 1871 and seemed destined to the profession of illustrator. The Free Library of Philadelphia has the set of scrapbooks about her career that she kept for her father, which contain at the very beginning several sketches done by him and one very early one done by Green. The scrapbooks attest to the fact that her "early inclinations were guided by a father devotedly fond of art."[27] After training at the Pennsylvania Academy of Fine Arts, she immediately set out to establish herself as an illustrator. In 1889 at age eighteen, her first published work appeared in the *Philadelphia Times*. Green was already a professional illustrator when she went to study with Howard Pyle at Drexel Institute. She explains in a 1948 letter that, although she was working full time at the *Ladies Home Journal* and the *Saturday Evening Post*, "I had made the stipulation that I might attend Mr. Pyle's lecture classes on composition on two afternoons each week and when he started a night class at the Institute for work from the costumed model. . . I managed to go to that also each night. That was steady work from 8:30 in the morning to ten at night for six days a week but it was so interesting and stimulating that it seemed more like play than work. . . ."[28] Green was to say of Pyle's influence: "In my own experience, it seems to me he did not so much teach me how to draw but he taught me how to interpret life. He taught me, I might say, what philosophy of life I possess."[29]

It was in Pyle's class that Green met Jessie Willcox Smith and Violet Oakley, and in 1897 she moved with them into a studio (which cost eighteen dollars a month). In 1902 the three women rented the Red Rose Inn and moved in along with Green's parents, Oakley's mother, Smith's brother, and a friend of Green's named Henrietta Cozens, who was to become an integral part of the household. In 1901 Green signed an exclusive contract with *Harper's* magazine, continuing her work with them until 1924. By 1905 she was comfortably sharing a restored country estate named Cogslea (C for Cozens, O for Oakley, G for Green and S for Smith) with the Red Rose girls and extended families, but this was their last common residence. At the age of thirty-six she met Huger Elliott. Although they became engaged in a short time, she would not marry until five years later, after her parents whom she had been supporting had died, since she didn't want to burden Elliott with their support.

After fourteen years of sharing a household with Smith and Oakley, Green moved about for some time when Elliott's career as director of various art schools took them first to Providence, then Boston, briefly back to Philadelphia, and on to New York City. During the short residence in Philadelphia, they bought a house that they called Little Garth close to Cogslea, and when Elliott died in 1951, Elizabeth Shippen Green returned to Little Garth and lived there until her death in 1954. Green proved to be one of Pyle's most prolific women students, producing more after her marriage than before. Her career spanned forty-four years and over twenty illustrated books.[30]

Green's elegance and attention to detail is immediately apparent in her drawings. Quilts, tapestries, gardens, and bookcases filled with elegant objects give them their texture and depth. Her skillfulness is demonstrated in the illustration, "Won't you eat just one more kernel, Thomas Jefferson?" (fig. 53) from *Rebecca Mary* (1905) by Annie Hamilton Donnell. Rebecca Mary is an orphan living with a seemingly hard-hearted spinster aunt named Olivia. Thomas Jefferson, her pet rooster, is her only real companion. In this illustration, he is ill and has stopped eating; Rebecca Mary is desperately trying to persuade him to try one more morsel of corn. The importance of the relationship between girl and rooster is emphasized by their stage center position. Thomas Jefferson seems to be almost bowing to his beloved owner, and Rebecca Mary is showing her profound concern and determination to save her one friend from dying. The image is framed by the arbor, with a gorgeous garden below, and a comforting landscape in the distance. In placing the central characters in the foreground, Green has given great poignancy to the relationship between the child and the unlikely recipient of her affection.

In August 1905, *Harper's* published Green's series of eight images for a pictorial essay entitled "The Mistress of the House." All eight illustrations extend irresistible invitations to the reader to enter a world that probably resembled the Cogslea commune. "The Library" (fig. 54), a self-portrait of Green in her own library, shows a woman sitting in a wicker chair with a large picture book on her lap and several at her feet, as she reaches out for more. She is positioned in front of a bookcase upon which we see a series of china objects. The bit of exposed wall exhibits lovely drawings, and the small part of a visible window is framed by floral curtains of a rich texture. Green might very well be at work doing research for a future art project, looking for inspiration amongst the established published artists who have found their place in the oversized art

Figure 53.
Elizabeth Shippen Green, "Won't you eat just one
more kernel, Thomas Jefferson?" from
Annie Hamilton Donnell, *Rebecca Mary*, 1905,
courtesy of Miriam Snow Mathes Historical Children's
Literature Collection, University at Albany,
State University of New York.

[261]

Figure 54.
Elizabeth Shippen Green, "The Library," from "The Mistress of the House," *Harper's*, August 1905, courtesy of Delaware Art Museum.

books that are scattered about the floor and shelves. Both of these images ask that the reader share in their intimate, honest emotions. The self-portrait conveys perfectly the satisfaction of a woman surrounded by books, art, and illustrations — in other words, a woman who can be seen enjoying both professional stature and personal serenity.

In a 1947 letter to Thornton Oakley, Green elaborates on her attraction to the field of illustration: "Painting - sculpture - architecture, naturally, always delighted me but illustration must somehow or other be my métier. For illustration embraces and covers the whole - landscapes, portraiture, character - interpretation - architecture -poetry - pathos - humor - beauty. . . design, color and form - a wide field for everything if one had the gift to interpret them fitly."[31] Green's art suggests she, indeed, possessed that gift, and her letter strongly asserts her love of narration and all the ways in which a picture can tell a story.

Although it has been suggested that Huger Elliott was originally introduced to Cogslea as a suitor for Violet Oakley, the youngest of the Red Rose girls, Oakley had other ambitions. Born in 1874 to a cultured, artistic family, Oakley was the youngest of three daughters. Oakley had studied abroad in Paris and London before returning to Philadelphia to enroll in Howard Pyle's class in 1897. She claimed that Pyle, along with the Pre-Raphaelites, were the two main influences on her work. Oakley began to work in illustration because it was lucrative, and she needed to help support her mother during her father's illness and after his death. With Pyle's encouragement, however, she turned to designing stained-glass windows and eventually murals and was never to return to full-time illustration.

Oakley's reputation today rests mainly on her murals, especially two cycles executed for the Pennsylvania State Capitol from 1902 to 1906. A Philadelphia reporter proclaimed the commission an extraordinary accomplishment, especially for such a young woman: "For the first time in the history of American Art, a woman is to be entrusted with the mural decoration of a great public building."[32] Her success was further feted in a 1912 *Good Housekeeping* article, "Violet Oakley and Her Vision of Life," by Charles Henry Caffin, who admired not just her technique but the fact Oakley's images do not ". . . tie us down to the temporal, the local and the personal, but extend outward in ever-widening circles that embrace the strivings of all men and women toward the universal."[33]

Oakley had always felt the artist had a responsibility to inspire and instruct, and throughout her life she supported the cause of universal peace and brotherhood. From 1927 to 1929 she went to Geneva to record the struggle of the League of Nations and to sketch portraits. Oakley continued her work on portraits, murals, and illuminated manuscripts until her death on 25 February 1961.

Although Oakley's contribution to illustration was limited by her ambitious glass and mural work, she, nonetheless, has a place alongside her Red Rose sisters. She used the pictorial skills she shared with Smith and Green to create her images on a grander scale. Her mural work broke down another set of barriers constructed to protect women from the strains of such large, demanding work. Even in the Caffin article, which purports to speak to Oakley's inner vision and depth, the author cannot resist pointing out that she is a ". . . womanly woman; eagerly receptive, very thoughtful, with eyes that gleam with intelligence and earnestness, yet have a lurking twinkle of quiet humor responding to the smile that hovers in the corners of her sensitive lips."[34] Clearly for Caffin, the power and magnificence of her interpretation of historical and biblical scenes might be thought to threaten her femininity; thus, he felt it important to assure the public that, however strong her work, she was still a "womanly woman." In 1922, Oakley published a portfolio of her Harrisburg murals and, in 1933, a sequel, entitled *Law Triumphant*, which reproduced the murals she had created for the Supreme Court Room and portraits of the League of Nations delegates. Although these are more books of illustrations than illustrated books, they demonstrate the power of Oakley's designs as well as her commitment to her political ideals.

Jessie Willcox Smith, the third member of the Cogslea trio, is probably the American woman illustrator with the most enduring reputation. Her dreamy images of children are reproduced in abundance even today. Smith was born 6 September 1863, the youngest daughter of an investment banker. Here is how Smith describes herself for an entry in *Who's Who*:

> I was born and educated and lived all my life in Philadel-
> phia. At the age of seventeen I began the study of kinder-
> garten as I was always keenly interested in children and
> wanted to do some work connected with them. It came
> purely by accident while in the kindergarten that I discov-
> ered that I had any talent in drawing. The children
> appealed to me more as pictures than as pupils and I was
> advised by an artist to give up teaching and go to art
> school — which I did. I made no mistake. . . .[35]

The story of Smith's accidental discovery of her artistic talent was frequently repeated, as if writers of newspapers and magazine articles about her couldn't resist the idea that without an accidental encounter with drawing, Smith might have lived out her life as another kindergarten teacher, undistinguished, and conceivably unhappy. The encounter happened thus:

> I was asked by my cousin — a young girl like myself, but
> quite an advanced art student — if I would chaperon her
> while she was teaching a friend of hers to draw. The friend

was a young professor in a boy's school who was anxious to learn enough drawing to illustrate on the blackboard his talks to the boys under his tutelage. . . . Friday, I remember it was — not a propitious day on which to discover one's life work. We sat at a large center-table on which a student-lamp was burning, and possibly because that was the most obvious thing in the room, our teacher suggested that we draw the lamp. . . . After two nerve-racking, intense evenings, the young professor gave up in disgust — while I was told to stop teaching kindergarten — at which, I may as well confess, I was not making a brilliant success — and go to art school. This I did, with deep gratitude in my heart to that young professor who wanted to learn to draw.[36]

In 1884 Smith enrolled in the School of Design for Women where she excelled. The next year, she continued her studies at the Pennsylvania Academy of Fine Arts where she learned a great deal about technique, but she found the Academy "stuffy and somber." She graduated in 1888, the year her first drawing was published. By 1889 Smith had begun work at the *Ladies Home Journal*, but in 1894 she enrolled in Drexel to study illustration with Howard Pyle. As happened with so many other of his students, Pyle was to be a primary force in her work. Smith said of Pyle as a teacher, "He seemed to wipe away all the cobwebs and confusions that so beset the path of the art student. . . and with his inspiration and practiced help, I was soon in the full tide of book illustration."[37]

In 1896 Pyle obtained for Smith and Oakley the commission for Henry Wadsworth Longfellow's *Evangeline* (1897). And it was not long before Smith was among the best paid and most sought after women illustrators in the country. By 1903 Smith's reputation was such that she was paid $3,600 to illustrate Robert Louis

Stevenson's *The Child's Garden of Verses*, $200 per full-page color drawing, $75 for the cover design and the lining design, $50 for the title page, and $1,000 for 100 small drawings to distribute throughout the book.[38] A letter from J. Chapin of the Charles Scribner's Sons art department in 1905 begins: "I have used up all my adjectives in acknowledging your various drawings for 'The Child's Garden of Verses' . . . so I will simply say that the last two drawings which reached me today are delightful examples of the sort of thing of which you are master."[39]

From 1906 to 1910 Smith dedicated herself to book illustration with Aileen Higgins's *Dream Blocks* (1908) and Carolyn Wells's *Seven Ages of Childhood* (1909), among the most sought after today. The illustration "Rainy Day" (fig. 55) from *Dream Blocks* demonstrates Smith's extraordinary ability for depicting the intimate relationship between mother and child. The accompanying poem is about the child's initial disappointment about the rainy day and her eventual happiness because "This whole day long had been just mine/And Mother's, in the fireplace glow./Because it rained, it made it so."[40] We can see in this image Smith's skill using realism to create the dreamy interior that so captured the imagination of her readership and still asserts itself as part of our definition of the prosperity and domestic tranquility in the United States in the early decades of the twentieth century. Mother and daughter nestle in a flower-patterned chair, partners in the reading of a book. In the most mundane of activities for a rainy day, Smith depicts both the child's intentness and the mother's patience. The easy elegance of the mother is shown in her flowing skirt and knotted tie. Her hand is wrapped gently around her daughter whose peaceful gravity lends a quiet pleasure to the activity.

The year 1911 was a difficult, transitional one for Smith. Elizabeth Shippen Green's parents died, and Green married Elliott and

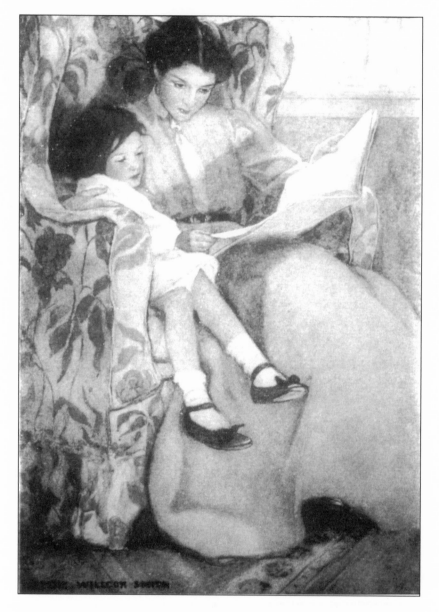

Figure 55.
Jessie Willcox Smith, "Rainy Day," from Aileen C. Higgins,
Dream Blocks, 1908, courtesy of Hyde Collection Art Museum.

[268]

left Cogslea. Violet Oakley was hard at work on another set of murals and was often gone to Harrisburg. And Howard Pyle died while traveling abroad to begin work on murals of his own. As a consolation, Smith acquired a parcel of land near Cogslea and began the project of building a house and studio for herself that she would call Cogshill, maintaining the importance of the Red Rose girls in her life. Smith continued to produce pictures at an extraordinary rate, and she illustrated a multitude of books including *Dickens' Children* (1912), *Jessie Willcox Smith Mother Goose* (1914), Louisa May Alcott's *Little Women* (1915), Charles Kingsley's *The Water Babies* (1916), and George MacDonald's *At the Back of the North Wind* (1919) among others. Simultaneously, she was responsible for a cover illustration for every issue of *Good Housekeeping* from December 1917 to April 1933. Throughout these years, Smith was receiving 10 percent royalties for her book sales and was engaged in doing private portraits of children. Her business savvy is found everywhere in the records of her transactions with publishers and galleries. Her undeniable financial success was clearly the result of the extraordinary popularity of her work and her business acumen.

The Smith archive at the Pennsylvania Academy is filled with letters from mothers wanting her to paint their children, offering their offspring as models, and lavishing praise upon Smith for her glorious illustrations. As Edith Emerson said of her after her death, "The ideals of Jessie Willcox Smith have been woven into the fabric of contemporary thought and impressed upon the consciousness of innumerable mothers who hope that their children will look like the children she paints."[41] There were also many mothers who approached Smith to paint their children as they actually looked. People from as far away as Colorado invited her to come to paint a series of portraits of children. A Mr. Willcox writes that his wife is named Jessie, and they must be related, so won't she please come

West?[42] Praise did not come from parents alone; writers, publishers, and other illustrators wrote letters to "My dear Miss Smith," marveling over her ability to capture and portray childhood and motherhood as no one else was able to do. Articles appeared about "Mother-love in Jessie Willcox Smith's Art." One journalist wrote to Smith to say "that really, whether you will or no, you *do* belong to the public! Teachers and mothers and children all over the country claim you as their own and *long* to hear about you — because of what Mark Sullivan calls in his new book 'the delightfully unsophisticated children immortalized by Jessie Willcox Smith.'"[43]

Smith captured and recreated in her art an essence of childhood and maternal love that could touch an entire generation. Smith remained unmarried by choice; often quoted is a 1932 interview in which she was asked if she ever regretted not marrying or her career? She said "no" to both, but she did go on to say, "To marry and have children is the ideal life for a woman. What career could ever be as fine?"[44] However, a written portrait of Smith, perhaps by Louise Armstrong, which is in the Pennsylvania Academy collection, suggests that: "[t]he hundreds of lovely picture children of Jessie Willcox Smith would never have been born if she had married and had babies of her own for she believes that though an unmarried woman's sphere is as wide as a man's, a married woman's is not. One may be an artist or mother but not both!"[45] This is further elaborated upon when Smith is quoted as saying:

> A woman's sphere is as sharply defined as a man's. If she elects to be a housewife and mother — that is her sphere, and no other. Circumstances may, but volition should not, lead her from it.
>
> If on the other hand she elects to go into business or the arts, she must sacrifice motherhood in order to fill successfully her chosen sphere.[46]

As a woman with a firm control over her personal and business life, Jessie Willcox Smith established a professional path for women artists to follow. Deferential though she might sound about motherhood, surely she is sincere when she says she does not regret her choice of a career over marriage and children. Cogslea, and later Cogshill, were constantly peopled with relatives, friends, and children. Violet Oakley lived close by, and Elizabeth Shippen Green spent what time she could at Little Garth. Most of the domestic aspects of the household were tended to by Henrietta Cozens, who was to live with Smith until Smith's death in 1935. This arrangement left Smith free to promote her art and her career and, judging from the quantity of correspondence in her archive, answer letters. If, as Henry Pitz claims, "her children were remote from sweat, dirt and savagery — dream younglings living in a world of improbable decorum," there were plenty of folks willing to subscribe to that image of childhood, and perhaps for many, that image of life.

In interpreting the work and presence of these women during the golden age of illustration, it is perhaps most difficult to find their voice. If art history has not been particularly helpful in discerning one for them, it is because they are twice-hampered, by both their medium and their gender. The archives and collections are sorely lacking in journals and diaries; what letters have come down to us involve for the most part the material concerns of the business of illustration. Yet this lack of a self-conscious reporting of their experiences points to a need obviated by community. Perhaps these women didn't need to put words on paper since their communal living arrangements gave them ready opportunity to share their ideas and feelings, their frustrations and triumphs, with members of their immediate or extended families of artists. Their principal mode of expression was a pictorial one. We assume at our peril that the vision presented in their art corresponds to their personal one,

Figure 56.
Jessie Willcox Smith, cover illustration, from Aileen C. Higgins, *Dream Blocks*, 1908, courtesy of Hyde Collection Art Museum.

or one commissioned by their publishers. This simplistic rationale has been used to diminish commercial artists for decades. It is, however, unquestionable, that theirs is a voice worth hearing, just as it is a vision worth seeing.

It is hard to deny the verdict that "none of these women achieved powerful intellectual, philosophical, or cultural insights. Most art historians persist in describing them as charming, anecdotal, and decorative."[47] The cover illustration by Jessie Willcox Smith for *Dream Blocks* (fig. 56) encodes several important issues connected to these women and their place in art history and could stand as emblematic of who they were and what they faced. Early illustrators worked engraving on wood blocks from which the prints were made, and it was not until a new, faster, cheaper process became available that women artists were sought out in the field of illustration. Until the proliferation of magazines for women became an economic factor, women were blocked from achieving professional status in such fields as illustration. Finally, economic independence through dignified and profitable professional work was slow in coming to women and must, for a long time, to have seemed a dream, similar to the castle in the sky we see the day-dreaming child building with his blocks. The art produced by these women speaks eloquently of their talent, vision, hard work, and success, and they deserve to be remembered as more than a footnote in American illustration's golden age.

Notes

1. Philip Rodney Pauling, "Illustrators and Illustrating," *Munsey's Magazine* 13, no. 2 (May 1895): 152.
2. Rowland Elzea, *Nostalgic Journey: American Illustration from the Collection of the Delaware Art Museum* (Wilmington, Del.: Delaware Art Museum, 1994), 3.

3. "Jessie Willcox Smith," *Good Housekeeping* 65 (October 1917): 190.

4. Helen Goodman, "Women Illustrators of the Golden Age of American Illustration," *Women's Art Journal* 8 (Spring/Summer 1987): 14.

5. Amos Stote, "The Illustrator and His Income," *Bookman* 28 (September 1908): 25.

6. Regina Armstrong, "Representative American Women Illustrators: The Child Interpreters," *The Critic* 36 (June 1900): 417.

7. Harold Payne, "American Women Illustrators," *Munsey's Magazine* 11 (May 1893): 47.

8. Walt Reed, *The Illustrator in America 1900–1960's* (New York: Reinhold Publishing Company, 1966), 6.

9. Cheryl A. Jones, "American Women and the American Woman Illustrator," *The American Personality: The Artist-Illustrator of Life in the United States, 1860–1930* (Los Angeles, Calif.: The Grunwald Center for the Graphic Arts, 1976), 27.

10. Susan E. Meyer, *America's Great Illustrators* (New York: Excalibur Books, 1978), 14.

11. Howard Pyle, "Why Art and Marriage Won't Mix," *The North American* (19 June 1904) section M, 8, Thornton Oakley Collection of Howard Pyle and his Students, Rare Book Department, Free Library of Philadelphia.

12. Michele H. Bogart, *Artist, Advertising, and the Borders of Art* (Chicago: University of Chicago Press, 1995), 31.

13. "Alice Barber Stephens, Illustrator," *Woman's Progress* 11, no. 2 (November 1893): 49.

14. Letter from A. Conan Doyle to Mr. Askell, 26 February 1895, Alice Barber Stephens Papers, Archives of American Art, Smithsonian Institution.

15. Letter from Edward Bok to Alice Barber Stephens, 23 October 1899, Alice Barber Stephens Papers, Archives of American Art, Smithsonian Institution.

16. Letter from Margaret Deland to Alice Barber Stephens, 6 November 1908, Alice Barber Stephens Papers, Archives of American Art, Smithsonian Institution.

17. Letter from Howard Pyle to Alice Barber Stephens, 2 February 1897, Alice Barber Stephens Papers, Archives of American Art, Smithsonian Institution.

18. Kate Douglas Wiggin, *Susanna and Sue* (Cambridge: The Riverside Press, 1909), 98.

19. Frances W. Marshall, "Qualities that Make for Success in Women Illustrators," *New York Times* (15 December 1912): 11.

20. Anne Barton Brown, *A Pioneer Woman Illustrator* (Chadds Ford, Pa.: Brandywine River Museum, 1984), 35.

21. Letter from Howard Pyle to Charlotte Harding, 15 June 1897, Brandywine River Museum Library.

22. Helen Hay Whitney, *Verses for Jock and Joan* (New York: Fox Duffield and Company, 1905), 18. Ironically, the model for Jock was Alexander Calder, a chubby seven-year-old neighbor whose reputation has far outstripped that of his sketcher.

23. Letter from Charlotte Adams Ganz to Ann Barton Brown, 28 August 1980, Brandywine River Museum Library.

24. Letter from Leicester B. Holland to Charlotte Harding Brown, 20 December 1934, Brandywine River Museum Library.

25. Letter from Charlotte Harding to Thornton Oakley, 15 July 1947, Thornton Oakley Collection of Howard Pyle and his Students, Rare Book Department, Free Library of Philadelphia.

26. Charlotte Herzog, "A Rose by Any Other Name," *Woman's Art Journal* 14 (Fall 1993/Winter 1994): 11.

27. Mary Tracy Earle, "The Red Rose," *The Lamp* 26, no. 4 (1903): 280.

28. Letter from Elizabeth Shippen Green to Mr. Sykes, 6 May 1948, Helen Farr Sloan Library, Delaware Art Museum.

29. Ibid.

30. Catherine Connell Stryker, *The Studios at Cogslea* (Wilmington, Del.: Delaware Art Museum, 1976), 19.

31. Letter from Elizabeth Shippen Green to Thornton Oakley, 12 July 1947, Thornton Oakley Collection of Howard Pyle and his Students, Rare Book Department, Free Library of Philadelphia.

32. "Capital Commission Names Artists," *Philadelphia Press* (23 July 1902) from Patricia Likos, "Violet Oakley, (1874–1961)," *Bulletin*, Philadelphia Museum of Art (June 1979): 5.

33. Charles Henry Caffin, "Violet Oakley and Her Vision of Life," *Good Housekeeping* 54 (October 1912): 477.

34. Ibid., 472.

35. Letter from Jessie Willcox Smith to Mr. Abbott, date unknown, Pennsylvania Academy of Art Archives.

36. "Jessie Willcox Smith," *Good Housekeeping* 65 (October 1917): 25.

37. Ibid., 190.

38. Letter from Charles Scribner's Sons to Jessie Willcox Smith, 23 December 1903, Pennsylvania Academy of Art Archives.

39. Letter from J. Chapin to Jessie Willcox Smith, 26 April 1905, Pennsylvania Academy of Art Archives.

40. Aileen Cleveland Higgins, *Dream Blocks* (New York: Duffield and Company, 1908), 14.

41. Edward D. Nudelman, *Jessie Willcox Smith: American Illustrator* (Gretna: Pelican Publishing Company, 1990), 46.

42. Letter from Orlando Willcox to Jessie Willcox Smith, 5 April 1907, Pennsylvania Academy of Art Archives.

43. Letter from Louise Armstrong to Jessie Willcox Smith, date unknown, Pennsylvania Academy of Art Archives.

44. Nudelman, *Jessie Willcox Smith*, 47.

45. Holograph manuscript (noted to be perhaps from Louise Armstrong), no date, Pennsylvania Academy of Art Archives.

46. Ibid.

47. Shelly Armitage, *Kewpies and Beyond* (Jackson, Miss.: University Press of Mississippi, 1994), 10.

"We All Sit on the Edge of Stools and Crack Jokes": Virginia Woolf and the Hogarth Press

David H. Porter

I. Introduction

I am a classicist, a book collector, and a Hogarth Press enthusiast, but a scholar neither of Bloomsbury nor the history of books. In one respect the very fact that I am an amateur is appropriate to my topic, for Leonard and Virginia Woolf always maintained that they had begun as amateur publishers, and remained such to the end. Virginia's 1930 response to an anonymous purchaser is typical (Letter, 10 December 1930):[1]

Dear Madam,

As one of the guilty parties I bow down to your strictures upon the printing of On Being Ill [a handprinted book by Virginia, published in November 1930]. I agree that the colour is uneven, the letters not always clear, the spacing inaccurate, and the word 'campion' should read 'companion'.

All I have to urge in excuse is that printing is a hobby carried on in the basement of a London house; that as amateurs
all instruction in the art was denied us; that we have picked
up what we know for ourselves; and that we practise printing in the intervals of lives that are otherwise engaged. . .

Yours, with apologies,
Virginia Woolf[2]

Although such claims may seem disingenuous, coming as they do
from proprietors of a publishing house that by this time was both
successful and widely respected, the fact remains that throughout
the history of the Hogarth Press the Woolfs did not see themselves
as professional publishers, as Leonard stresses in his autobiography:

> The organization and machinery of the Press were ama-
> teurish; it was, so far as Virginia and I were concerned, a
> hobby which we carried on in afternoons, when we were
> not writing books and articles or editing papers.

(Downhill All the Way 78)

Yet another parallel between my involvement with the Hogarth
Press and the Woolfs is that neither of us could have guessed
where this would lead us. I fell into collecting Hogarth Press books
because in 1986 I happened upon a nice copy of The Years, purchased it as a gift for my late wife, and in the next few months
picked up a few other Hogarths that caught my fancy. But at the
time I had no idea of building a Hogarth Press collection, nor of
the magnitude of such an undertaking. I also had no notion as to
how absorbing this project would become once I was launched on
it, nor of the fascinating byways into which it would lead me.[3]

In the same way, when the Woolfs purchased the handpress in
1917, they clearly had little thought of becoming proprietors of a

major publishing house, or of the complexities and burdens such a business would entail for the rest of their lives. Nor, I suspect, could they have imagined the delights that would come with this unexpected calling — "it gets ever so much quicker, and the fascination is something extreme," comments Virginia just a month after they have begun printing[4] — or the remarkable new directions in which the Hogarth Press would lead them.

In retrospect, of course, one can see that many of these unexpected outcomes developed naturally, even inevitably, from the Woolfs' backgrounds and interests. While in 1917 the Woolfs would not have expected that by the 1930s they would be publishing a stream of pamphlets on political, economic, and social themes, their decision to undertake such a series is scarcely surprising, given their own interests, and Leonard's political involvements. Similarly, as they printed their first small "paperback" in 1917, they cannot have imagined that within ten years they would be commissioning artists to create dust jackets for numerous substantial hardbound volumes. But Virginia's active involvement in finding papers with which to bind that first book clearly foreshadows their subsequent interest in using a book's cover to enhance its impact. Even the financial success of the Hogarth Press, a success they could not have dreamed of in 1917 but that was to have a major impact on their lives, is implicit in the meticulous accounts Leonard kept from the beginning, and in his satisfaction that their first publication entailed expenditures of three pounds, seven shillings, and realized income of ten pounds, eight shillings — a profit of seven pounds, one shilling (an amount that represents over one-third of their initial capital expenditure for the Press).

It is this counterpoint between the surprises that the Press brought the Woolfs on the one hand, the ways in which these surprises grew naturally from their own interests and personalities on the other, that provides a common thread in the musings that follow.

[279]

II.". . . TO BUY A PRINTING PRESS": A BRIEF OVERVIEW

Accounts of the Hogarth Press often begin with that day in March 1917 when Leonard and Virginia Woolf, walking on London's Farringdon Street, see in a shop window a handpress for sale, with printing instructions included. Leonard captures their delight vividly: "[W]e stared through the window at them rather like two hungry children gazing at buns and cakes in a baker shop window" (*Beginning Again* 234). They return on a subsequent day and for about twenty pounds purchase the press and a supply of type, set up operations in the dining room of their Richmond home, Hogarth House (hence the Press's name), and at once begin teaching themselves how to print. With astonishing rapidity they progress to printing and selling their first book, *Two Stories*, one by each of them, and within weeks they are planning future publications and lining up a list of subscribers.

This familiar account is not incorrect — just incomplete, as Leonard himself makes clear in the section of his autobiography from which I have excerpted the passage above.[5] In fact, the Woolfs had been contemplating this purchase for more than two years. In her diary entry for her thirty-third birthday, 25 January 1915, Virginia writes, "Sitting at tea we decided three things: in the first place to take Hogarth, if we can get it; in the second, to buy a Printing press; in the third to buy a Bull dog, probably called John." From that moment on, printing was on their minds. Leonard hoped that the more manual, rote activities of printing might offer a useful break for Virginia from the intensity of her writing — and from its tendency to precipitate her violent fits of depression,[6] and almost immediately he begins looking for a press.[7] During the same period Virginia asks Roger Fry if she and Leonard may have access to Fry's list of Omega Workshop subscribers — a foretaste of the active interest she will later take in this side of the Press's operation.[8] And Virginia's letters in the fall of 1916 refer to an expected tax refund of £35 that will enable them to purchase a press — and to their disappointment when the refund turns out to be only £15, leaving them five pounds short (i.e., of the £20 needed for the Farringdon Street press).[9] Finally, a letter from Virginia to Vanessa Bell on the very day they bought the Press — 23 March 1917 — makes it clear that the purchase was but the final step in a long process: "I must stop — as we are going to the Farrington Rd. (sic) to buy our press."

While it is thus clear that the Woolfs' purchase was no momentary whim, the press, once owned, proved a constant source of surprise — as well as more than occasional frustration — and a repeated spur to improvisation. The childlike delight they felt as they viewed the press through the shop window colors their days once it arrives in late April. Almost immediately they print a small notice, awkwardly typeset but to the point, announcing their intention to publish their own "two stories," and soliciting subscriptions.[10] Shortly thereafter, Virginia writes Ottoline Morrell for suggestions as to possible subscribers; by 22 May she is printing Leonard's "Three Jews," and sixty orders are in;[11] and on 8 June she writes her sister that she is looking for paper in which to wrap the book. By early July [Dora] Carrington's illustrations for the book are in hand, and by mid-July the covers are printed and the book is off to subscribers — less than three months after the press arrived at Hogarth House.

Virginia's 13 July letter to Carrington suggests the improvisatory tenor of these early days, as the Woolfs simultaneously taught themselves the craft and printed 150 copies of their first book:

We like the wood cuts immensely. It was very good of you to bring them yourself — We have printed them off, and they make the book much more interesting than it would have been without. The ones I like best are the servant girl and the plates, and the Snail.

Our difficulty was that the margins would mark; we bought a chisel, and chopped away, I am afraid rather spoiling one edge. . .

[The Press] is specially good at printing pictures, and we see that we must make a practice of always having pictures.

The challenges Virginia describes here were nothing, however, in comparison with what they encountered in their next major project, Katherine Mansfield's *Prelude*.[12] Not only was this book far longer than *Two Stories* — sixty-eight pages compared to thirty-one — but the Woolfs also decided on a print run of 300, twice that of their first book. The process stretched over nine months — from October 1917 to July 1918 — and outstripped the capacity of their handpress, so that Leonard ended up carrying the chases to a nearby shop where he could print them on a treadle press.[13] Many years later he commented on the unanticipated magnitude of this early undertaking:

When I look at my copy of *Prelude* today, I am astonished at our courage and energy in attempting it and producing it only a year after we had started to teach ourselves to print. (*Beginning Again* 237)

A more pleasant surprise was to come approximately a year later, about a month after their publication on 12 May 1919 of Virginia's story, *Kew Gardens*. The book's bold mingling of text, illustration, and book design — covers hand painted by Roger Fry with strokes and dabs of blue, green, and dusky rose on a black background (Plate 2 fig. 57); woodcuts by Vanessa Bell that magically echo the story's interplay of animate nature with the flowers and plants of Kew Gardens — caught the attention of the *Times Literary Supplement*, as Virginia recalls (Diary, 10 June 1919):

> . . . [W]e came back from Asheham to find the hall table stacked, littered, with orders for Kew Gardens. They strewed the sofa, & we opened them intermittently through dinner, & quarrelled, I'm sorry to say, because we were both excited . . . All these orders — 150 about, from shops & private people — come from a review in the Lit. Sup. presumably by Logan, in which as much praise was allowed me as I like to claim.[14]

From this time on, the Hogarth Press was a public success such as the Woolfs could never have anticipated — and brought corresponding demands, also unanticipated, on their time and energy. Within days, for instance, in order to capitalize on the unexpected interest in *Kew Gardens*, they arranged with a commercial printer to produce a second edition, this time of 500 copies, and rushed into print as well a 1,000-copy second edition of *The Mark on the Wall*, Virginia's contribution to *Two Stories*. They also soon embarked on an ambitious series of further publications, most of them commercially printed. The numbers document their ever-accelerating level of activity: whereas from 1917 through 1920 they produced a total of eleven books, they published six in 1921, nine in 1922, and fourteen in 1923; by 1925 they were publishing at least twenty-five books each year, many of them far more substantial in scope than they would have dreamed of in the early days.[15]

Some of the directions in which they moved in this first decade are predictable — books, many of them hand printed, by Bloomsbury writers and associates such as Roger Fry, Clive and Vanessa Bell, John Maynard Keynes, E. M. Forster — and, of course, themselves.[16] But one doubts that a few years earlier the Woolfs could have imagined that from 1920 to 1924 they would publish nine translations from the Russian by authors such as Tolstoy, Dostoevsky, Chekhov, Bunin, Gorky, and Andreev — even the Archpriest Avvakum; that beginning in 1921 they would take over the English publications of the International Psycho-Analytical Library and produce within the 1920s alone twelve works by Sigmund Freud, Ernest Jones, and other leaders in the field; or that by 1924 they would be embarked on the first of two series of Hogarth Essays (thirty-five in all, including essays by T. S. Eliot, Robert Graves, Edith Sitwell, John Maynard Keynes, and Gertrude Stein); by 1928 on the Hogarth Living Poets (twenty-nine books in all, including poets such as Robinson Jeffers, Edwin Arlington Robinson, C. Day Lewis, and John Lehmann); and by 1930 on the Hogarth Day to Day Pamphlets (forty in all, featuring authors as diverse as Harold Laski, Benito Mussolini, H. G. Wells, and W. H. Auden).[17] And even those who know the Hogarth Press and its history well are amazed by later entries such as the following:

Adventures in Investing by "Securitas"[18] (1936)

Diet and High Blood Pressure, by Dr. I. Harris (1937)

Can I Help You? Your Manners — Menus — Amusements — Friends — Charades — Make-Ups — Travel — Calling — Children — Love Affairs, by Viola Tree (1937)[19]

****

Since the larger story of the Press has been well covered in a number of other accounts, in what follows I shall focus on two specific areas — Virginia's own day-by-day involvement in the Press, and some different ways in which the Woolfs used visual means to enhance their books.

III. "A FURY OF FOLDING AND STAPLING" :
VIRGINIA WOOLF AND THE PRESS

The degree to which the Press intrudes on the lives of the Woolfs and on their writing, and their frustration and even anger with these intrusions, is a frequent leitmotif in the writings of both Virginia and Leonard, and from time to time they seriously considered selling the Press. They also tried repeatedly, usually with but modest success, to find appropriate assistants to help meet its unending demands. At the same time, both of them were passionately involved in the Press — and consequently unwilling to let go to the degree necessary for them either to sell it or to make full use of the assistance others could give. This was notoriously true of Leonard, who was both brilliant at managing the Press — at seeing the larger picture — and also inextricably involved in its minute operational details. His constitutional inclination to micromanage at times infuriated everyone with whom he worked, but it was undoubtedly also one reason that the Press succeeded as it did, and maintained such a high qualitative level.

Virginia was no less involved. She and Leonard had hoped the Press might entail some rote, nonliterary activities that would benefit her physically and mentally; neither of them can have imagined, however, just how many, varied, and onerous such activities would be for her. With the hand-printed books, she took part in virtually every aspect of production, from typesetting and proofreading to finding, stitching, and sewing the covers. And for the larger Hogarth list she was constantly involved in getting books to the public — identifying possible subscribers, answering inquiries, "traveling" the books to dealers throughout England, and wrapping and mailing copies to purchasers. And, perhaps most time-consuming, throughout the rest of her life Virginia devoted long hours to reading manuscripts sent for possible publication, an activity that became increasingly onerous as the Press gained public recognition but that even in the early days was a drain on her time and energy.

By far the best way to understand the range of these activities and their impact on Virginia's daily life is to let her speak for herself through the words of her letters and diary. She constantly refers, for instance, to the challenges encountered in producing the early hand-printed books. On Hope Mirrlees's *Paris. A Poem* she comments in 1920:

> Half blind with writing notices, & corrections in 160 copies of Paris, a Poem, by Hope Mirrlees. (Diary, 24 April 1920)

The following year finds her working for months on Roger Fry's *Twelve Original Woodcuts* — with Roger himself frequently part of the action:

> Roger again last night, scraping at his woodcuts while I sewed; the sound like that of a large pertinacious rat.
> (Diary, 12 April 1921)

> Roger's woodcuts, 150 copies, have been gulped down in 2 days. I have just finished stitching the last copies — all but six. (Diary, 25 November 1921)

In 1923 she comments on the travails involved for both Leonard and her in producing Clive Bell's *The Legend of Monte Della Sibilla* and T.S. Eliot's *The Waste Land*:

> But I must descend to the basement, & see whats doing with Clive's cover; which Leonard does for 8 hours daily.
> (Diary, 3 November 1923)

I have just finished setting up the whole of Mr Eliots poem
with my own hands: You see how my hand trembles.
(Letter, 8 July 1923, to Barbara Bagenal)

The books once produced had to be marketed, and Virginia
showed from the beginning a perhaps surprising taste and talent
for this entrepreneurial side of the operation. In an undated letter,
apparently written in May 1917 just weeks after the arrival of the
handpress, she writes Ottoline Morrell to enlist her assistance in
finding subscribers for the Press's first publication, *Two Stories*:

We find we have only 50 friends in the world — and most
of them stingy. Could you think of any generous people —
they need not be very generous — whose names you would
send me? If so, I should very grateful.

The initial excitement wears off in time, of course, and by the
mid-twenties and early thirties Virginia's comments reveal the
strain of the continuing pressure to market and sell the books the
Press is now pouring forth:

We are having rather a grind at the moment to get Viola
going again [the Woolfs had just published Viola Tree's
Castles in the Air. The Story of My Singing Days]. Twenty
four sandwichmen are parading the West End today, and I
have just travelled Kensington High Street . . . (Letter, 19
May 1926, to Vanessa Bell)

We have been driving all day from Taunton over Dart-
moor in a storm, and selling books where we saw a shop,
but its disheartening business. No one reads, no one wants
books, the booksellers say, and they keep us hanging about.
(Letter, 6 May 1930, to Ethel Smyth)

[287]

"Traveling books," the phrase Virginia uses for these marketing efforts, was at least only an intermittent obligation, one that fluctuated with the seasons, and that could upon occasion be combined with recreational travel. The same could not be said for another activity that rapidly became part of Virginia's and Leonard's daily routine — reading manuscripts. From surprisingly early on in the history of the Hogarth Press, the Woolfs found themselves bombarded by manuscripts, usually unsolicited, from authors and would-be authors eager to have their work appear under the Hogarth Press imprimatur.[20] Some of Virginia's most delightful comments on the Press grow out of her understandable impatience over this constant invasion on her time and energy:

> I am weighed down by innumerable manuscripts. Edith Sitwell; 20 dozen poets; one man on birth control; another on religion in Leeds; and the whole of Gertrude Stein, which I flutter with the tips of my little fingers, but dont open. I think her dodge is to repeat the same word 100 times over in different connections, until at last you feel the force of it.[21] (Letter, 24 August 1925, to V. Sackville-West)

> I am sitting over the fire with masses of virgin — what d'you think I'm going to say? — typescript by my side; novels six foot thick to be read instantly or I shall be knived by cadaverous men at Bournemouth whose life depends on my verdict; and amorous typists. They write because they cant have their nights to their liking. This is hard on me. They write to revenge themselves upon the young man at the fish shop, or the young woman in red at the flower shop.
> (Letter, 17 February 1930, to Quentin Bell)

> I thought I should feel in the mood for letter writing between tea and dinner, after a walk over the downs. But I

16. George Cruikshank, *Ah! Sure Such a Pair*, colored etching, 23 June 1820.

[Plate 1]

57. Cover, hand painted by Roger Fry, for Virginia Woolf,
Kew Gardens, 1919.

[Plate 2]

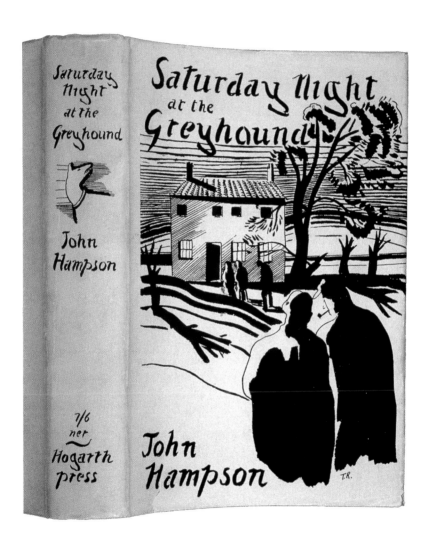

58. Jacket, designed by Trekkie Ritchie, for John Hampson,
Saturday Night at the Greyhound, 1931.

[Plate 3]

60. Jacket, designed by Anthony Butts, for Laurens Van der Post, *In a Province*, 1934.

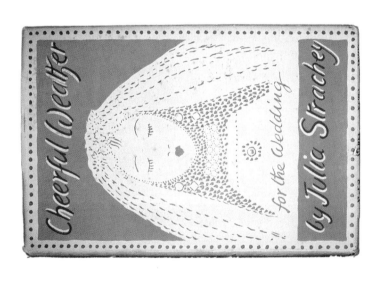

59. Jacket, designed by Duncan Grant, for Julia Strachey, *Cheerful Weather for the Wedding*, 1932.

[Plate 4]

62. Jacket, designed by Vanessa Bell, for Virginia Woolf, *Jacob's Room*, 1922.

61. Jacket, designed by John Armstrong, for William Plomer, *Sado*, 1931.

[Plate 5]

64. Jacket, designed by E. McKnight Kauffer, for Leonard Woolf, *Quack, Quack!*, 1935.

63. Jacket, designed by Vanessa Bell, for Virginia Woolf, *To the Lighthouse*, 1927.

[Plate 6]

66. Cover, designed by Dora Carrington, for Leonard Woolf, *Stories of the East*, 1921.

65. Cover paper, Roger Fry, *Twelve Original Woodcuts*, 1921.

[Plate 7]

67. Four covers, for Fredegond Shove, *Daybreak*, 1922.

68. Two covers, for Hope Mirrlees, *Paris. A Poem*, 1920.

[Plate 8]

have wasted the time reading a manuscript — the slow sickliness of which, falling on me drop by drop, has completely extinguished my love of words. And I have at least six more to read. When you analyse my moods, make allowance for the pervasion of bad fiction or do I mean perversion? (Letter, 22 March 1931, to Ethel Smyth)

Given the burden of these unending labors, one is surprised less by Virginia's occasionally acerbic tone than by the generous seasoning of wit. Indeed, the comments evoked by her constant assessment of authors often reveal Virginia at her lapidary best:

Mr Eliot is an American of the highest culture, so that his writing is almost unintelligible.[22] (Letter, 8? May 1919, to Violet Dickinson)

We are. . . busy printing a new long poem by a short fat poetess [Ruth Manning Sanders], who came to correct her proofs the other day and stayed for 2 hours and a half, like a baby sucking a coral, discussing her genius. But she was very nice, and very modest. Poetry is not like prose. Clearly these poets feel themselves the mouthpiece of God in a way which I certainly dont.[23] (Letter, 6 February 1922, to Lady Robert Cecil)

Devil that you are, to vanish to Persia and leave me here! — dabbling in wet type, which makes my fingers frozen; and setting up the poems of Mrs Manning Sanders, which the more I set them, the less I like. (Letter, 17 February 1926, to V. Sackville-West)

. . . Miss Winter has asked us to ask Mr Robinson Jeffers to tea because he is only in London for a week and will then return to a cave in California and write immortal poetry

for ever. Mr Jeffers is a genius so one must see him. (Letter,
4 October 1929, to Gerald Brenan)

Whatever its burdens and frustrations, the reading of manuscripts clearly also challenged Virginia's literary sensibilities and
brought its own fascinations. And there were those welcome
occasions where she could respond with enthusiasm, as she does in
her reactions to Mirrlees's *Paris* and Eliot's *Waste Land*, or with
compassion, as in her comment on John Hampson, a homosexual
author who had risen from the lowest classes and survived a spell
in prison to publish two novels with the Hogarth Press:[24]

> She [Hope Mirrlees] knows Greek and Russian better than
> I do French; is Jane Harrison's favourite pupil, and has
> written a very obscure, indecent, and brilliant poem,
> which we are going to print. (Letter, 17 August 1919, to
> Margaret Llewelyn Davies)

> Eliot dined last Sunday & read his poem. He sang it &
> chanted it rhythmed it. It has great beauty & force of
> phrase: symmetry; & tensity. What connects it together,
> I'm not so sure. But he read till he had to rush — letters to
> write about the London Magazine — & discussion thus was
> curtailed. One was left, however, with some strong emo-
> tion. The Waste Land, it is called; & Mary Hutch, who has
> heard it more quietly, interprets it to be Tom's autobiogra-
> phy — a melancholy one.[25] (Diary, 23 June 1922)

> The Saturday night man [John Hampson, whose *Saturday
> Night at the Greyhound* the Woolfs published in 1931] is
> most curious — ravaged, exhausted, has been a bootboy, a
> waiter, also in prison — but so shy its difficult to catch
> him. (Letter, 26 June 1931, to Ottoline Morrell)

IV. ". . .A PRACTICE OF ALWAYS HAVING PICTURES":
HOGARTH PRESS COVERS AND ILLUSTRATIONS

In an earlier section I quoted Virginia's comment to Carrington about her illustrations for *Two Stories:* ". . . we see that we
must make a practice of always having pictures." A number of
Hogarth publications respond to this intention, many of them —
interestingly — books with close ties to Bloomsbury. Vanessa Bell,
for instance, created woodblock prints not only for *Kew Gardens*
but also for another early book by Virginia, *Monday or Tuesday.*[26]
Roger Fry contributed four significant illustrated books — *Twelve
Original Woodcuts* (1921) and *A Sampler of Castile* (1923), both
featuring his own work; and important studies of Duncan Grant
(1923) and Cézanne (1927), the latter of special interest because
of Fry's role in the First Post-Impressionist Exhibition of 1910,
which had so focused English attention on Cézanne. Fry and Virginia Woolf herself wrote introductions to a handsome 1926 volume on the art of Julia Margaret Cameron (Virginia's great aunt),
Victorian Photographs of Famous Men & Fair Women.[27] Duncan
Grant and Vanessa Bell together illustrated Clive Bell's 1923 *jeu
d'esprit*, *The Legend of Monte Della Sibilla*,[28] and Vanessa provided
elegant illustrations and page decorations for a limited edition of
Kew Gardens in 1927 as well as line drawings for *Flush*, Virginia's
1933 "biography" of Elizabeth Barrett Browning's spaniel. V.
Sackville-West's two early travel books, *Passenger to Teheran*
(1926) and *Twelve Days* (1928), have numerous illustrations; and
Orlando, Virginia's "love letter" to V. Sackville-West,[29] has wonderful photographic illustrations, some featuring Vita posing as the
novel's hero/heroine. Two of the Press's more idiosyncratic publications, Ernst Benkard's *Undying Faces. A Collection of Death
Masks* (1929) and Ralph Brewster's *The 6,000 Beards of Athos*
(1935), contain numerous photographs, as do several family
chronicles and travel books.[30]

Nonetheless, the Woolfs did not come close to fulfilling their intention "always to have pictures." Only about one in seven of the books they published between 1917 and 1946, when Leonard sold out his share of the Press, is illustrated, and a similar ratio obtains even among the hand-printed books: of the thirty-four published between 1917 and 1932, only five are illustrated. There are two other ways, however, in which the Woolfs richly fulfilled their intention to enhance their publications by visual means — the dust jackets they commissioned for their books, and the covers and labels they created for the smaller publications.

The list of those who created dust jackets for Hogarth books includes many leading artists and illustrators of the time. The jackets illustrated in this volume (Plates 3-6 figs. 58–64) are representative of Hogarth jackets in the artistic distinction and evocative power their designers brought to this ephemeral art form. Just as Virginia Woolf's words provide the best entrée into the daily life of the Press, so these illustrations are the best testimony to the Woolfs' attention to this way of "always having pictures."

Trekkie Ritchie (subsequently married to Eric Parsons, and in later years Leonard Woolf's close associate) designed a jacket for John Hampson's *Saturday Night at the Greyhound* (1931) that powerfully evokes the loneliness, even lostness, of the people who congregate at the country inn named in the novel's title (Plate 3 fig. 58). The elongated, groping silhouettes and shadows of the trees dwarf the building and stretch their long fingers toward the two hunched men in the foreground; the design continues onto the book's spine in the figure of a lone dog, head raised, teeth slightly bared, who lurks outside the inn — Ritchie's version of the punning Press device, a wolf's-head, that typically appears on Hogarth spines.

In contrast to the dark tones and mood of Ritchie's jacket, Duncan Grant's piquant jacket for *Cheerful Weather for the Wedding* limns in pinks and light aqua a doll-like bride with rosebud lips and closed eyes — a figure whose not-quite innocent demureness perfectly echoes the blithe insouciance of Julia Strachey's 1932 novel (Plate 4 fig. 59). Anthony Butts's jacket for Laurens Van der Post's *In a Province* (1934), done entirely in somber browns and tans, superimposes a transparent Caucasian face in profile on a solid but mask-like African-American face, seen head-on, and places both against the backdrop of the map of Africa (Plate 4 fig. 60). John Armstrong's striking jacket for *Sado* (1931) uses a bold, stylized, Art Deco Asian figure, drawn in deep purplish blue on a white background, to lead the reader into William Plomer's fictionalized account of a relationship he had had with a young Japanese man (Plate 5 fig. 61).

Perhaps the most characteristic Hogarth jackets are those Vanessa Bell created for Virginia's books, though Leonard points out that the first one they commissioned, for *Jacob's Room* (Plate 5 fig. 62), was far from an immediate success:

> It is, I think, a very good jacket and today no bookseller would feel his hackles or his temperature rise at sight of it. But it did not represent a desirable female or even Jacob or his room, and it was what in 1923 many people would have called reproachfully post-impressionist. It was almost universally condemned by the booksellers, and several of the buyers laughed at it.[31]

Leonard slightly overstates the case, since the jacket's curtains and vase of flowers at least hint at Jacob's room, but he is right in identifying the jacket's nonliteral, design-oriented character. The same indirection is typical of Vanessa's jackets in general. She begins with a strong, emotionally evocative design, often somewhat symmetrical; only when one studies the design more closely does one catch her allusions to the story — e.g., the powerful burst of light that erupts from the tree-like lighthouse on her jacket for *To the Lighthouse* (Plate 6 fig. 63).

Both thematically and visually, Hogarth Press publications throughout the 1930s bespeak the Woolfs' keen awareness of the rising threat of fascism. In 1932, a year before Hitler came to power, they published Louis Golding's *A Letter to Adolf Hitler*, a powerful indictment of Hitler's antisemitism, and the following year they brought out an English translation of Mussolini's *The Political and Social Doctrine of Fascism*. In 1935 Leonard published his own *Quack, Quack!*, a devastating attack on the mob mentality that was fueling the rise of Hitler and Mussolini; he followed this in 1936 with *The League and Abyssinia*, a short book on the League of Nation's inept response to Italy's invasion of Abyssinia. Dust jackets commissioned by the Woolfs during this period make their concern poignantly visible. The unsigned jacket for Libby Benedict's 1938 novel, *The Refugees*, for instance, has a tan jacket literally covered with small black swastikas — on front, back, and spine — and both the front and the back of the jacket also have large swastikas, again black, superimposed on the others and fashioned out of barbed wire. E. McKnight Kauffer's jacket for Leonard's *Quack, Quack!*, in stark black, blue, red, and white, juxtaposes a terrifying image of the savage war-god Kukailimoku with photographs of Mussolini and Hitler, each with arms outstretched in demagogic poses (Plate 6 fig. 64). John Banting's jacket for Christopher Isherwood's *Mr. Norris Changes Trains* (1935) is more subtle in approach, but its muted brown and tan tones, the spidery, shaded lettering of its title, and the juxtaposition at the foot of its cover of a cross-like pair of stockinged legs with a swastika and a hammer and sickle all ominously foreshadow the tale of escalating international espionage the reader will find within.[32]

The Woolfs devoted similar attention to commissioning wrappers for their smaller publications, most of which did not have dust jackets. For the Hogarth Essays and Hogarth Living Poets, Vanessa Bell created a variety of highly decorative designs. John Banting provided a bold cover template for the Hogarth Letters, realized on the various letters in different bright colors on a cream background — red, blue, green, brown, purple, yellow. And E. McKnight Kauffer created for the covers of the Day to Day Pamphlets a modernized, Art Deco version of the characteristic wolf's-head device.[33]

Above all, however, there are the unique covers the Woolfs themselves created for many of their early books, and their own constant involvement in this aspect of book production. Leonard refers in his autobiography to the special attention they paid to finding appropriate papers with which to wrap their books:

> For many years we gave much time and care to finding beautiful, uncommon, and sometimes cheerful paper for binding our books, and, as the first publishers to do this, I think we started a fashion which many of the regular, old established publishers followed. We got papers from all over the place, including some brilliantly patterned from Czechoslovakia, and we also had some marbled covers made for us by Roger Fry's daughter in Paris. (*Beginning Again* 236)

This aspect was always of particular interest to Virginia. We have seen that in early June of 1917, as she and Leonard completed the printing of the first of their two stories, she was already looking for special paper with which to bind the book,[34] and that two years later Fry's hand-painted covers played a major role in the dazzling success of her *Kew Gardens*. Characteristically, though, Virginia's involvement in this latter instance focused on economic as well as aesthetic considerations. Just weeks before *Kew Gardens* was to appear, she asked Duncan Grant if he and Vanessa Bell could create covers for a substantial portion of the run. "We have bought 25/- worth off Roger [Fry], but they only cover 80 copies, and there are 150," she wrote, then continued:

> [T]he price seems to me extortionate — at anyrate impossible, so I have told him to do no more. The size is 12 inches across and 9½ the other way. We should want enough for 70 copies. Perhaps you could send me a sample if you would do it, and could do it cheaper than Roger. It ought to be on as stiff and thick paper as possible. We are only waiting now for the covers: and there need be no likeness between one cover and another. (Letter, 17 April 1919)

A couple of years later she pointed out to her sister that the cover paper for Fry's *Twelve Original Woodcuts*, one of their most handsome books (Plate 7 fig. 65), "was not designed by Carrington; I get it from a little man in Holborn; it is clearly an imitation of the Kew Gardens cover" (Letter, 13 November 1921). By the following year she was yet more closely involved, as she tells Vanessa in a 10 August 1922 letter: "I have been employing myself in making coloured papers, with wild success."

The Woolfs' special attention to covers occasioned a dispute with Katherine Mansfield over *Prelude*. Mansfield wanted the cover to carry a stylized picture of a woman by her friend J. D. Fergusson; the Woolfs did not like it (the design "makes our gorges rise," wrote Virginia on 24 May 1918 to Ottoline Morrell) and ended up printing a few copies with the Fergusson design for Mansfield and her close friends but replacing this cover with plain dark-blue wrappers on subsequent copies.[35]

[296]

They were to be involved in a similar, even more petty dispute a few years later with the poet Laura Riding, though this time the focus was on a book's title page, not its cover. During the period when the Woolfs were handsetting her *Voltaire. A Biographical Fantasy* (1927), Riding divorced her husband, Louis Gottschalk, and requested that her name appear on the book's title page as "Laura Riding," with "Gottschalk" in parentheses. Her request came late enough in the process, and after enough other difficulties between Riding and Leonard Woolf, that Leonard complied only to the extent of leaving the name as it had been but placing two thick black cancel bars through the offending portion of the name: LAURA RIDING ~~GOTTSCHALK~~. The result is a thoroughly ugly title page — one of those rare instances where personal animus apparently blunted the Woolfs' aesthetic sensibilities!

Though many of the early books are covered with handsome but generic paper that is marbled or has bright, repeated designs, some covers reflect more specifically the contents of the book. For Leonard Woolf's *Stories of the East* (1921), Carrington crafted a bold woodblock, printed in red ink on the tan covers, showing a stalking, teeth-bared tiger framed by two palm trees (Plate 7 fig. 66). Vanessa Bell and Duncan Grant's cover design for Clive Bell's *The Legend of Monte Della Sibilla* (1923) features a sensuous nymph rising from the sea. Delicate black feathers float across the pink paper covers of Robert Graves's *The Feather Bed* (1923). Nancy Cunard's *Parallax* (1925) has cover drawings by Eugene McCown — tilted buildings on the front, distorted trees on the back — that, as one critic puts it, "show splendidly the skewed perspectives of the poem" (Willis 117).

Virginia's comment to Duncan Grant that "there need be no likeness between one cover and another" is apropos for many early Hogarth Press books, for the Woolfs seem to delight in using different papers for different copies of the same book. Their very first publication, *Two Stories*, sets the pattern by using at least three different covers within its run of just 150 copies. The most familiar paper, and perhaps the earliest, features a complex linear design in bright red on a white background, but some copies of the book have simple dull-yellow wrappers, still others a woven, fabric-like blue paper. The small 1919 collection of seven T. S. Eliot *Poems*, published at the same time as *Kew Gardens*, appears at times in its own hand-painted paper by Roger Fry — bright oranges, greens, browns — at others in the blue woven or red patterned papers the Woolfs had used for *Two Stories*. Fredegond Shove's *Daybreak*, a book of rather undistinguished poems published in 1922 in a print run of only 250, appears in a riot of different bindings (four of which are illustrated in Plate 8 fig. 67).[36] Of the thirty-four hand-printed books, close to half appear in at least two different covers, and quite a few of the early, commercially printed books show similar variations.[37]

An apparently rare variant of another early book, Hope Mirrlees's *Paris. A Poem*, is especially intriguing. Like other copies, it contains Virginia's inked-in corrections of the two misprints in the text. But it differs from most other copies in that where the usual binding has red, gold, and *blue* diamonds, this variant has the same pattern — but with bright *green* diamonds (Plate 8 fig. 68).[38] It is of particular interest that Virginia apparently used this same variant paper to bind the notebook, now in the Berg Collection of the New York Public Library, which contains her holograph draft of the first portion of *Jacob's Room*.[39] It's a touch that carries one straight back to the Woolfs' home *cum* workshop, at a time when Virginia is both beginning *Jacob's Room* (the holograph is dated 15 April 1920) and also binding and correcting misprints in *Paris* (as she mentions in her diary on 24 April — just nine days later): one day, in the midst of handling the many copies of *Paris*, she chooses (or happens?) to use for a few copies the slightly different paper with which she has just bound the notebook in which she will compose her new novel.[40]

In the earliest hand-printed books — *Two Stories* and *Prelude* — the Woolfs printed the title and other basic information directly on the covers of the book, a procedure that often proved not very successful. The cover printing on *Two Stories* works well enough on the drabbest (and perhaps least frequent) of the three papers used to bind this book, the dull yellow, but gets lost amidst the busy design of the red paper and shows up poorly on the blue. The cover of Mansfield's *Prelude* is an even deeper blue — and the printing on it consequently even harder to see.[41] The Woolfs rapidly realized that in such cases paper labels affixed to their books would more effectively highlight the title and other important information, and they adopted this procedure for their next books — Eliot's *Poems, Kew Gardens*, Mirrlees's *Paris* — and for most subsequent hand-printed books, often with great success (see, for instance, the brilliant effect achieved by the combination of cover paper and decorated label on Fry's *Twelve Original Woodcuts* [Plate 7 fig. 65]). As might be expected, intriguing variations appear also in these early labels. Those for the T. S. Eliot *Poems*, for instance, are in red ink for a time, then shift to black; those for Eliot's *The Waste Land* (published by the Woolfs soon after the first edition appeared in 1922) appear in three different forms, as do those for E. M. Forster's *The Story of the Siren*, another early publication (with one version of the Forster label sporting brilliant gold borders against the marbled sea-blues and sea-greens of the two variant covers).[42]

V. CONCLUSION: FREEDOM — AND "RIDING A GREAT HORSE"

We have seen that Virginia and Leonard had high hopes that work on the Press might afford Virginia a change of pace and of focus, a measure of daily freedom from the intensity of her writing.

[299]

That it would in fact provide her a far more important freedom — one central to her life as a writer — had not been in their minds, but such indeed proved to be the case. In a diary entry of 22 September 1925, Virginia calls herself "the only woman in England free to write what I like." The basis for this claim, as Virginia explicitly indicates in the same entry, is that from 1919 on she could publish virtually everything she wrote through the Hogarth Press. This "Press of Her Own," as we might call it, brought her a rare and valued degree of artistic freedom:

> How my handwriting goes down hill! Another sacrifice to the Hogarth Press. Yet what I owe the Hogarth Press is barely paid by the whole of my handwriting. Haven't I just written to Herbert Fisher refusing to do a book for the Home University Series on Post Victorian? — knowing that I can write a book, a better book, a book off my own bat, for the Press if I wish! To think of being battened down in the hold of those University dons fairly makes my blood run cold.

As to the Woolfs' hope that the Press would provide Virginia daily respite from stress and strain, we have seen that its impact was frequently just the opposite, a point underscored by an 8 July 1923 letter from Virginia to Barbara Bagenal:

> I assure you the Press is worse than 6 children at breast simultaneously . . . Leonard and I live apart — he in the basement, I in the printing room. We meet only at meals, often so cross that we can't speak, and generally dirty.[43]

And yet, despite the associated stress on both of them, in a strange way the Press did indeed have a salutary impact on Virginia. A diary entry of 9 July 1918, written at the very time when Virginia was desperately working to complete Mansfield's *Prelude*, suggests some considerable satisfaction amidst the pressure:

> I cant fill up the lost days, though it is safe to attribute much space in them to printing. The title page was finally done on Sunday. Now I'm in the fury of folding & stapling, so as to have all ready for glueing & sending out tomorrow & Thursday. By rights these processes should be dull; but its always possible to devise some little skill or economy, & the pleasure of profiting by them keeps one content.

And during the similarly intense period when Virginia was struggling to complete Eliot's *Waste Land* — and finding the Press comparable to six children at breast — she writes:

> As for the press, we have finished Tom, much to our relief. . . [W]e have worked at full speed since May. & that is I'm persuaded the root & source & origin of all health & happiness, provided of course that one rides work as a man rides a great horse, in a spirited & independent way; not a drudge, but a man with spurs in his heels. (Diary, 28 July 1923)

A letter of 22 October 1929 to V. Sackville-West conveys even more vividly Virginia's contentment with the daily Press routine and also evokes an earthy everyday-ness that contrasts sharply with the frequent image of Virginia as an esoteric genius somehow disconnected from the real world. Her description of herself drinking tea and bantering with colleagues amidst the clutter and bustle of the Press is an appropriate place to leave her, suggesting as it does the degree to which, in ways the Woolfs could not have imagined when they began printing books, the Hogarth Press had

[301]

indeed given Virginia daily duties that proved both enjoyable and restorative — and that took her away from the terrifying privacy of her writing:

> Yes I would very much like to see you on Wednesday, but I cant manage a matinée — for one thing I always snore; then we're very brisk at the Press, and my services are in demand — how I like it! doing up parcels, please remember open ends, Mrs Woolf, with bagmen coming in and out and saying Well good bye all when they leave; and we all say good bye. And then I'm given a cup of pale lemon tea, and asked to choose what biscuit I like; and we all sit on the edge of stools and crack jokes.

Notes

1. Of the many studies that have informed my work on this essay, two have been of particular use: J. Howard Woolmer, *A Checklist of the Hogarth Press 1917-1946* (Revere, Pa.: Woolmer Brotherson Ltd., 1986); and J. H. Willis, Jr., *Leonard and Virginia Woolf as Publishers: The Hogarth Press, 1917-41* (Charlottesville, Va.: University Press of Virginia, 1992). For any study of the Hogarth Press, the most important primary sources are Virginia Woolf's diary and letters (*The Diary of Virginia Woolf*, ed. Anne Olivier Bell, 5 vols. [London: Hogarth Press, 1977-84]; *The Letters of Virginia Woolf*, ed. Nigel Nicolson and Joan Trautmann, 6 vols. [London: Hogarth Press, 1975-80]) and Leonard Woolf's autobiography, especially the following volumes: *Beginning Again. An Autobiography of the years 1911 to 1918* (London: Hogarth Press, 1963); *Downhill All the Way. An Autobiography of the Years 1919-1939* (London: Hogarth Press, 1967); and *The Journey Not the Arrival Matters. An Autobiography of the Years 1939-1969* (London: Hogarth Press, 1969). Subsequent references to these sources are usually cited in the text of the chapter.

2. Cf. Leonard's retrospective comment in 1963: "Ten years after we started printing *Two Stories* The Hogarth Press was a successful commercial publishing business. It remained for Virginia and me, and has always remained for me, a half-time occupation" (*Beginning Again*, 254).

3. For a fuller account of my entrapment, see "In Defense of Bibliomania," *AB Bookman's Weekly* 93.2 (10 January 1994): 5-12; reprinted in *A Catalog of the David and Helen Porter Collection of Books from the Hogarth Press* (Saratoga Springs, NY: Skidmore College, 1998).

4. Letter, 8 June 1917, to Vanessa Bell, quoted in fuller detail below, note 34.

5. *Beginning Again*, 233ff. For a good account of the origins, see Willis, 1ff.

6. *Beginning Again*, 233: "The difficulty with Virginia was to find any play sufficiently absorbing to take her mind off her work. We were both interested in printing and had from time to time in a casual way talked about the possibility of learning to print. It struck me that it would be a good thing if Virginia had a manual occupation of this kind which, in say the afternoons, would take her mind completely off her work." With the same thought in mind, Virginia had in 1914 undertaken to type Lytton Strachey's racy novelette, *Ermyntrude and Esmeralda*; see Willis, 4, and Virginia's letter of 7 February 1914 to Strachey: "I shall be delighted to do Esmeralda — and anything else chaste or otherwise."

7. Just over two weeks after Virginia's birthday, Leonard writes Lytton Strachey, "[W]e think of setting up a printing press in the cellarage. Now Ray [Rachel Strachey] tells us you know all about printing presses. Is this true & can you tell us how & where one gets them & what they cost?" (letter of 10 February 1915, in *Letters of Leonard Woolf*, ed. Frederic Spotts [New York: Harcourt Brace Jovanovich, 1989]).

8. Letter, 10 September 1916: "I meant to ask whether you have a list of possible buyers at the Omega which you would lend us when it comes to sending post cards about the press."

9. See letters of 24 October 1916 and 3? December 1916 to Vanessa Bell, in the latter of which Virginia specifically refers to the £20 needed for the press.

10. See Virginia's letter of 2 May 1917 to Margaret Llewelyn Davis: "After 2 hours work at the press, Leonard heaved a terrific sigh and said 'I wish to God we'd never bought the cursed thing!' To my relief, though not surprise, he added 'Because I shall never do anything else'. You can't think how exciting, soothing, ennobling and satisfying it is. And so far we've only done the dullest and most difficult part — setting up a notice, which you will recieve [sic] one day. We cant print it off yet, because, to our horror, the press arrived smashed, and it will take some time to get it mended. Meanwhile our brains buzz with all sorts of works. . . ."

11. Letter, 22 May 1917, to Vanessa Bell: "We have just started printing Leonards story; I haven't produced mine yet, but there's nothing in writing compared with printing."

12. *Prelude* in fact ended up being the Woolfs' third publication, since during the time they were working on it they also published in a very small edition, for private circulation, a memorial volume of youthful poems by Leonard Woolf's brother Cecil, who had been killed in the war: see Willis, 23-24.

13. Leonard gives a full account in *Beginning Again*, 237-39. Before long the Woolfs were turning to commercial publishers for assistance with other projects which they could not handle on the handpress — e.g., J. Middleton Murry's *The Critic in Judgment* (which came out in May 1919, at the same time as two hand-printed books, Virginia's *Kew Gardens* and Eliot's *Poems*); the second editions of *Kew Gardens* and *Mark on the Wall* slightly later that same year; and the various translations from the Russian which began in 1920 with Maxim Gorky's *Reminiscences of Leo Nicolayevitch Tolstoi*.

14. "Logan" is Logan Piersall Smith, a transplanted American who published two books with the Hogarth Press and appears occasionally as a guest or correspondent of the Woolfs. His somewhat precious *TLS* review had said, "But here is 'Kew Gardens' — a work of art, made,

'created' as we say, finished, four-square . . . with its own 'atmos-phere,' its own vital force. Quotation cannot present its beauty, or as we should like to say, its being. . . . [T]he more one gloats over 'Kew Gardens' the more beauty shines out of it; and the fitter to it seems this cover that is like no other cover, and carries associations; and the more one likes Mrs. Bell's 'Kew Gardens' woodcuts" (Woolmer, xxiv). On Smith, see also note 37.

15. Numbers again document the point: none of the eleven books pub-lished through 1920 reaches 100 pages, and six have less than 25; of the 28 books published in 1925, six again have less than 25 pages, but eight run to 100 pages or more; of the 30 published in 1930, 22 exceed 100 pages.

16. In Virginia's case, the list is extraordinary, including, among others, *Jacob's Room* (1922), *Mrs. Dalloway* (1925), *To the Lighthouse* (1927), *Orlando* (1928), *A Room of One's Own* (1929), *The Waves* (1931), *The Years* (1937), and *Between the Acts* (1941).

17. Other series include the Hogarth Lectures on Literature (sixteen books), the Merttens Lectures on War and Peace (eight books), and World-Makers and World-Shakers, four biographies (Joan of Arc [by V. Sackville-West]; Socrates; Darwin; and Mazzini, Garibaldi and Cavour) aimed at teen-age readers.

18. Pen name of the financial editor of *Time and Tide*.

19. In style, if not always in substance, Tree's book rises well above the usual instance of this type, as in her comments on after-dinner activ-ities (44): "You come down for coffee. The tray is placed on a low table or chintz stool near the fire. The men are assembled or assem-bling. You pour out, coffee first, into each cup. As you pour black you say 'White?' The guest hesitates and says 'Black.' After a little muddle of this kind it is settled amicably all round. Everyone loves coffee sugar (crystals). It has the merit of confetti. At a dull dinner party it acts as a drug. Everyone cheers up."

20. Among the manuscripts reviewed and rejected in the early years was James Joyce's *Ulysses*, a portion of which Harriet Shaw Weaver showed to the Woolfs in 1918; Leonard tells the story in *Beginning Again*, 245-47. Virginia's 17 May 1918 letter to Weaver focuses on

the book's length as an "insuperable difficulty" to their publishing it and tactfully does not mention their other, and deeper, concerns about its quality and the possible threat of censorship. For a good account of Virginia and Leonard's reading of manuscripts, see Willis, 369-372.

21. The Woolfs published Stein's *Composition as Explanation* as a Hogarth Essay in 1926.

22. The context of this remark is important. Virginia mentions in her letter three imminent Hogarth publications — *Kew Gardens*, Eliot's *Poems*, and J. Middleton Murry's *The Critic in Judgment* — and contrasts her own *Kew* ("as simple as can be") with Eliot's complexity and Murry's "obscurity."

23. The poem in question is *Karn*, published by the Woolfs in 1922. One wonders why the Woolfs hand printed so many books by minor authors such as Manning Sanders. In the case of *Karn*, Virginia seems to have seen some merit in the poem, which the author had sent to them for review (see Virginia's letter of 2 December 1921 to Katherine Arnold-Forster). The Berg Collection of the New York Public Library has a fragment (presumably the second page) of the letter which must have accompanied the submission. "I should be extraordinarily happy if you could undertake 'Karn' for me," writes Manning Sanders, and adds in a postscript, "I have not submitted Karn to anyone else." By 1926, when the Woolfs were hand printing a second of her poems, *Martha Wish-You-Ill*, Virginia has revised her opinion, as is apparent from the next letter I quote, written during the period when Virginia was trying to complete *To The Lighthouse*.

24. Virginia is characteristically candid even about the poetry of Leonard's brother Cecil (see above, note 12): "I began setting up Cecil's poems this afternoon. They're not good; they show the Woolf tendency to denunciation, without the vigour of my particular Woolf" (Diary, 8 March 1918).

25. With Virginia's comments on Eliot, compare the following passage from Leonard's autobiography: "[A]s an amateur printer and also the publisher of what I was printing, I found it impossible not to attend

to the sense, and usually after setting a line and then seeing it appear again and again as I took it off the machine, I got terribly irritated by it. But I never tired and still do not tire of those lines which were a new note in poetry and came from the heart of the Eliot of those days (and sounded with even greater depth and volume in the next work of his which we published, the poem which had greater influence upon English poetry, indeed upon English literature, than any other in the 20th century, *The Waste Land*)" (*Beginning Again*, 243).

26. The Woolfs set *Monday or Tuesday* by hand, but Leonard took it for printing to the same local printer, McDermott, who had helped with Mansfield's *Prelude*. The result, he comments, is "one of the worst printed books ever published, certainly the worst ever published by The Hogarth Press" (*Beginning Again*, 239). After describing the messy and laborious process by which he and McDermott produced the thousand copies, he concludes, ". . . at the end we sank down exhausted and speechless on the floor by the side of the machine, where we sat and silently drank beer until I was sufficiently revived to crawl battered and broken back to Hogarth House" (*loc. cit.*, 240).

27. Cameron's photographs, including a number of those in the Hogarth book, were the subject of a recent major show at New York's Museum of Modern Art.

28. Grant was far less active than Bell as a Hogarth illustrator, but he did provide illustrations for the 1923 publication of the *Poems* of G. H. Luce.

29. Cf. Nigel Nicolson, *Portrait of a Marriage* (Chicago: University of Chicago Press, 1973), 202: ". . . *Orlando*, the longest and most charming love letter in literature."

30. In a way, the Woolfs' initial interest in "having pictures" comes full circle with John Lehmann, who joins Leonard as co-publisher in 1938 and includes numerous illustrations in the volumes he edits under the titles *Daylight* and *New Writing and Daylight*.

31. *Downhill All the Way*, 76. A 10 August 1922 letter from Virginia to her sister discusses the then-evolving design for this jacket with a

characteristic attention to detail: "We think your design lovely — Our only doubts are practical. L. thinks the lettering isn't plain enough, and the effect is rather too dazzling. Could you make the r of Room into a Capital? And could the lettering be picked out in some colour which would make it bolder?" Vanessa also produced jackets for books by other Hogarth authors, among them Susan Buchan's *Funeral March of a Marionette*. *Charlotte of Albany* (1935), Edward Upward's *Journey to the Border* (1938), and Henry Green's *Back* (1946).

32. Concern over the rising threat of fascism and especially of Nazi Germany is focal or implicit in many other Hogarth Press publications throughout the 1930s. The topic attains particular poignancy in three publications that appear in 1939: E. M. Forster's *What I Believe*, Christopher Isherwood's *Goodbye to Berlin*, and Herbert Rosinski's *The German Army*. The jacket blurb for the last, a historical account written by a German refugee, begins, "This book was planned and written some time before the outbreak of war, but the present situation can only enhance its importance as a unique study of the army which we are facing in the field today." The book's evocative jacket, in dark red and black, features a photograph of the tomb of the unknown soldier in Munich.

33. The other version of the device, by Vanessa Bell, is more realistic in style and first appears on books published in 1925. From 1930 on, both devices are used (e.g., Ivan Bunin's *The Well of Days*, published in 1933, has Kauffer's device; his *Grammar of Love*, published two years later, has Bell's). Woolmer's *Checklist* contains good illustrations both of these devices and of Bell's and Banting's covers for the Hogarth Essays, Living Poets, and Letters.

34. Letter, 8 June 1917, to Vanessa Bell: "I have heard of a shop where you can get wonderful coloured papers. We're half way through L's story — it gets ever so much quicker, and the fascination is something extreme." In a letter written some two weeks earlier, on 22 May 1917, Virginia tells Vanessa, "I want your advice about covers." And Leonard leads into the passage quoted above by referring to the

trouble they took to find "some rather unusual, gay Japanese paper for the covers" of *Two Stories* (*Beginning Again*, 236).

35. One wonders to what degree the Woolfs' testiness over the design reflects Virginia's somewhat ambivalent feelings toward Katherine Mansfield (see especially her retrospective remarks in a letter of 8 August 1931 to V. Sackville-West). As for Mansfield's husband, J. Middleton Murry, Virginia describes him in a letter of the same period as "the one vile man I have ever known" (15 April 1931, to Ethel Smyth).

36. In addition to those shown in figure 11, another variant appears in an illustration in Woolmer's *Checklist* (14, upper panel), and a copy in the British Library represents yet one more. One suspects there are others as well.

37. E.g, several of the early translations from the Russian (Gorky, Woolmer #14; Dostoevsky, Woolmer #20; Goldenveizer, Woolmer #32, et al.). The most notable instance of multiple bindings in a book that was not hand printed is Logan Piersall Smith's *Stories from the Old Testament*. I myself have copies with three different covers, and I suspect there are other variants as well. Interesting circumstances surround the publication of this book. It came out in 1920 but was already on the Woolfs' minds in 1919. Indeed, just before Logan wrote his *TLS* review of *Kew Gardens*, Virginia records a visit from him in which "his real object in coming was to ask us to print some of his works" (Letter, 18 May 1919, to Vanessa Bell). The publication of *Stories from the Old Testament* the next year clearly continues the saga, and one wonders to what degree both Logan's effusive review, and the special care the Woolfs subsequently lavished on his modest book, are part of the story. Virginia was less forthcoming many years later when Logan asked her to become a member of the BBC "Pronouncing Committee," mentioning that "Bernard Shaw" was chairman of this committee, and commenting, "We want a woman on the Comtee, and ought of course to have one (or more); and who could 'voice' her sex better than you?" (Letter, 1 December 1933, Berg Collection, New York Public Library). After

initially indicating she might accept, Virginia wrote Logan to say that she had decided against it: "I have never sat on a Comtee. in my life, and feel it is too late to begin" (Letter, 4 March 1934).

38. I know of only two copies of this type — one that I own, and a copy in the Berg Collection. The variant is not noted by Woolmer in his *Checklist*, nor I have seen it mentioned elsewhere.

39. I say "apparently" since the diamonds that are gold in the two *Paris* copies mentioned in note 38 appear slightly more brown in tone in the paper used for *Jacob's Room*. This possible distinction does not, however, change the fact that the two *Paris* copies in question differ from all others I have seen in having green diamonds where others have dark blue — a characteristic they share with the *Jacob's Room* holograph.

40. Hope Mirrlees around the same time gives another glimpse into the daily life of the Press, and the surprisingly intimate scale of its operations: "When I was staying with [the Woolfs] on one occasion . . . I asked if I might see the Hogarth Press, expecting to be taken to a room full of mysterious machinery. We were in the dining-room when I asked & they pointed to something behind my chair about the size of a radio, and informed me that that was the Hogarth Press" (Donna E. Rhein, *The Handprinted Books of Leonard and Virginia Woolf at the Hogarth Press, 1917-1932* [Ann Arbor: UMI Research Press, 1985], 42).

41. Their memorial volume of Cecil Woolf's poems also has the title printed directly onto the cover, but in this case, the printing shows up relatively well since the paper used for binding is near-white and without design (cf. the copies of *Two Stories* that are bound in plain yellow paper).

42. A copy I have with the sea-green cover contains an interesting inscription from Forster to his close friend Forrest Reid: *F. R. amico hanc editionem principissimam d. d. amicus E. M. F. 10.5.23* ("To my friend Forrest Reid E. M. Forster gives and dedicates this very first edition"). I have wondered whether its reference to *hanc editionem principissimam* may suggest that this was the earlier state of the binding.

43. A 25 July 1924 letter, also to Barbara Bagenal, strikes an even more manic note: "Our Mrs Joad [the Woolfs' current assistant at the Press], God damn her, has been away with pneumonia these four weeks, and will take another six before she is back: with the result that we all run about the basement, distracted, henlike, with wisps of string, labels, brown paper, now answering the door — Please come in. Yes I'm the advertising manager. Yes we give you 33½% on numbers over twelve — No; we don't keep Songs of Sunrise. . . The Press has suddenly become monstrous, kicking and sprawling. We have a drawer full of manuscripts which the authors deposit and the seediest old bankrupts arrive who won't go away till Leonard, whose heart is of gold, gives them five pounds, which they lavish on drink, but, as he says, we shall all come to it one of these days. I dwell on these glories to make you regret your marriage."

INDEX

---- ◄◄►►► ----

Index

Index

3791023

DATE DUE

OCT 31 2009			